THE REFORMATION UNSETTLED

PROTEUS: STUDIES IN EARLY MODERN
IDENTITY FORMATION

Previously published volumes in this series are listed at the back of this book.

VOLUME 3

THE REFORMATION UNSETTLED
British Literature and the Question
of Religious Identity, 1560–1660

Edited by

Jan Frans van Dijkhuizen
and Richard Todd

BREPOLS

British Library Cataloguing in Publication Data

The Reformation unsettled : British literature and the
question of religious identity, 1560-1660. - (Proteus :
studies in early-modern identity formation ; 3)
1. Donne, John, 1572-1631 - Criticism and interpretation
2. English literature - Early modern, 1500-1700 - History
and criticism 3. Religion and literature - Great Britain -
History - 16th century 4. Religion and literature - Great
Britain - History - 17th century 5. Religion in literature
6. Reformation - Great Britain 7. Identification (Religion)
I. Dijkhuizen, Jan Frans van, 1970- II. Todd, Richard
820.9'3823'09032

ISBN-13: 9782503526249

© **2008, Brepols Publishers n.v., Turnhout, Belgium**

D/2008/0095/168
ISBN: 978-2-503-52624-9

Printed in the E.U. on acid-free paper

CONTENTS

Acknowledgements

The editors would like to thank the following sponsors for their generous support in organizing the conference from which the papers in this volume emerged:

Leids Universiteits Fonds (LUF)
PALLAS, Instituut voor historisch, kunsthistorisch en letterkundige studies

The editors have made efforts to contact all copyright-holders. If there should be any omissions, please contact the editors, who will endeavour to rectify this on the occasion of the publisher reprinting the work.

ILLUSTRATIONS

Fig. 1, p. 61. Lucas Cranach the Elder, *Calvary*, 1502. Department of Prints and Drawings — Metropolitan Museum, New York.

Fig. 2, p. 62. Lucas Cranach the Elder, *Calvary*, c. 1500–04. Berlin, Kupferstich-kabinett. Reproduced with the permission of the Bildportal der Kunstmuseen/ Kupferstichkabinett — Staatliche Museen zu Berlin.

Fig. 3, p. 63. Bohemian Master, *Calvary*, c. 1360. Berlin, Gemäldegalerie. Repro-duced with the permission of the Bildportal der Kunstmuseen/Gemäldegalerie — Staatliche Museen zu Berlin.

Fig. 4, p. 68. Lucas Cranach the Elder, *Crufixion with Centurion*, 1539. Staats-galerie Aschaffenburg.

INTRODUCTION

Jan Frans van Dijkhuizen and Richard Todd

R ecent historical studies have emphasized that the English Reformation can no longer be seen as an inevitable response to abuses within the late-medieval Catholic Church, or an increasingly powerful nationalism and sense of resentment against spiritual colonization at the hands of an Italian prince of that church. Contrary to Protestant stereotypes, the late-medieval church catered, and did so effectively, to the spiritual needs of its members. What is more, the English Reformation was anything but a complete process, and even after the Elizabethan Settlement of 1559, English religious culture was full of continuities with the past, with pre-Reformation religious culture only partially displaced. As Robert Whiting perceptively suggests, even if the Reformation decades witnessed a partial 'destruction of Catholicism', this 'owed considerably less to the rise of Protestant convictions than to the motive power of essentially secular compulsions'.[1] Indeed, as Christopher Haigh crisply argues, 'legislative destruction proved easier than evangelical construction' until well into our period.[2] As a result, England after the Elizabethan Settlement found itself in a transitional phase in which a new, emergent religious culture had not yet fully established itself, while an older, residual culture was still present. In Haigh's words, 'church-goers [in the English Church] were de-catholicized but un-protestantized'.[3]

Though these claims represent something of an academic consensus as they stand here, they are of necessity rather boldly stated. The contributors are naturally

---

[1] Robert Whiting, *The Blind Devotion of the People: Popular Religion and the English Reformation* (Cambridge: Cambridge University Press, 1989), p. 266.

[2] Christopher Haigh, *English Reformations: Religion, Politics, and Society under the Tudors* (Oxford: Oxford University Press, 1993), p. 288.

[3] Haigh, *English Reformations*, p. 290.

well aware that there were certain incontrovertible discontinuities in terms of theological doctrine, church government, and liturgical practice. In the second half of the twentieth century, the work of Patrick Collinson, more than that of anyone else, showed how a distinctively Protestant culture was forged during the late sixteenth and early seventeenth centuries.[4] Yet Collinson has also argued that this Protestant culture was the product of a gradual, accretive process of change that involved the initial appropriation of existing Catholic cultural forms. Moreover, while this process led, by a series of steps, to what Collinson terms 'an authentically protestant literary culture' in the second quarter of the seventeenth century, it is worth noting that, at the same time, the identity of the English Church was being subjected to possibly the most intense doctrinal scrutiny it would receive before the Oxford Movement of the nineteenth century.[5] Furthermore, to place exclusive emphasis on the discontinuities that accompanied the Reformation would be to overlook what this book is at pains to examine, that is the extent to which literary and cultural expressions of religious matters do not always immediately reflect the major institutional and theological changes in a predictable or uniform fashion. Eamon Duffy's *The Voices of Morebath* presents, in the figure of the remarkably long-lived Sir Christopher Trichey, a fascinating case study. Others are provided in a fine chapter, 'Choosing Reformations', in Norman Jones's *The English Reformation*, while Alexandra Walsham has shown how 'church papists' managed to avoid the obligatory fine for not attending the English Church weekly.[6]

The purpose of the following collection of essays, which originated as conference papers for the Leiden October Conference in 2004, is to examine the issues outlined above from a number of perspectives. This book centres around the question of how the literature of the first century after the Elizabethan Settlement dealt with issues of religious and cultural ambivalence. The essays in this book investigate how pre-Reformation religious culture was addressed in a variety of literary texts dating from the period between 1560 and 1660, that is,

[4] See Patrick Collinson's *The Religion of Protestants* (Oxford: Clarendon Press, 1982).

[5] Patrick Collinson, 'Protestant Culture and the Cultural Revolution', in *Reformation to Revolution: Politics and Religion in Early Modern England*, ed. by Margo Todd (London: Routledge, 1995), pp. 33–52 (p. 36, emphasis added).

[6] Eamon Duffy, *The Voices of Morebath: Reformation and Rebellion in an English Village* (New Haven: Yale University Press, 2001); Norman Jones, 'Choosing Reformations', in *The English Reformation: Religion and Cultural Adaptation* (Oxford: Blackwell, 2002), pp. 7–33; Alexandra Walsham, *Church Papists: Catholicism, Conformity and Confessional Polemic in Early Modern England* (London: Royal Historical Society, 1993).

from Elizabeth I's accession to the throne to the Restoration of the monarchy. These literary texts demonstrate the religious hybridity of early modern England in a concentrated form. As opposed to writers on, for instance, church government or theology, literary writers were not obliged to choose sides, although, as is uniformly accepted, they in effect printed under censorship. In spite of the undeniable politico-religious pressures to which it was subject, literary discourse could confront incompatible doctrinal perspectives within a single text, or forge a hybrid spiritual sensibility out of competing religious traditions. Literature, sometimes in spite of writers' avowed denominational allegiances, embraced, explored, and deepened the ambivalence of early modern English religious culture in a manner perhaps less readily available in other kinds of texts. The essays focus on a mixture of canonical texts (by Shakespeare, Donne, Herbert, and others) as well as less canonical ones (seventeenth-century Irish drama, manuscript elegies, works by women).

The book concentrates on four thematic fields. Part I investigates how literary texts addressed the notion of religious identity in early modern England. Literary writers of the period were both sensitive to the genuine differences between religious cultures and acutely aware that fixed doctrinal identity is a chimera; they were also alert to the often violent consequences of religious identity politics. Part II is devoted to the theology of word and image, and to explorations of the word-image polarity in poetry. Part III examines the religious significance of geographical and spatial locations in early modern theatre: drama in early modern Catholic Ireland, Shakespeare's imagining of Catholic Spain, and theatrical appropriations of the evacuated space of the late-medieval monastery. Part IV, finally, looks at how English culture after the Elizabethan Settlement dealt with the relations between the living and the dead, and looks at post-Settlement attitudes toward physical remnants of the Catholic past.

In the opening essay, Helen Wilcox examines the hybrid doctrinal nature of post-1559 Protestant poetry. In spite of the prevailing anti-Catholic rhetoric of the period, English Protestant poets were in many ways indebted to Catholic traditions, and it is often unhelpful to read their work with clear-cut denominational categories in mind. However, rather than embracing irenic ideals of unification, spiritual poetry formed a platform in which religious difference was confronted, enacted, and examined in all its complexity and ambivalence.

Approaching the politics of religious identity from a different perspective, Richard Todd looks at contemporary scholarly debates about John Donne's 'apostasy'. Donne's shift from Catholicism to the Church of England continues to cause unease among critics today because notions of Protestant Britishness that were promoted in the century after Donne's death, but had not yet been sharply defined during his lifetime, also co-determined twentieth-century British and American views of religious identity. Donne's own hybrid denominational identity is explored by Hugh Adlington. Adlington looks at the neglected significance of pre-Reformation legal traditions to the scriptural exegesis of conformist Jacobean preachers such as Donne. On the one hand, consistent with the exegetical principle of *sola scriptura*, Donne's sermons, poems, prose, and familiar letters appear to comprise an unequivocal rejection of the 'Decretals and Extravagants' of the *Corpus iuris canonici* (1503). On the other hand, Donne preached in conformity with the English Church's *Code of Canons* (1603). Adlington examines how Donne's reading of pre-Reformation canonists (such as Ivo of Chartres, Gulielmus Durandus, Baldus and Turrecremata) contributes to the methods and principles of his exegetical style. He also shows how Donne's reading of 'humanist' ecclesiastical historians, such as Severin Binnius, informs his attitude to, and understanding of, canon law.

The ambiguities of religious difference are also explored by Jan Frans van Dijkhuizen, who traces changing early modern theological views on the meaning, and especially the soteriological effect, of physical pain, and shows how John Donne and George Herbert responded to these shifts in their religious poetry. Both poets explored the conflicting Catholic and Reformed understandings of pain that were available to them. In Donne these different conceptions are often locked in opposition, while for Herbert the medium of poetry, because of its formal properties, offered a way of formulating a hybrid religious understanding of physical suffering. Claudia Richter argues that the satirical attacks on Protestant nonconformists in Thomas Nashe's *Unfortunate Traveller* (1594) and the long poem *Hell's Broke Loose* (1605), attributed to Samuel Rowlands, reveal how much conformist discourse owed to the very Catholic practices which it rejected as 'magical' and superstitious, in this case exorcism rituals. Nashe and Rowlands present radical Protestantism as a demonic threat to the sacred order of the state that needs to be expelled by means of ritual linguistic formulae akin to the speech acts that characterize an exorcism.

Theological debates about the visual and the textual were at the heart of the Reformation, and the essays in Part II of this volume look at the position of poetry and of the genre of the emblem book within these controversies. Frances Cruickshank shows how John Donne and George Herbert responded in their spiritual poetry to the Protestant distrust of the visual, and its concurrent promotion of the written and spoken word. In spite of their Protestant allegiance, the work of both poets betrays a strong interest in the visual apprehension of the doctrines of Christianity. Indeed, they employ the medium of devotional poetry as a privileged religious space in which word and image can be joined. Since poetry could draw extensively on visual imagery without incurring charges of idolatry, it offered a way of bypassing the theological opposition between word and image. Bart Westerweel investigates the sacred emblem book, a genre with clearly Protestant origins. Jan van der Noot, a Protestant refugee who had fled to England, published *Het Theatre* (The Theatre) in 1568/69 in Dutch, French, and English. In France Georgette de Montenay published her *Emblemes, ou devises chrestiennes* (1571) at the Protestant court of Navarre. It is well known that emblem books, and the emblematic mode in general, were a strong influence on English devotional poets of the first half of the seventeenth century. Yet the models for a poet like George Herbert, and for an early-seventeenth-century emblem writer like Francis Quarles, were Jesuit rather than Protestant emblem books, for example Hugo's *Pia Desideria* (1624) and Benedictus van Haeften's *Schola cordis* (1629). Westerweel demonstrates why this type of emblem book was congenial to English poets writing at the time.

In the first essay of Part III John Kerrigan widens the scope of this volume to include the archipelagic context of the English Reformation. Kerrigan investigates the role of drama within the complex religious politics of Ireland during the 1630s and 1640s. He shows that, although the Henrician Reformation had some administrative impact on the Church in Ireland, there was no significant drive to reform popular beliefs and attitudes until the end of the sixteenth century. As a result of this delay, English and Scottish Protestant settlers encountered a confident Counter-Reformation Catholicism imported from the Continent, as well as a live array of indigenous, unreformed beliefs. The potency of the clash between late, zealous Calvinism, and popular, often unreformed Catholicism goes some way toward explaining the bitterness of the Irish Rebellion of 1641 and the subsequent wars in Ireland. What is more, the mixed nature of the Catholic inheritance, and its tendency to correlate with ethnic groups, helps explain why the wars became so fractiously complicated. Kerrigan focuses on Anglophone plays by James Shirley, Henry Burnell, and Henry Burkhead, written for audiences of New English incomers as well as for the Old English, usually Catholic descendants of the Anglo-Norman colonists. The latter group's difficult position as Royalists estranged from the king by their faith, and as traditional enemies of the Gaelic Irish driven into alliance with them from 1641, drew them to literature as an outlet for their apologia but also as a medium in which they could explore the historical and contemporary dimensions of their predicament.

Kristine Steenbergh addresses the ambivalent relation of the London theatre to the religious past. Steenbergh assesses the implications of the fact that Blackfriars, the seventeenth-century private theatre of the King's Men, was situated in a former Dominican priory, and investigates how early modern plays represent monasteries. Although monasteries figure frequently in the drama, they are rarely employed as an onstage setting. Moreover, in plays, monasteries have often been stripped of their religious function. Seldom featured as actual communities of monks or nuns, monasteries operate as imagined locations exterior to the play's action that function as an outlet for social and political problems addressed in it.

The final section opens with Andrea Brady's investigation of grief in Reformation England. Protestant views on grief downplayed the emotional ties between the living and the dead, for example in their rejection of purgatory, and of the obit and month's mind or anniversary Mass. Instead Reformed theology emphasized the edification of the bereaved and was suspicious of 'excessive' mourning (although it was also dismissive of emotional coldness in the face of death). In the absence of pre-Reformation ways of managing grief, early modern elegists, mourning the deaths of their loved ones, adopted a variety of poetic strategies for mourning and commemoration, for example an emphasis on time, including the time it takes to compose a poem, as a crucial factor in the process of grief. These poems show how the psychological need to maintain bonds with the dead led elegists to re-create rituals of service in elegies themselves.

Kevin Laam shows how Robert Persons's devotional work *The First Booke of the Christian Exercise, Appertayning to Resolution* (1582), later published as *A Christian Directorie*, relies heavily on Ignatian models of consolation. Its popularity outside recusant circles testifies to the continuing cultural relevance of the traditional church, and to the often fluid nature of religious identity in the early modern era. The concept of consolation — rooted in medieval piety and subsequently codified into Ignatian orthodoxy — adapted efficiently to the religion of Elizabethan England partly because no alternative models were available: until well into the seventeenth century, the *Christian Directory* was the premier work of its kind in English. Oliver Harris, finally, analyses the relation between the Reformation and the rise of antiquarianism in the sixteenth century. Antiquarianists attempted to limit what Harris calls the 'collateral damage of reform' by salvaging medieval manuscripts and recording church monuments and glass as material remnants of the Catholic past. Interestingly, they frequently did so not because they were practising Catholics. Antiquarianism was widely practised, united by its desire to record and celebrate the past — even if, in concrete terms, this was the past of the Catholic Church.

Textual Note

In quotations from early modern texts, original spellings are retained, but 'long *s*', *u*/*v*, and *i*/*j* have been modernized.

Part I
The Poetics and Politics of Religious Identity

'SHE ON THE HILLS': TRACES OF CATHOLICISM IN SEVENTEENTH-CENTURY ENGLISH PROTESTANT POETRY

Helen Wilcox

It may be stated with some certainty that Renaissance England bore multiple marks of the pre-Reformation culture of Catholicism.[1] Indeed, it has recently been asserted that Catholic thought was so important to the young Protestant nation that historians 'cannot understand the Elizabethan state and its Jacobean successor without it'.[2] There is no doubting the political impact of continuing Catholic ideologies and loyalties in post-Reformation England. However, it is not so easy to discern just how prevalent the *doctrines* of the old faith still were among non-Catholics in this period. One early-seventeenth-century English bishop, John Cosin, so thoroughly played down the impact of the Reformation that he stated: '[W]e [in the Church of England] have continued the old religion.'[3] To what

---

[1] As this view is the premise for the current volume, it is appropriate to acknowledge here the scholarly initiative of the editors in organizing the conference at which an earlier version of this essay was presented, and to thank them for their constructive editorial comments.

[2] Gerard Kilroy, *TLS*, 13 January 2006, p. 25, reviewing *Catholics and the 'Protestant Nation'*, ed. by Ethan H. Shagan (Manchester: Manchester University Press, 2005).

[3] John Cosin, *Notes and Collections on the Book of Common Prayer*, in *The Works of John Cosin: Now First Collected*, ed. by Rev. John Sansom and Rev. John Barrow, 5 vols (Oxford: John Henry and James Parker, 1843–55), v, 13. For an exploration of the political reasons for making a bold statement of ecclesiastical allegiance such as this, in the context of the widening gulf between pro-Catholic leaders of the Church of England and their Puritan critics in the run-up to the Civil War, see Achsah Guibbory, *Ceremony and Community from Herbert to Milton* (Cambridge: Cambridge University Press, 1998).

extent might such a claim to continuity also have been applied to the devotional poetry of the period? How did the possible influence of Catholic doctrines and traditions reveal itself in the imagination and the rhetoric of individual English poets? This essay enquires into the traces of the 'old religion' to be found in the devotional poetry of Protestant writers in approximately the first half of the seventeenth century. The central writer in my investigation is George Herbert, but the poetry of John Donne, An Collins, 'Eliza', and Robert Herrick will also feature, along with references to their contemporaries Thomas Browne, Andrew Marvell, William Austin and Joseph Beaumont.[4] The discussion will raise two fundamental issues concerning the interpretation of early modern texts: the difficulty of assigning poetry to theological pigeonholes, both then and now, and the possibility of rethinking the function of devotional verse in seventeenth-century English culture.

It is essential to begin by acknowledging the prevailing context of anti-Catholicism in England in this period.[5] Outspoken allegiance to Catholic tradition had been considered an act of political treason during the reign of Elizabeth I, and came to a head again in 1605 with the furore surrounding the foiled Catholic conspiracy known as the Gunpowder Plot. While official Church of England allegiance during the later part of the reign of James I, and under Charles I, moved increasingly toward sympathy with Rome, Puritan anti-Catholic rhetoric intensified at an equivalent rate. Even the most measured early-seventeenth-century English Protestant texts tended to depict Catholicism in an unflattering guise. Take, for example, the widely used biblical metaphor of the church as a woman, observed by the (implicitly male) believer, likening the Catholic Church and the Protestant reformed churches to two females of extremely contrasting outward appearance. In his poem 'The British Church', George Herbert gave this ecclesiastical duo a particularly vivid representation:

> She on the hills, which wantonly
> Allureth all in hope to be
> By her preferr'd,

---

[4] The work of writers from the period who were — or who seem to have been — Catholic at some point in their lives, including Robert Southwell, William Alabaster, John Donne, William Shakespeare, Ben Jonson, Elizabeth Cary, Richard Crashaw, Patrick Carey, and Gertrude More, will largely not feature in the discussion, since the central questions of this essay specifically concern the work of non-Catholic poets.

[5] This phenomenon — and its continuation to some extent in modern critical practice — is documented by Alison Shell in *Catholicism, Controversy and the English Literary Imagination, 1558–1660* (Cambridge: Cambridge University Press, 1999).

> Hath kiss'd so long her painted shrines,
> That ev'n her face by kissing shines,
>   For her reward.
>
> She in the valley is so shie
> Of dressing, that her hair doth lie
>   About her eares:[6]

The Catholic Church, easily identified as the woman standing on the seven hills of Rome, is presented as an alluring prostitute (akin to the biblical 'great whore' of Babylon in Revelation 19. 2) who 'wantonly' attracts and corrupts her customers by raising in them false hopes of preferment. She is associated with colourful idolatry — the kissing of 'painted shrines' — and is herself, by implication, dangerously sensuous in appearance. Herbert's lines recall John Donne's description of the Catholic Church as 'she' who is 'richly painted',[7] linking Catholicism with a woman who is excessively made up in order to deceive those who look upon her. The shining face of Herbert's personification of Catholicism is also reminiscent of the false glow of the House of Pride in *The Faerie Queene*: a 'stately Pallace' covered with bright 'golden foile', with 'hinder parts' that were 'painted cunningly' to disguise the fact that they were 'ruinous and old'.[8] The anti-Catholicism of the early modern period is not to be underestimated: 'she on the hills' is an ancient ruin disguised as a tempting beauty.

In contrast to the whore of Rome, Calvin's church in the Genevan 'valley' is portrayed by Herbert as totally unselfconscious, so oblivious of presenting herself to the world that she lets her hair 'lie | About her eares'. However, lest we might think that the purity of Protestantism is wholly to be favoured over the artifice of Rome, Herbert goes on to suggest that Calvinist practice is equally extreme:

> While she [in the valley] avoids her neighbours pride,
> She wholly goes on th'other side,
>   And nothing wears.
>
>   (p. 391)

---

[6] George Herbert, 'The British Church', in *The Temple*, from *The English Poems of George Herbert*, ed. by Helen Wilcox (Cambridge: Cambridge University Press, 2007), p. 391. All further references are to this edition, cited by page number.

[7] John Donne, 'Holy Sonnet XVIII' ('Show me deare Christ, thy Spouse'), in *Complete English Poems*, ed. by C. A. Patrides (London: Dent, 1985), p. 446.

[8] Edmund Spenser, *The Faerie Queene*, I.4.4–5, in *Poetical Works*, ed. by J. C. Smith and E. de Selincourt (Oxford: Oxford University Press, 1970), p. 19.

The two symbolic females appear to be almost as bad as each other — for is not nakedness just as immodest as over-paintedness? And while Calvinism lurks in the valley, Catholicism stands out on the hills — interestingly, not unlike 'Truth' itself which, according to Donne's third 'Satyre', is also a female figure to be seen 'on a huge hill'.[9] This introduces a further element of ambiguity into the tension between the two extremes of Christian practice. Indeed, the unstable attractions of both the woman 'on the hills' and 'She in the valley' function in Herbert's poem as foils for the reliable, maternal 'British Church' who represents the middle way or 'mean' between Rome and Geneva:

> But dearest Mother, (what those misse)
> The mean thy praise and glorie is,
>   And long may be.
>
> Blessed be God, whose love it was
> To double-moat thee with his grace,
>   And none but thee.
>   (p. 391)

Holding the middle ground between overdressed Catholicism and undressed Calvinism, Herbert's church wins 'praise and glorie'; already safe on her island surrounded by the sea, the 'British Church' has an additional protective 'moat' of divine grace. These images assert that the blatant sensuality of Catholicism was seen as not only potentially corrupting but also decidedly foreign; the church he praises, by contrast, is a national mother-figure whose identity is linked with that of the island nation itself. Politically as well as doctrinally, the Catholic tradition suffered from a doubly negative reputation, associated as it was with a dubious nostalgia for past festivals and superstitious traditions on the one hand, and the danger of invasion or collusion from abroad on the other.[10]

A closer look at the work of Protestant poets from the period, however, can alert us to the profound knowledge of Catholic theology and the Church Fathers implicit in their writing — indeed, reference to the Catholic tradition was a widespread and accepted aspect of early modern English religious writing. George Herbert advised his well-trained 'Country Parson' not only to know the 'secrets of God treasured in the Holy Scripture', as a good Protestant would, but to read 'the Fathers also, and the Schoolmen, and the later

[9] Donne, *Complete English Poems*, p. 228.

[10] See Thomas Browne on the spirituality 'which misguided zeal termes superstition', cited below.

Writers'.[11] Sometimes, familiarity with Catholic doctrine came about for the strangest of reasons; as a young man in a Calvinist household, Richard Crashaw read the theological works that were kept by his father only for the purposes of anti-Catholic propaganda.[12] Sir Thomas Browne, a man of notable toleration who nevertheless clearly described himself as being 'of that reformed new-cast Religion', defined his faith as 'the same belief that our Saviour taught, the Apostles disseminated, the Fathers authorised, and the Martyrs confirmed'.[13] Browne's generosity was unusual for his day: few could have shared his commitment that he would 'never divide' himself 'from any man upon the difference of an opinion' (1.6), and he did admit that Catholicism was likely to be more acceptable to a person such as himself who was 'naturally inclined to that, which misguided zeale termes superstition' (1.3). However, Browne still insisted on his fundamental principle that 'there is between us one common name and appellation, one faith, and necessary body of principles common to us both' (1.3). This statement at the very least indicates the *possibility* that his fellow-Protestant contemporaries might also think — and write — a little in this vein.

Although Browne asserts here that the old and new faiths have a basis of common or shared belief, he does proceed to note some of the doctrines and devotional practices which marked Catholics as distinctive (and in his view misguided), including 'Holy water and Crucifix', 'the fruitlesse journeys of Pilgrims', and 'the miserable condition of Friers' (1.3). Underlying these practical or visible signs of Catholicism, I would suggest that five basic issues typifying the Catholic tradition may be seen repeatedly emerging in the work of Browne's Protestant contemporaries. The first subject on which Catholic sympathies become clear is the theology of the Eucharist, and particularly the extent to which the consecration of the bread and wine is regarded as a re-enactment of Christ's sacrificial offering on the Cross. In contrast to the Protestant understanding of the Eucharist as an act of memorial (to generalize from the variety of reformed positions on this matter that proved so crucial to the Reformation),[14] the Catholic doctrine of

[11] George Herbert, *A Priest to the Temple or The Country Parson*, in *Works*, ed. by F. E. Hutchinson (Oxford: Clarendon Press, 1941), p. 229.

[12] Crashaw himself not only made use of Catholic traditions in his poetry but eventually converted to Catholicism.

[13] Sir Thomas Browne, *Religio Medici*, I.2, in *The Major Works*, ed. by C. A. Patrides (Harmondsworth: Penguin, 1977), p. 62. All further references are to this edition, identified by section and paragraph number.

[14] See R. V. Young, *Doctrine and Devotion in Seventeenth-Century Poetry* (Cambridge: Brewer, 2000), p. 83.

the Mass centres on the conviction that the elements of the bread and wine change their nature into the body and blood of Christ — a belief which led, as Donne expressed it when preaching in 1630, to 'that heresie of Rome, That the body of Christ may be in divers places at once, by the way of Transubstantiation'.[15] At the heart of Catholic devotion is the Mass, and at the centre of the Mass is the bodily presence of Christ.

This leads to the second key quality of early modern Catholicism, its emphasis on the sensual experience of religion, not only discerned in the physical environment of worship (such as the visible and tangible crucifixes and statues, the smell of incense, and the colours of the 'painted shrines' referred to by Herbert) but also in the attitude to faith that this materiality expresses. Catholic devotion is understood in terms of the senses — 'O taste and see that the Lord is good'[16] — whereby the bodily experience of external beauty forms a sign of, and inspiration to, inner spirituality. Thomas Browne confessed to being in sympathy with this aspect of Catholicism, since 'at my devotion I love to use the civility of my knee, my hat, and hand, with all those outward and sensible motions, which may expresse, or promote my invisible devotion' (I.3).

The third defining feature of Catholicism — and source of early modern controversy — is not unconnected to this emphasis on sensual (or 'sensible') devotional experience: it concerns the greater attention paid to the sacraments and ritual in Catholic worship, and the equivalently greater importance of hearing the word read and preached in Protestantism. As Ramie Targoff has noted, 'In place of the Latin Mass, whose crucial moment of collective experience was the sight of the elevation of the Host, the Reformed English service was designed specifically to be heard.'[17] From communally witnessed to individually interpreted devotion, from visual to verbal experience, from Latin to vernacular liturgical texts — these were the cultural shifts, both inside and outside the church, brought about by the Reformation.

---

[15] *The Sermons of John Donne*, ed. by George R. Potter and E. M. Simpson, 10 vols (Berkeley and Los Angeles: University of California Press, 1953–62), I, 8.20. See also M. M. Ross, *Poetry and Dogma: The Transfiguration of Eucharistic Symbols in Seventeenth-Century English Poetry* (New Brunswick: Rutgers University Press, 1954).

[16] Psalm 34. 8, in *The Bible: Authorized King James Version*, ed. by Robert Carroll and Stephen Prickett (Oxford: Oxford University Press, 1997).

[17] Ramie Targoff, *Common Prayer: The Language of Public Devotion in Early Modern England* (Chicago: University of Chicago Press, 2001), p. 22.

The fourth major doctrinal difference between the Catholic and reformed churches is the prominent role given to the Virgin Mary and the saints in Catholicism. William Perkins commented that Catholicism turned the 'Saints in heaven' into 'idols', urging Christians to 'kneele downe to them, and to make prayer to them', thus acknowledging that saints 'have power to heare and help'.[18] Sir Thomas Browne is self-righteously Protestant in his attitude to the '*Ave Marie* Bell': while Catholics who heard the bell ring 'directed their devotions to her, I offered mine to God, and rectified the errours of their prayers by rightly ordering mine owne' (1.3). The Catholic practice of prayers to the Virgin, and the sense of the saints as examples and intercessors, differed fundamentally from the Protestant commitment to Christ as the only mediator between God and humanity, and the redefinition of the saints in reformed religion as those who are saved.

Finally in this brief survey of recognizable features of Catholicism, the fifth recurring issue defining early modern doctrinal allegiances was the fundamental question of agency in the matter of redemption. Is it possible to effect one's own salvation by devotional activity and good works, or are the elect predestined from the beginning of time? While aspects of a doctrine of predestination have always been a part of the Christian faith,[19] the total inability of individuals to influence their spiritual fate was a particular emphasis of Calvinism — a 'decree' that Calvin himself admitted was 'dreadful'.[20] Meanwhile, Catholic practice continued to stress the relative agency of each Christian, and therefore their responsibility for activity in spiritual matters. The Protestant theology of the elect as irrevocably chosen implies a significant contrast from the emphasis on spiritual fitness and energy implied, for example, in the title as well as the practice of the *Spiritual Exercises* of Ignatius Loyola, the founder of the Jesuits and a leading figure in the Catholic Counter-Reformation.

These elements of Catholicism will all recur in the following discussion of some English devotional poems from the first half of the seventeenth century. This will not, however, be an exercise in the discovery of 'popish' echoes where we least expect to find them, just for the sake of proving that there were Catholic influences on Protestant verse. Rather, the traces of a recent Catholic past to be discerned in early modern Protestant poetry can help us, first, to understand the

[18] William Perkins, *Warning against the Idolatrie of the Last Times*, in *Workes* (London: Iohn Haviland, 1631), I.679.

[19] Young, *Doctrine and Devotion*, p. 55.

[20] Jean Calvin, *Institutes of the Christian Religion*, trans. by Henry Beveridge (1845; repr. Grand Rapids: Eerdmans, 1957), III.23.7.

nature of everyday devotional experience in the period. They demonstrate that the
distinctions between different religious traditions, though apparently crystal clear
to the polemicists, were unclear, even murky, to most early modern believers,
including many ministers and poets. John Donne was not the only early modern
Christian to be defined by a 'constant habit' of 'inconstancy' when it came to
religious doctrine.[21] Indeed, the poet and priest of the 'British Church', George
Herbert, is himself an intriguing example of the doctrinal uncertainty inherent
in the era. In an early poem on 'The H. Communion', Herbert raises the key question of how a believer knows what is going on at the moment of the consecration
of the 'gifts' of bread and wine:

> O gratious Lord how shall I know
> Whether in these gifts thou bee so
>   As thou art evry-where;
> Or rather so, as thou alone
> Tak'st all ye Lodging, leaving none
>   ffor thy poore creature there.[22]

The perplexed believer has no doubt about the basic fact that the 'gratious
Lord' is present, but is uncertain as to whether Christ takes 'Lodging' in the
Eucharistic host in an exclusive way, in a manner unlike the generally reassuring
sense that Christ is 'evry-where'. Taking a commonsense approach, the speaker
then asserts the things that are indeed certain about the consecrated bread:

> ffirst I am sure, whether bread stay
> Or whether Bread doe fly away
>   Concerneth bread, not mee.
> But yt both thou, and all thy traine
> Bee there, to thy truth, & my gaine
>   Concerneth mee & Thee.
> And if in comming to thy foes
> Thou dost come first to them, yt showes
>   The hast of thy good will.

---

[21] Donne, 'Holy Sonnet XIX', in *Complete English Poems*, p. 447.

[22] 'The H. Communion', Williams MS Jones B62, fol. 30ᵛ (*English Poems*, p. 8). The poem
as a whole is to be found on fols 30ᵛ–31ᵛ. This manuscript may have been compiled as early as
1615, and certainly substantially predates the 1630s (Herbert died in 1633 and *The Temple* was
published posthumously). See *The Williams Manuscript of George Herbert's Poems*, ed. by Amy
M. Charles (Delmar, NY: Scholars' Facsimiles and Reprints, 1977).

> Or if that thou two stations makest
> In Bread & mee, the way thou takest
>   Is more, but for mee still.
>   (fol. 30ᵛ, p. 8)

The speaker's tone and argument are supremely reasonable: since we cannot know all the answers to spiritual puzzles, we should not try to settle the issue but leave it to the 'Bread' itself (whose nature it alone 'Concerneth'). Whichever way we interpret what is happening — as memorial or transubstantiation — the net result is shown to be the same, a declaration of God's 'good will'. The poem is remarkably candid, demonstrating a kind of naive honesty in the face of the mysterious workings of divine love.

The poem, Herbert's earliest on the subject of Eucharist, does not conclude at this point but changes its tone from the third stanza onward, taking up a cheekier and more combative approach:

> Then of this also I am sure
> That thou didst all those pains endure
>   To' abolish Sinn, not Wheat.
> Creatures are good, & have their place;
> Sinn onely, wᶜʰ did all deface,
>   Thou drivest from his seat.
>
> I could beleeve an Impanation
> At the rate of an Incarnation
>   If thou hadst dyde for Bread.
> But that wᶜʰ made my soule to dye
> My flesh, & fleshly villany,
>   That allso made thee dead.
>   (fol. 31, p. 9)

Using the logic of a public debate on the subject, the speaker argues against transubstantiation on the grounds that Christ did not come to wipe out 'Wheat' but rather 'Sinn', and did not die to save 'Bread' but human beings. This technical method of defeating the notion of transubstantiation continues for a further two stanzas, but in the final stanza a less strident and more familiar Herbertian serenity is achieved:

> This gift of all gifts is the best,
> Thy flesh the least yᵗ I request.
>   Thou took'st that pledg from mee:

> Give me not that I had before,
> Or give me that, so I have more
>   My God, give mee all Thee.
>   (fol. 31ᵛ, p. 9)

The last line leaves debate and controversy behind, discovering a rhetoric of acceptance and inclusive adoration: 'give mee all Thee'. This is a plea for everything that Christ has to offer in this 'gift', whether bread or body, wine or blood.

Herbert's early poem 'The H. Communion' thus demonstrates the traces of Catholicism in early-seventeenth-century devotional poetry, not by an acceptance of Catholic doctrines but through the unavoidable necessity of the debate. More significantly, however, the several poems that Herbert wrote on this topic show his own shifting perspective and increasing uncertainty. Leaving behind the combative mode, Herbert replaced the early poem with a completely new lyric (sharing the same title) in *The Temple* (1633):

> Not in rich furniture, or fine aray,
>   Nor in a wedge of gold,
>   Thou, who from me wast sold,
> To me dost now thy self convey;
> For so thou shouldst without me still have been,
>   Leaving within me sinne:
>
> But by the way of nourishment and strength
>   Thou creep'st into my breast;
>   Making thy way my rest,
> And thy small quantities my length;
> Which spread their forces into every part,
>   Meeting sinnes force and art.
>   (p. 182)

Instead of enquiring and rationalizing, as in the earlier poem, the speaker here quietly but confidently addresses Christ, marvelling at the generosity of a God who will fight 'sinnes force and art' by reducing himself to 'small quantities' and creeping inside the body of his creature. The fact that the Eucharistic host cannot transfer from the route of 'nourishment' to the spiritual realm of the soul does not now trouble the speaker as it did in the earlier poem, leading then to a rejection of transubstantiation. In this later poem, the answer lies in grace:

> Yet can these not get over to my soul,
>   Leaping the wall that parts
>   Our souls and fleshly hearts;

But as th'outworks, they may controll
My rebel-flesh, and carrying thy name,
          Affright both sinne and shame.

Onely thy grace, which with these elements comes,
          Knoweth the ready way,
          And hath the privie key,
Op'ning the souls most subtile rooms;
While those to spirits refin'd, at doore attend
          Dispatches from their friend.

                              (p. 183)

In this confident and celebratory poem, every aspect of the Eucharist is seen as a bonus. Even if the bread itself is unable to leap into the soul, then it can function as a protective force to keep the 'rebel-flesh' under control. Meanwhile, it is grace that is able to enter the 'most subtile rooms' of the soul — the grace which 'with these elements comes', a teasingly elusive phrase which could be interpreted as sympathetic to either Protestant or Catholic doctrine (or both at once). If the grace comes *along with* the elements, the poem suggests that the bread and the wine are memorials or signs of redemption, firmly keeping their original nature, to which the individual recipient must respond spiritually and thereby receive grace. If, on the other hand, the grace is understood to come integrally with — that is, *within* — the elements themselves, it suggests a Catholic emphasis on the inherent efficacy of the transubstantiated bread and wine.

Herbert's two poems are strikingly different in their tone — the first pugnacious and technical, the second gentler and more subtle — but to what extent do they represent a development in doctrinal terms? Janis Lull claims that, despite their contrasting modes, 'both poems present the same line of reasoning'.[23] I would suggest, rather, that the later of the two poems hints at a move toward a more Catholic position, with its strong sense of the incarnate Christ who conveys himself to the believer in the elements of bread and wine. This increasingly Catholic tendency seems to be confirmed by the tone of some of the poems added to *The Temple* which were not in the earlier Williams manuscript, such as 'The Banquet':

Welcome sweet and sacred cheer,
          Welcome deare;
With me, in me, live and dwell:

[23] Janis Lull, *The Poem in Time: Reading George Herbert's Revisions of 'The Church'* (Newark: University of Delaware Press, 1990), p. 104.

> For thy neatnesse passeth sight,
>   Thy delight
> Passeth tongue to taste or tell.
>
> O what sweetnesse from the bowl
>   Fills my soul,
> Such as is, and makes divine!
> Is some starre (fled from the sphere)
>   Melted there,
> As we sugar melt in wine?
>   (p. 627–28)

In this Eucharistic poem the speaker is overwhelmed by the luscious 'sweetnesse' of the sacrament and praises its holiness in sensual terms. The subsequent stanzas refer not only to the senses of sight and taste but also of smell, suggesting the use of incense in the Mass with an evocation of the sweet scents imparted by 'Flowers, and gummes, and powders' (p. 628).[24] Ultimately the true sweetness is not that of bread but of the God who 'Flesh assumes, | And with it perfumes my heart' (p. 628).

Can we speak here of increasing traces of Catholicism in Herbert's work as he matured? Moving from an argumentative early poem which seeks to understand the technical workings of the sacrament, through a poem of praise addressed to Christ, to one which adores the elements of bread and wine in all their sweetness, would seem to imply a trend toward a more Catholic interpretation of the Eucharist. As we saw earlier, there is certainly no doubt that Herbert was familiar with Catholic doctrine.[25] His lyrics echo the devotional tradition of François de Sales, and his links with Nicholas Ferrar brought him into contact with the work of Catholic writers such as Juán de Valdés and Luigi Cornaro.[26] However, this impression must be countered by Herbert's own comment concerning de Valdés's work, that it was a notable sign of how 'God in the midst of Popery should open the eyes of one to understand and expresse so clearly and excellently the intent

[24] In *A Priest to the Temple*, Herbert also advises that churches should be 'perfumed with incense' during 'great festivalls' (*Works*, p. 246).

[25] See *A Priest to the Temple*, in *Works*, p. 229, quoted above, p. 14–15.

[26] For a discussion of the links between Herbert and Salesian spirituality, see Louis L. Martz *The Poetry of Meditation: A Study in English Religious Literature of the Seventeenth Century* (New Haven: Yale University Press, 1954), pp. 249–59; for de Valdés and Cornaro, see Herbert, *Works*, pp. 291–320.

of the Gospell'.[27] In addition to this negative view of 'Popery', Herbert also shows strongly Calvinist sympathies by actively aligning himself with the extreme doctrine of predestination in his poem 'The Water-course'. In this short lyric, souls are shown to be irrevocably en route for either salvation or damnation, as God 'sees fit', just as water can be divided and rerouted as it approaches its destination.[28] This is another late poem found in *The Temple* and not in the earlier Williams manuscript, thus challenging any straightforward sense of a developing Catholic sensibility in Herbert's attitudes during his lifetime. Indeed, these poems together demonstrate that Herbert, like so many other early modern writers and believers, did not have a clear-cut position on the essential (and often controversial) aspects of the Christian faith such as the Eucharist, the sensual experience of religion, and the extent to which the fate of an individual is predestined. Herbert mingled aspects of Catholic and reformed doctrine in and between his poems, just as the lyrics also reflect a range of moods and relationships with God. Indeed, we might view *The Temple* as a whole as an extended meditation on the opening question of his early poem on 'The H. Communion', applied to an understanding of true faith and devotional practice: 'how shall I know?'

Individual poets, then, were often unsure of their doctrinal positions, and open to a variety of ecclesiastical influences. Like many of his contemporaries, Donne asked for divine assistance in the perplexing business of knowing which was the true faith, as he wrote in his 'Holy Sonnet XVIII':

> Show me deare Christ, thy Spouse, so bright and clear.
> What! is it she, which on the other shore
> Goes richly painted? or which rob'd and tore
> Laments and mournes in Germany and here?
> Sleepes she a thousand, then peepes up one yeare?
> Is she selfe truth and errs? now new, now outwore?
> Doth she, and did she, and shall she evermore
> On one, on seaven, or on no hill appeare?[29]

---

[27] Herbert, *Works*, p. 304.

[28] See Herbert, *English Poems*, p. 583. The inspiration for the metaphor of the water pipes may well derive from Calvin, who writes of grace as water which 'abundantly flows out for us' down a 'pipe' from the divine fountain (*Institutes*, III.24.3).

[29] Donne, 'Holy Sonnet XVIII', in *Complete English Poems*, p. 446. Like Herbert in 'The British Church', Donne also makes use of the metaphor of the churches as females of contrasting styles.

Donne's questions are deeply troubling: if the church manifests herself in these different forms, then what is her relation to truth and tradition? The probing uncertainty of this poem is, I would suggest, typical of the way in which devotional poetry could function in this period: as a place of exploration and a site for the confession of not knowing. His metaphors also recall those used by Herbert — Donne's 'richly painted' Catholic Church on the 'seaven' hills is very similar to Herbert's 'She on the hills' with her 'painted shrines' — but the difference is that Herbert ascribes the true position to the 'British Church', who stands midway between the two extremes. In his other lyrics, however, as we have seen, Herbert's rejection of Rome and Geneva was less confident, and his doctrinal positions were complex and shifting.

If the issue of finding Christ's true 'Spouse' or fully understanding her practices in early modern England was so challenging for the poets themselves, it is no surprise that modern critics and historians also struggle to pin down the theological allegiances of the devotional poets from the period. The debate about the poets' sources and doctrinal emphases is typified by the opposed interpretations of two pioneering critics, Louis Martz and Barbara Lewalski, each of whom claimed to have found clear evidence of the ecclesiastical traditions forming the basis of English devotional poetry in the late sixteenth and early seventeenth centuries.[30] While Martz stressed the influence of the Catholic practice of meditation, Lewalski claimed a Protestant and biblical basis for the work of virtually the same group of poets. The arguments may be seen particularly intensely in critical writing on Herbert's poetry. On the one hand, *The Temple* is seen as deeply Catholic (as in Rosemond Tuve's reading of 'The Sacrifice'), but on the other it is interpreted as thoroughly Calvinist (as in Richard Strier's analysis of 'The Holdfast').[31] And if this range of opinions is to be found in responses to the poetry of George Herbert, about whose life and views we know a considerable amount, then there is sure to be even more uncertainty of interpretation when it comes to the work of poets about whose lives we know less.

The case of An Collins, author of *Divine Songs and Meditacions* (1653), is very interesting in this respect. We know nothing of the life or allegiances of Collins other than the tantalizing snippets that can be gleaned from her single volume of

---

[30] Martz, *The Poetry of Meditation*, p. 11; Barbara Kiefer Lewalski, *Protestant Poetics and the Seventeenth-Century Religious Lyric* (Princeton: Princeton University Press, 1979).

[31] Rosemund Tuve, *A Reading of George Herbert* (Chicago: University of Chicago Press, 1952), pp. 23–99; Richard Strier, *Love Known: Theology and Experience in George Herbert's Poetry* (Chicago: University of Chicago Press, 1983), pp. 65–78.

poetry. What, then, was the nature of her faith? She, too, was searching for certainty, for the answer to questions such as Herbert's 'how shall I know?' and for clarity such as requested by Donne's 'Show me deare Christ, thy Spouse'. The first poem of her collection (apart from a preface in verse) is 'The Discourse', a long, discursive examination of her experience and beliefs, in which she speaks of seeking 'carefully to understand, | The grounds of true Religion' with 'Divine Discreshion'.[32] Among her insights into these 'sacred principles' far beyond 'All civill policy or humane Art' (ll. 206–07) is the following account of the feminized soul, which perceives

> that nothing can afford
> Her either finall rest, or full content,
> But saveing Graces, and Gods holy word,
> Which is a means those Graces to augment;
> With Praier, and the blessed Sacrament:
> Which means with reverence my soul affects
> And former pleasing vanities rejects.
>
> (ll. 134–40)

What is the modern reader to make of this passage? The first three lines appear to build Collins's 'true Religion' on the cornerstones of Protestantism: grace, the word, and the dependence of the soul upon God's intervention. However, the subsequent phrases 'the blessed Sacrament' and 'with reverence' take on a much more Catholic tone. As these few lines alone indicate, Collins is very difficult to 'pigeonhole' in doctrinal and denominational terms, and the critical accounts of her work confirm this. She has been variously described as 'if not actually a Catholic, [then] devoutly anti-Calvinist'; as a moderate Calvinist; as 'a Puritan of some kind'; and as possibly a Quaker.[33] Fascinatingly, there is evidence in her poems to support each of these interpretations of her standpoint. In particular,

[32] An Collins, *Divine Songs and Meditacions*, ed. by Sidney Gottlieb (Tempe: Arizona Center for Medieval and Renaissance Studies, 1996), p. 14, ll. 204–06. Further references to Collins's other poems are taken from this edition, and indicated by page number; further quotations from 'The Discourse' are indicated by line numbers in the main text.

[33] *Kissing the Rod: An Anthology of Seventeenth-Century Women's Verse*, ed. by Germaine Greer and others (London: Virago, 1988), p. 148; *Her Own Life: Autobiographical Writings by Seventeenth-Century Englishwomen*, ed. by Elspeth Graham and others (London: Routledge, 1989); and An Collins, *Divine Songs and Meditations*, ed. by Stanley Stewart, Augustan Reprint Society Publication, 94 (Los Angeles: Clark Library, 1961); *Early Modern Women Poets: An Anthology*, ed. by Jane Stevenson and Peter Davidson (Oxford: Oxford University Press, 2001), p. 337; Sidney Gottlieb, in Collins, *Divine Songs*, p. xvii.

the traces of Catholicism in her work include frequent references to Christ's saving blood in connection with the 'blessed Sacrament' (as mentioned in the above passage) and an intensely personal application of the biblical metaphor of the 'enclosed garden' traditionally linked with the Virgin Mary.[34] It is also tempting to assume an aspect of Catholicism in Collins's emphasis on the 'trancendant ravishing delights' of holy 'merth' in 'The Discourse' (ll. 169–71), but these phrases are also directly linked with 'godlynesse' (l. 172), a term more readily associated with Puritanism. She also refers to 'Saints', not in the Catholic sense of specific holy men and women of the past who now intercede for sinners, but as the 'Elect' in the Calvinist tradition,[35] and insists that those who think that good 'works' can lead to spiritual justification are misguided and 'vainly [...] surmise' (ll. 579–80). Her use of the term 'Friends', as well as her experience of a personal inner light, makes it possible to suggest that Collins had Quaker tendencies.[36] In other words, Collins's *Divine Songs and Meditacions* give such varied signals of the nature of her devotional allegiance that modern readers cannot be sure to which Christian church or sect she belonged — nor will they ever be sure, unless further biographical discoveries are made which corroborate some of the textual hints.

The instability of modern interpretations of Collins's religious position is, in my view, not a problem but a helpful phenomenon — that is, a warning to us as to how devotional poetry actually functioned in this period. The rhetorical context offered by poetry can significantly loosen the relationship between doctrine and spirituality. As Margaret Ezell has put it, such creativity 'often will not fit neatly into theological, literary or canonical spaces'.[37]

In his *Religio Medici*, Sir Thomas Browne condemned those who 'confine the Church of God, either to particular Nations, Churches, or Families', since they have 'made it farre narrower than our Saviour ever meant it' (I.55). In a somewhat similar way I would suggest that critics are in danger of confining early modern poets too narrowly to particular churches or doctrinal positions. As we have seen, the allegiances of devotional poets in early modern England were not so clear-cut

---

[34] Song of Songs, 4.12; see Collins, *Divine Songs*, 'Another Song', p. 55.

[35] See, for example, Collins, *Divine Songs*, pp. 3, 4, 5, 27.

[36] Gottlieb, in Collins, *Divine Songs*, p. 95.

[37] Margaret Ezell, *Writing Women's Literary History* (Baltimore: Johns Hopkins University Press, 1993), pp. 132–38, neatly paraphrased by Michael Rex, 'Eyes on the Prize: The Search for Personal Space and Stability through Religious Devotion in *Eliza's Babes*', in *Discovering and (Re)Covering the Seventeenth Century English Religious Lyric*, ed. by Eugene R. Cunnar and Jeffrey Johnson (Pittsburgh: Duquesne University Press, 2001), pp. 205–30 (p. 206).

as we have tended to assume. Nevertheless, it should be borne in mind that these writers were active at a time when religious loyalty could be life-threatening, and when fulfilling the obligations of membership of a church or sect could (and did) lead to prosecution, civil unrest, and personal martyrdom. How can we reconcile these apparently contradictory perspectives? It would be wrong to resolve them by regarding poetry simply as an escape from the controversies of the age. The examples of both Herbert and Collins have demonstrated that poetry provides a space in which dilemmas can be teased out, in a rhetorical context poised between the private and the communal. All the texts being considered here were published in print or circulated in manuscript, thereby entering the 'common' sphere,[38] yet they were not public in the same way as, for example, a play performed in the theatre. Ben Jonson was called before the Privy Council and accused of popery in *Sejanus*, but not in his verse. The devotional lyric had a unique cultural position and could enable writers to enjoy a rare freedom by means of the language of personal spirituality. Louis Martz has recently commented on the 'generous ambiguities'[39] of Herbert's verse, a useful phrase which draws attention to the impulse behind devotional rhetoric, as well as the effects of this feature of his poetry. Kate Narveson has similarly pointed out how the poetic work of William Austin suggests

> that it was quite possible for a devout lay person in the 1620s to be both a typical Jacobean Protestant, with a comfortable anti-popish bias, a concern for fellowship in edification, and a Scripture-centered devotion, and to be interested in the church fabric and in patristic and later Roman Catholic writings.[40]

The place in which to bring these varied approaches together was lyric poetry. In his edition of Marvell's poems, Nigel Smith identifies at least three Catholic sources (all of them Jesuit texts) for this Protestant poet's famous lyric, 'The Garden'.[41] If we listen attentively to the 'echoing song'[42] of devotional verse, then

[38] See Targoff, *Common Prayer*.

[39] Louis L. Martz, 'Donne, Herbert, and the Worm of Controversy', in *Wrestling with God: Literature and Theology in the English Renaissance*, ed. by Mary Ellen Henley and others (Vancouver: private publication, 2001), p. 18.

[40] Kate Narveson, 'William Austin, Poet of Anglicanism', in *Discovering and (Re)Covering* (see n. 37, above), pp. 140–63 (p. 148).

[41] Andrew Marvell, *Poems*, ed. by Nigel Smith (London: Longmans, 2003), pp. 152–59. See also Nigel Smith, 'The Boomerang Theology of Andrew Marvell', *Renaissance and Reformation*, 14.4 (2001), 142.

[42] The phrase is from Marvell's 'To his Coy Mistress', l. 27.

we may learn more about the accepted presence of Catholic traits in English religious culture than we would by reading the tracts and treatises of the era.

A wide range of echoes of doctrinal allegiance may be heard in another early modern collection of devotional poetry that has recently become the focus of critical and historical interpretation: *Eliza's Babes* (1652). As with An Collins, we know nothing definite about the author of this volume of verse — in this case, not even her name — though we assume from the perspective of the text, as well as the title, that she was female. The tone of the prose pieces included in *Eliza's Babes* is resistant to Catholic influences, to which she refers as 'the contrary Religion'.[43] However, in her poetry, as Michael Rex has pointed out, she uses 'elements of Catholicism, Calvinism and Anglicanism without admitting or attempting to reconcile the differences'.[44] Among the traces of Catholicism in her verse is an attraction to the cult of the Virgin Mary. The full title of the volume is *Eliza's Babes: Or The Virgins-Offering*, and in a poem which is itself called 'The Virgins Offring' Eliza sets herself alongside the Virgin Mary as she worships her 'King'. Unlike the adherents of the 'contrary' tradition, who would perhaps prefer to worship with the assistance of the Blessed Virgin, Eliza sees herself as in parallel with the Virgin — but this feminine identification itself sets her in the Catholic tradition:

> With thee, blest Virgin, I would bring
> An Offering, to please my King.
> Two Turtle Doves, thou didst present,
> Can there be better by me sent.
> A Lambe more pure, then they could be,
> I heard was thither brought by thee.
> These two small Turtles now of mine,
> To him, I do present with thine.
> The Lambe will serve for thee and mee,
> No better offering, can there be.
> Thus with thee, Virgin doe I bring
> An offering will please my King.
>
> (p. 62)

---

[43] 'The Support', in *Eliza's Babes: Or The Virgins-Offering (1652): A Critical Edition*, ed. by L. E. Semler (Madison: Fairleigh Dickinson University Press, 2001), p. 115. All further references are taken from this edition and indicated by page number in the main text.

[44] Rex, 'Eyes on the Prize', p. 206.

The Virgin Mary brought two doves to the temple (as required after childbirth according to Jewish tradition, recounted in Luke 2. 22–24) along with the young Christ himself, referred to symbolically by Eliza as the sacrificial 'Lambe' who will now 'serve for' them both, by means of his act of redemption on the Cross. Eliza deliberately likens herself to Mary, since the poet, too, is a virgin and a mother, having just given birth to the 'babes', her poems; therefore she also offers 'two small Turtles' (doves) to her 'King' in this lyric, in thanksgiving for the childbirth that is her poetic creativity. Though the approach of Eliza is quite different from mainstream Catholic responses to the Virgin,[45] she has inherited and appropriated a Catholic inheritance in the chosen vocabulary and the attitudes expressed in this poem.

As we read on through *Eliza's Babes*, it becomes evident that the poet wishes her likeness to the Virgin Mary to be more than merely symbolic. Many of her poems express a desire for earthly celibacy, in order to remain free to be betrothed to God. Indeed, what Eliza seeks is something akin to the life of a Catholic nun, devoted to the service of a heavenly Lord. However, this was not an option for a Protestant woman in the mid-seventeenth century, and several of the lyrics negotiate her feelings of disappointment at her apparent abandonment by Christ, her 'lover', whose place has been taken by her prospective earthly husband.[46] In her short poem 'The Life', Eliza celebrates the continuation of her relationship with God in an alternative, spiritual mode of living:

> If as men say, we live not, where we are,
>   But where we love,
>   I live above.
> For what on earth, or yet in heaven is there,
>   Desir'd can be,
>   'Tis none but thee.
> Great God, thou onely worth desiring art,
> And none but thee, then must possess my heart.
>   (pp. 67–68)

In the vision of the virgin-mother-poet, God is the only worthy object of desire and thus the only proper 'Lord' who can take possession of her heart. The function of the devotional poem, set free from denominational constraints, is to construct a cloister of the heart in the work of a Protestant poet.

[45] See *Eliza's Babes*, p. 142.
[46] See 'The Lover', p. 77, and 'The Gift', p. 92.

The rhetorical space of devotional poetry may thus serve many functions in a time of intense doctrinal disputes: it allows for questioning and searching, negotiation and celebration, commitment and fulfilment. Finally, with its formal patterns and linguistic structures, it can also offer a frame in which to experience ritual. This key feature of Catholic liturgical tradition, also reflected in the surviving Anglican calendar of festivals but outlawed in mid-seventeenth-century Puritan England,[47] was commemorated by Robert Herrick in his poem 'Ceremonies for Candlemasse Eve', published in *Hesperides* in 1648:

> Down with the Rosemary and Bayes,
>> Down with the Misleto;
> In stead of Holly, now up-raise
>> The greener Box (for show.)
>
> The Holly hitherto did sway;
>> Let Box now domineere;
> Untill the dancing Easter-day,
>> Or Easters Eve appeare.
>
> Then youthfull Box which now hath grace,
>> Your houses to renew;
> Grown old, surrender must his place,
>> Unto the crisped Yew.
>
> When Yew is out, then Birch comes in,
>> And many Flowers beside;
> Both of a fresh, and fragrant kinne
>> To honour Whitsontide.
>
> Green Rushes then, and sweetest Bents,
>> With cooler Oken boughs;
> Come in for comely ornaments,
>> To re-adorn the house.
> Thus times do shift; each thing his turne do's hold;
> *New things succeed, as former things grow old.*[48]

The poem proclaims the importance of ritual, not only in its title — 'Ceremonies' — but also in its very nature: the structure of repeated rhetorical sequences and interlocking stanzas, the reassuring framework of metre and rhyme, and the basic

---

[47] See Leah S. Marcus, *The Politics of Mirth: Jonson, Herrick, Milton, Marvell, and the Defense of Old Holiday Pastimes* (Chicago: Chicago University Press, 1986).

[48] Robert Herrick, *Poetical Works*, ed. by L. C. Martin (Oxford: Clarendon Press, 1956), p. 285.

pattern of the cycle of seasons and festivals. The parallels between this pastoral lyric and the liturgy that it implicitly celebrates are surely not coincidental.

What are the sources of this poem? As in the work of Herbert, Browne, Donne, Collins, Marvell, 'Eliza', and many more early modern writers, a number of traditions converge: in Herrick's case, these include classical, Catholic, and Laudian Church of England. Taking its starting point from the tradition of pagan rituals (whose laurels seem to lie behind all Herrick's greenery), the poem surveys the liturgical year from Christmas, past Candlemas (the day celebrated in Eliza's 'Virgins Offring'), and beyond Easter to the late-spring festival of Whitsuntide with its 'fresh and fragrant' adornments of the house. It is hard to separate the old Catholic calendar here from the post-Reformation version tactically revived as an act of resistance to Puritan restrictions; but that overlap, too, is part of the blurring of layers of church practice to be discerned in the seventeenth century and honoured in devotional poems such as this. There is no retreating here — this poem's celebration is defiance — and the nostalgia for the pre-Reformation structure of the year has a constructive and forward-looking effect in the end. The final couplet is a reminder of the cycles of change that have structured the past and, by implication, will give shape to the future, too: 'each thing his turne do's hold'. This is a spiritual as well as political observation, and Herrick's apparently secular poem about the decoration of a house deserves to be considered as a spiritual work. Achsah Guibbory has argued convincingly that we must 'enlarge the limits' of the early modern devotional lyric by admitting Herrick, who himself regarded his whole poetic oeuvre as religious, a 'Temple' in the tradition of Herbert's poems.[49] Herrick's 'Ceremonies' enriches the genre, with its sense of poetry itself a site of ritual. Among the 'new things' that his closing line promises, we might suggest, is a devotional mode which has found the means to explore Catholic traditions in a Protestant world. Other examples of such transformations and absorptions of a Catholic poetic inheritance during the period would include the adaptation of Continental emblem books by English Protestant poets and publishers, and the adoption of the literature of tears by non-Catholic poets.[50] If,

---

[49] Achsah Guibbory, 'Enlarging the Limits of the "Religious Lyric": The Case of Robert Herrick's Hesperides', in *New Perspectives on the Seventeenth-Century English Religious Lyric*, ed. by John R. Roberts (Columbia: University of Missouri Press, 1994), pp. 28–45, and Guibbory, *Ceremony and Community*, pp. 79–118.

[50] See Bart Westerweel, '"The Sweet Cement ... is Love": George Herbert and the Emblem Books', in *George Herbert: Sacred and Profane*, ed. by Helen Wilcox and Richard Todd (Amsterdam: Free University Press, 1995), pp. 155–71, and Alison Shell, 'Catholic Poets and the Protestant Canon', in her *Catholicism*, pp. 56–104.

in the terms of Herbert's 'British Church', these are all cases of the poets' looking up from their position near or in the 'valley' of Protestantism and adapting what 'She on the hills' had to offer, then perhaps the resulting cultural topography was a comfortable plateau between the two, with a wide-ranging view over the religious landscape.

We have seen that early modern spiritual poetry is not a retreat from doctrinal issues but a rhetorical negotiation of them. For a concluding instance of this vital function of early modern devotional verse, let us return to George Herbert, whose lyrics do not hide his longings and uncertainties but give voice to them in controlled aesthetic form. In 'To all Angels and Saints' we see George Herbert confronting his fear, as a Protestant, of praying to the saints or the Virgin Mary:

> Oh glorious spirits, who after all your bands
> See the smooth face of God, without a frown
>   Or strict commands;
> Where ev'ry one is king, and hath his crown,
> If not upon his head, yet in his hands:
>
> Not out of envie or maliciousnesse
> Do I forbear to crave your speciall aid:
>   I would addresse
> My vows to thee most gladly, blessed Maid,
> And Mother of my God, in my distresse.
>
> Thou art the holy mine, whence came the gold,
> The great restorative for all decay
>   In young and old;
> Thou art the cabinet where the jewell lay:
> Chiefly to thee would I my soul unfold:
>
> But now (alas!) I dare not; for our King,
> Whom we do all joyntly adore and praise,
>   Bids no such thing:
> And where his pleasure no injunction layes,
> ('Tis your own case) ye never move a wing.
>
>   (p. 281)

With rhetorical poise worthy of the former public orator of Cambridge University, Herbert declares that it is no longer deemed proper to 'addresse' the Virgin Mary and other saints, even as he proceeds to do precisely that in this prayerful and affectionate lyric. The 'glorious spirits' are the intended first audience, to whom the speaker apologetically explains that he is unable to invoke their 'speciall

aid'. He goes on to express unqualified praise for Mary as the 'cabinet' which once
enclosed the 'jewell' of the incarnate Christ, but in the fourth stanza the antici-
pated 'But' announces the counter-argument: it is Christ who should receive
all our adoration. The post-Reformation world is 'now', and the speaker's 'alas!'
declares his regret at the loss of that Catholic freedom to 'unfold' his soul to Mary.
However, the rebellious moment is brief, giving way to a sense of the higher duty
of praising God 'joyntly' with the angels and saints. Old devotional pleasures and
new spiritual priorities can co-exist in this poem.

The inevitable interconnection of politics and spirituality in the early modern
period is also evident in 'To all Angels and Saints', particularly in the use of the
phrase 'our King' in the fourth stanza.[51] Which King is this who insists that Christ
is the only intercessor and forbids the believer to 'crave' the help of the saints? On
the one hand it is God who decrees it — 'no man cometh unto the Father, but by
me', says Christ in John 14. 6. On the other hand, the king is the earthly monarch,
supreme head of the Church of England, the statutes of which specifically declare
that the 'Romish doctrine' of the 'invocation of saints' is 'a fond thing vainly
invented, and grounded upon no warranty of Scripture'.[52] Herbert's poem, far
from evading controversy, incorporates it in this double language of heavenly
and earthly authority: is it God who controls the doctrine of the saints, or the
English monarchs who have taken power over doctrinal issues that were formerly
the 'prerogative' of the Church? The remaining two stanzas deftly explore this
dilemma, not only in relationship to Christ and the saints but also in the tensions
between sacred and secular authorities:

> All worship is prerogative, and a flower
> Of his rich crown, from whom lyes no appeal
> At the last houre:
> Therefore we dare not from his garland steal,
> To make a posie for inferiour power.
>
> Although then others court you, if ye know
> What's done on earth, we shall not fare the worse,

[51] In the version of this poem in the earlier Williams manuscript, Herbert used the phrase 'my
King' instead of 'our King'. The 'my' in the early draft implies a more private and spiritual bond,
less politically overt than the later 'our'; the revised version, on the other hand, could also be seen
as doctrinally bolder in linking the speaker with the angels and saints who all worship the same
('our') God.

[52] Thirty-Nine Articles of the Church of England (1562ff.), article xxii.

> Who do not so;
> Since we are ever ready to disburse,
> If any one our Masters hand can show.
> (p. 281–82)

The reference to 'inferiour power' is typically double-edged: it could describe the saints in relation to their superior, Christ, but it could also set the worldly monarch in his place under the infinitely greater power of God. The final stanza makes clear that religious practice may vary — some 'court' the saints in prayer, and others like this speaker 'do not so' — but God is the ultimate figure of toleration: whichever practice is our tradition, 'we shall not fare the worse'. After this striking affirmation of God's open-mindedness, the equally unexpected last lines remind us of how temporary all doctrinal positions must always be: the speaker is ready to resume the practice of invocation to the saints, if it can be shown that Christ authorized it with his 'hand'.[53] The decisive move here is not that of an earthly king but of Christ, the 'Master' whose touch and revelation will make all things new.[54]

Achsah Guibbory has rightly commented that Herbert's poetry does not transcend doctrinal differences and polemical conflicts but 'inscribes' them.[55] This poem, I would suggest, is a fine example of the wit and imagination that might be called a rhetoric of engagement: the poem engages with Catholicism and ecclesiastical politics by means of the practice of devotion itself. The difficulties of religious allegiance in post-Reformation England are not evaded but inscribed in Herbert's rhetoric; devotional verse at its most creative can allow Catholic sympathies space and constraint simultaneously. Joseph Beaumont wrote in his lyric 'Loves Mysterie' that divine love is a 'secret open thing',[56] which is a fine phrase for the phenomenon that I am attempting to evoke here: pre-Reformation Catholic doctrine is both 'secret' and 'open', rhetorically embedded yet not evaded in these post-Reformation Protestant poems. I suggest that, just as these early modern poets could not limit their faith neatly within the bounds of either

[53] The last line suggests not only a permit or authorizing signature, but also a hand of cards, symbolic of Christ's power and intentions yet to be revealed.

[54] See Revelation 21. 5: 'Behold, I make all things new'. Herbert's lyric 'The Odour' makes clear that the title 'My Master' belongs to Christ (p. 604), and the poem ends on a note of expectation, awaiting a clarifying of the doctrine in relation to saints.

[55] Guibbory, *Ceremony and Community*, p. 78.

[56] Joseph Beaumont, 'Loves Mysterie', in *The Minor Poems of Joseph Beaumont, D.D.*, ed. by Eloise Robinson (London: Constable, 1914), p. 11.

sacramental, feminized, and material Catholicism or biblical, predestined, and textual Protestantism, so neither should we modern readers fall into the trap of unnecessarily constraining the poets by the imposition of restrictive denominational labels of our own. To do so is to misconstrue the aesthetic impact, as well as the devotional function, of early modern religious verse.

As a much more recent poet, R. S. Thomas, has put it,

> History showed us
> He was too big to be nailed to the wall
> Of a stone chapel, yet still we crammed him
> Between the boards of a black book.[57]

In Thomas' Protestant Wales, the idea of the sacrificial Christ 'nailed' to a crucifix has been rejected, but the poet recognizes how the 'black book' of Protestantism, with its emphasis on word and judgement, can also stultify the faith. The seventeenth-century devotional poets steered their own course between these and other dichotomies of Christian belief, with a great deal more creative and spiritual freedom than we have perhaps acknowledged hitherto. We modern readers might also learn to resist a temptation to which R. S. Thomas's metaphors alert us — the danger of nailing down or limiting our understanding of the faith and poetry of early modern England.

[57] R. S. Thomas, 'A Welsh Testament', in *Collected Poems, 1945–1990* (London: Dent, 1993), p. 117, ll. 16–19.

WAS DONNE REALLY AN APOSTATE?

Richard Todd

T he idea that John Donne was an apostate was spectacularly revived with the publication in 1982 of John Carey's *John Donne: Life, Mind and Art.* This book appears to enjoy a poor reputation among American scholars of the early modern period, and repeated visits to the annual conference of the John Donne Society have reminded me of this fact. One guest speaker at the Donne Conference, none less than Heather Dubrow, made it clear in an answer to a question I put that she found Carey's idea of apostasy hard to come to terms with, and that this was the main reason she disliked the book. Robert Young, however, who doubles as both a distinguished seventeenth-century scholar and a Catholic apologist, recalls how in the second of these incarnations he found himself in conversation with the late G. E. M. Anscombe. Not, apparently, having grasped the finer implications of her being a 'staunch' co-religionist as well as an Englishwoman, Young had happened to mention that he and Thomas Hester had just founded a new scholarly journal, the *John Donne Journal*, at North Carolina State University. Anscombe's reply was, apparently, to 'fix [Young] with a steely gaze: "Henry Donne, his brother, was a martyr, but John Donne was an *apostate*! We don't like him very much at all."'[1]

The Catholic Church holds that there are three kinds of apostasy. We should be clear that these are tight definitions excluding the wider concepts of disobedience or heresy. It is fair to say that consensually the Catholic Church recognizes: firstly, apostasy *a fide*, or *perfidiae* ('complete and voluntary abandonment of the Christian religion' as the *Catholic Encyclopedia* puts it);[2] secondly, apostasy *ab ordine* (abandonment of the clerical state by those who have received major

---

[1] R. V. Young, 'John Donne, Richard Crashaw, and the Mystery of God's Grace', <www.catholic.net/rcc/Periodicals/Dossier/2002-04/article.html> [accessed 8 September 2005].

[2] *Catholic Encylopedia*, 'apostasy' <http://www.newadvent.org/cathen/01624b.htm> [accessed 20 August 2008].

orders); and thirdly, apostasy *a religione*, or *monachatus* (in the case of 'the cul-
pable departure of a religious from his monastery with the intention of not
returning to it and of withdrawing himself from the obligations of the religious
life' [for 'his' etc., read also 'her']). Clearly the last two definitions do not apply
here, although all posit some major act of defection, and so we are obliged to
consider just the first, 'complete and voluntary abandonment of the Christian
religion'.

Before going further, we should be clear that this first definition, complete and
voluntary abandonment of the Christian religion, is not a child of the ecumenical
or at least reforming spirit of Vatican II (1962–65). All three definitions I have
mentioned were set down finally by Benedict XIV in the mid-eighteenth century,
and I think it would be fair to say that they represent the spirit of Tridentine
doctrine as it would have been understood in the age of Donne. So what intrigues
me about the whole question about Donne and apostasy is not a crude black-and-
white argument that would have Carey (and indeed Anscombe) throwing the
term apostasy clumsily around. Nor do I have much sympathy for the equally
crude if well-meant efforts of those who would seek to shelter Donne under the
umbrella of a Protestant poetics without admitting the phenomenal debt Donne
the preacher (like virtually all his Protestant contemporaries, from Richard
Hooker to George Herbert) owed to the Church Fathers and pre-Reformation
thinking in general.[3]

What interests me more is, firstly: why should the fact that Donne left the
Catholic Church of his ancestors for the fledgling English Church arouse such
evident passion now, in an ecumenical and (in terms of the inner workings of the
Christian Church) relatively irenic age? Secondly, I will suggest that this question
has to do with a conception of Englishness, or Britishness, that arose, and was
deliberately promoted, during the century after Donne's death, a conception that
has made it extremely difficult for sixteenth- and seventeenth-century scholars to
look back at the period as the period saw itself. What follows will *not* be another
neo-historicist reading of Donne's work — or at least, it is not meant to be — but
it *will* involve us in the effort to understand what we are doing when we
historicize what we do, in keeping with the subject of this volume.

Why did Carey, and he is clearly not alone in doing so, use the word *apostate*
as late as the late twentieth century? When Pius V excommunicated Elizabeth I
in 1570, his bull *Regnans in excelsis* clearly termed her, in what is actually a
formulaic expression, 'a heretic and favourer of heretics'. The term *heretic*, as

---

[3] It is evident that I refer here to the Lewalski and Strier school of Protestant poetics.

used by Aquinas, is, one might argue, a milder one than *apostate* — although it is much more commonly used nowadays and its sense has been widened away from matters of religious belief to mean simply 'very wicked' or even 'depraved'. But for Aquinas, a 'heretic' was one who (in the words of the *Catholic Encyclopedia*)[4] practises 'a species of infidelity in men who, having professed the faith of Christ, corrupt its dogmas': in other words, this is precisely not a complete and deliberate abandonment of Christianity altogether. Indeed, the Catholic Church teaches that the difference between the apostate and the heretic is that the former rejects all forms of Christianity in their entirety, whereas the heretic merely denies one or more tenets of revealed religion. It is as though the term *heretic* by its very overuse has become no longer sufficiently specific; so that although Aquinas's definition is much closer to what Carey means (the abandonment of the Catholic faith of his ancestors), it is as though Carey needed a more unusual word, a more intense and arresting one, to make his case. Yet in choosing 'apostasy' Carey denies Donne's eclectic approach to matters of theology as to so much else. Donne is just as capable of 'negative capability' as is Shakespeare. It is this that enables him not just to write the poetry he does but, as Jeanne Shami, focusing on the Sermons, has recently put it, to preach in such a way as to 'present him[self] as an ethical model of integrity and a force of cohesion in a fractured institution'.[5] We need, Shami argues, to be aware of heterodoxy not just across the boundary between the Catholic and the English churches, but within the English Church itself; and we need also to be aware that this heterodoxy is *both theological and political*. It is true that every Englishman (the word is deliberately gendered) who wished to stay within the Elizabethan and (in due course) Jacobean establishment was obliged to accept the authority of the English Church as enshrined in the Elizabethan settlement. There were those — Shakespeare may have been among them — who kept their Catholic faith but outwardly conformed: these have been termed *Church Papists*.[6] The term refers to the obligation to attend church once a week.

So what is Carey's case? A hint can be gained in Anscombe's remark that Henry Donne was a martyr. In fact Henry Donne was relatively fortunate in dying of

[4] *Catholic Encyclopedia*, 'heretic' <http://www.newadvent.org/cathen/07256b.htm> [accessed 20 August 2008].

[5] Jeanne Shami, *John Donne and Conformity in Crisis in the Late Jacobean Pulpit* (Cambridge: Brewer, 2003), p. 274.

[6] Alexandra Walsham, *Church Papists: Catholicism, Conformity, and Confessional Polemics in Early Modern England* (Woodbridge: Boydell & Brewer, 1993).

disease in a squalid prison cell on a charge of harbouring a Catholic priest. Had this not happened, he would certainly have died much more painfully and unpleasantly, whether or not the charge was true in fact. He might have recanted on the scaffold but he didn't get the chance. We can even argue that the term *martyr* is inappropriate — Henry Donne died as it were by (perhaps providential) accident and not as a result of deliberate choice. The Protestant martyrdoms chronicled by John Foxe, however unhistorical some of them were, are sufficient to remind us that sixteenth-century martyrdom was no light matter, and they make a point of the victims' composure at the stake or scaffold. In Foxe's world martyrdom could mean excruciating physical pain, mutilation, and degradation: in the next, having schooled oneself for it (as many English Jesuits did) could mean the difference between heaven (whether or not reached by means of purgatory) and hell.[7] Let us not dare to patronize our predecessors.

Donne was indirectly descended, through his mother's family, from Sir Thomas More, known to us now (but not then) as one of England's, and indeed London's, two post-Conquest saints. More was canonized four hundred years after his death, in 1935. Various members of Donne's mother's family, the Heywoods, were priests and exiles. There is, then, a rich tradition of suffering and dying for one's principles in Donne's background. This is all well known. Carey even asks, rather as Stephen Greenblatt has more recently asked, how much the unwilled or unexpected death of a father can spark off profound thoughts about what happens when we die, although we know little about Donne's father.[8] Donne, 'a great frequenter of plays', could very well have seen a performance of *Hamlet* or a lost predecessor and been struck by the appearance of the ghost of Hamlet's father in the opening scenes of the play, along with the vivid portrayal of purgatory that Hamlet senior gives his son.

Donne did not, in fact, throw out every piece of Catholic dogma when he took Holy Orders in the English Church: on the contrary. There is ample evidence of the retention of his Catholic learning both in the *Sermons* and in relatively late poems (late, that is, on the evidence of existing in few manuscript versions) such as 'The Litany', one of Donne's least read poems — perhaps because

---

[7] In interviews, the British poet Geoffrey Hill (1932) has declared himself both fascinated and chilled by this schooling for martyrdom, and has paid tribute to the Jesuit martyr Robert Southwell (1561–95) in his sonnet sequence 'Lachrymae', in the collection *Tenebrae* (London: André Deutsch, 1978).

[8] Stephen Greenblatt, *Will in the World: How Shakespeare Became Shakespeare* (New York: Norton, 2004).

of its daunting length at over 250 lines. Written, in all likelihood, about a decade after Donne's apostasy, or as I shall now term it, act of heresy, 'The Litany' does not shrink (as both Annabel Patterson and Dayton Haskin have recently shown) from mentioning the Patriarchs, the Martyrs and the Virgin Mary in elevated terms that no child of the Reformation would have intellectual access to.[9] Louis Martz, whom I shall mention again shortly, found an Ignatian pattern of meditative exercise structuring the *Holy Sonnets*, although the Donne Variorum's 2005 presentation of three distinct sequences ('Devine Meditations': 12 sonnets; the 'Westmoreland': 19 sonnets; and a 'Revised Sequence': 12 sonnets) obliges us to nuance this argument.[10]

What Carey seems to be arguing is that Donne's achievement can to a large extent be accounted for in terms of a tremendous struggle, between on the one hand a huge debt of guilt in abandoning a faith for which his ancestors had died (and let us not forget that his mother, still a Catholic, would only predecease him by a few weeks, as a constant reminder of that faith, in his own residence) and on the other an absolutely unflinching realization that if he were to achieve anything at all in the kind of public life he envisaged, he would have to change with the times even if this meant fawning and abasement toward better-placed patrons. Carey is remarkably unjudging about all this. He draws attention to Donne's repeated fantasies of power and subjection, the relative disregard for his constantly pregnant wife (she is nowhere physically described — nor, indeed, are the mistresses addressed in his poems), and his apparent coolness in the face of the deaths of his children. But, we may ask, do these attitudes, or some of them at least, translated into traits of personality, not derive from *Realpolitik* rather than apostasy, or even heresy?

It follows, I shall now argue, that we need to distinguish between 'heresy' in the sense of treachery to one's church, and treachery to one's nation, a dilemma into which Pius V's bull *Regnans in excelsis* thrust every English Catholic in 1570. Apart from Henry VIII, no head of state other than Elizabeth had attempted to reverse the Catholic status quo in usurping the pope's place as supreme head. It is worth pausing to reflect on an observation made in a conference paper some years ago by the bibliographer John R. Roberts, who noted that Donne is one of

[9] See Annabel Patterson, 'A Man Is to Himself a Dioclesian: Donne's Rectified Litany', *John Donne Journal*, 21 (2002), 35–49, and Dayton Haskin, 'Is There a Future for Donne's "Litany"?', *John Donne Journal*, 21 (2002), 51–78.

[10] *The Variorum Edition of the Poetry of John Donne*: VII, pt 1, *The Holy Sonnets*, ed. by Gary Stringer (Bloomington: Indiana University Press, 2005).

those writers, scholarship on whom often tells us more about the position and even identity of the scholar than about that of Donne.

From here it is not a large step to the overstatement that American commentary presupposes a kind of secular *dissenting* Protestantism, whereas British (and specifically English) commentary presupposes a secular *established* Anglicanism. The difference is that the former, because deriving from a revolution that led to a republic, enshrines a constitutional view of the sanctity of the state, whereas the latter does not. One might offer Hywel Williams's insight, in an intervention into the *Guardian*'s ongoing debate on the British monarchy, that after 1701, England was

> [s]anctified by time's passage and Anglicanism's power, [and] ossified as a network of associations, of clubs and regiments, of schools and colleges, of JPs, high sheriffs and lord lieutenants, of Jane Austen-ish county society. It remains a place where loyalties are local and particular and are owed to the dynastic power which originally underwrote these loyalties. The state, that progressivist dissolver of prejudice, has had no English home.[11]

This is another critique of Whiggish interpretations of history, which are generally understood to be both teleological or essentialist, and optimistic, in nature. A typical expression might go like this: because England or Britain (it is ideologically helpful to blur the distinction) experienced no major revolution in 1776, or 1789, or 1830, or 1848, England, or Britain, was somehow predestined to produce a leader of Churchill's stature at Europe's moment of deepest crisis. Furthermore, Macaulay, who is generally credited with 'codifying' Whiggish historiography, saw the 1832 Reform Act above all as its justification. Iris Murdoch once wrote of the 'phenomenal luck of the English-speaking peoples' but seems to have been thinking more of Britain and the Commonwealth than of the United States.[12] We may cite the view that Helen Gardner, for instance, re-created Donne as a twentieth-century Anglo-Catholic inheritor of the tradition of the nineteenth-century Oxford Movement, because that is what she herself was. Carey notes Gardner's tendency to claim as 'dubia' works that did not suit this conception of Donne.

I want to nuance this view slightly. By the end of the seventeenth century, as everyone knows, the likelihood of the Stuart lineage dying out in its Protestant form was so strong that the English Parliament was conveniently ignoring primogeniture and looking to the Hanoverian, Protestant, descendants of James's

---

[11] Hywel Williams, 'Nursery Nation', *The Guardian*, 16 December 2000.

[12] I am unfortunately unable to trace this quotation, but it is engraved on my mind.

daughter Elizabeth to 'save' the British monarchy. It is not always appreciated how chilling the wording of the 1701 Act of Settlement actually is. It is addressed to William III of Orange, whose wife Mary II Stuart, joint head of state, had died in 1695, and reminds us of legislation enacted in the first year of his reign:

> [I]t was thereby further enacted, that all and every person and persons that then were, or afterwards should be reconciled to, or shall hold communion with the see or Church of Rome, or should profess the popish religion, or marry a papist, should be excluded, and are by that Act made for ever incapable to inherit, possess, or enjoy the Crown and government of this realm, and Ireland, and the dominions thereunto belonging, or any part of the same, or to have, use, or exercise any regal power, authority, or jurisdiction within the same: and in all and every such case and cases the people of these realms shall be and are thereby absolved of their allegiance: and that the said Crown and government shall from time to time descend to and be enjoyed by such person or persons, being Protestants, as should have inherited and enjoyed the same, in case the said person or persons, so reconciled, holding communion, professing or marrying, as aforesaid, were naturally dead.[13]

Legitimating the position of the Hanoverian monarchs involved a 'sleight of thought' whereby 'heresy' became confused with 'foreignness' or even 'otherness'. The anti-Spanish and anti-French postures of the English were justified, sometimes retrospectively: even the anti-Scottish (anti-Jacobite) position taken (when taken) in the eighteenth century is a politico-religious one. Defining 'otherness' helps one to define oneself. The first Hanoverian to visit Scotland was George IV in 1822, over a century after the 1707 Act of Union. By the time the 1673 Test Act had been repealed in 1828 the damage had been done. To this day the 1701 Act of Settlement holds in the United Kingdom. (This, incidentally, is what makes it impossible for Sinn Féin MPs to take their seats in the Westminster Parliament, since they are obliged to swear an oath of loyalty to the queen. This, as Catholics and Republicans, they cannot do.) Although under the United States Constitution and its First Amendment the 1701 Act would be illegal, it is nonetheless the case that the first Catholic to be elected US president was John F. Kennedy as late as 1960, and 2004, close though it came to doing so, failed to echo that precedent.

The queens consort of James VI & I, and Charles I were Catholics. Admittedly Anne of Denmark converted from Lutheranism. In 1623 Charles I's original Spanish match failed to go through because it required his conversion: yet when he did marry — to the French Princess Isabella — it was to a Catholic. As was Charles II's wife, Catherine of Braganza. It is only because that union was

---

[13] 'The Act of Settlement', <www.guardian.co.uk/monarchy/story/0,2763,407239,00.html> [accessed 6 July 2006].

childless that Charles II's brother James VII & II acceded to the throne in the first place. Because James's first wife Anne Hyde, and thus his surviving daughters Mary and Anne, were Protestants, there was always a Protestant 'safety net' under the succession after James VII & II. It was the birth of a male heir, favoured by the terms of primogeniture, to James's second, Catholic, wife, Mary of Modena, that precipitated James's flight and exile. But these daughters failed to produce viable progeny (the case of Mary Stuart and William of Orange is a genealogical night-mare that lifted inbreeding into an art form not seen on the English throne since before 1485; amazingly they managed to have three children, all of whom died at birth without being named). The fix that we term the Hanoverian settlement involved the refusal to recognize the better claims, not just of James and his son James Edward, but of between forty and fifty-three other Stuart *rejetés* (solely on the grounds that they were Catholic). Better than whose claims? Than those of James VI & I's granddaughter through the distaff side, Sophia, who predeceased Anne in 1714, so that the throne eventually passed to her elderly middle-aged son George I.

This much belongs to the realm of general knowledge. But the implication — that what it meant to be British, and Protestant, meaning above all the practice of conformity to the Church of England if one were (as a man, of course) to aspire to any kind of professional career, was defined under a regime that was genetically increasingly German — was rarely considered before the appearance of Linda Colley's *Britons 1707–1837: The Forging of a Nation* (1992). To look back through an accumulation of historical baggage is not easy, but it is also all too often not attempted. As Diarmaid MacCulloch has recently argued, a case can be made for regarding the United States and Canada, in their different ways, as constructions of the Reformation.

One is therefore obliged to ask, when British and American scholars approach the late sixteenth and early seventeenth century, whether it is possible to discard what appear to be the ideological shackles of monarchism and republicanism, respectively. The ideologies in question now may have little to do with active professions of faith (although in some cases they clearly do). If we accept the revisionist position that British historiography depends for its narrative design on the development of a chance rather than providential form of Protestant Episcopal belief and practice — a consequence of which is to mythologize island status, impregnability, a dormant (Catholic or 'other') enemy 'out there', a barely developed concept of the nation as 'state' and one associated with sinister leftist forces — it is not surprising that historical figures such as Donne will be in a way demonized by those holding very different agendas. One tactic, whether or not expressed by practising Catholics, is to problematize Donne's having left the Catholic Church. If we try to view the problem with transatlantic eyes, Donne's move away from the Catholic Church is more easily seen as a matter of freedom of choice, regrettable if you are a Catholic but to be applauded if your 'default setting', if not actual background, is Protestant.

It is possible to argue that an influential study such as the late Louis Martz's *The Poetry of Meditation* could not have been written by a Briton — but it could have been written by someone (almost certainly a man) who was Irish or with an Irish background or a Briton who had been brought up by Jesuits. Martz knew that Donne was familiar with the work of Ignatius Loyola, and his book filled an important lacuna. It did not suit later critics such as Barbara Lewalski or Richard Strier — but that, I'm afraid, is their problem.

I think, in conclusion, that this volume proposes a very timely reconsideration of its subject. I also think it is vital that we abandon 'either/or' patterns of thinking, and make an attempt to understand, on its own terms, the complexity of religious thinking and practice as it has evolved between Donne's time and our own. In answer to the question embodied in my title, I think John Carey was ill-advised to think of Donne as an apostate, but from the view of the Catholic Church which he left, Donne was certainly a heretic. In an age where heterodox beliefs (of whatever kind) could mean a painful, undignified, and prolonged death, there was clearly much to fear. Today there is not, but the handicaps under which Donne laboured persisted so long (in many ways intensifying for more than a century after his death) that it is hard to detach our critical culture from them. I do think that Carey shows pretty convincingly how — and the ways in which — Donne was empowered by his heterodoxy, and I think (in conclusion) this raises interesting questions about what it would take to empower a writer with a similar mindset today.

'NO RULE OF OUR BELEEF'?
JOHN DONNE AND CANON LAW

Hugh Adlington

This essay considers John Donne's engagement in his religious prose with both pre- and post-Reformation canon law.[1] Writing in 1610, John Boys, the Dean of Canterbury, refers directly to Donne's learning in canon law, praising him for discrediting the obfuscation of post-Tridentine Catholic canonists: 'I will not meddle [...] with the distorted and idle glosses of the Canonists: he that list may burthen his memory with a shipfull of their fooleries, accuratly collected by the penner of Pseudomartyr, cap 10.'[2] Yet at the same time as deprecating the 'idle glosses' of Romanist canonists, Donne also held fast — as Divinity Reader at Lincoln's Inn (1616–21) and as Dean of St Paul's (1621–31) — to the canon law of the Jacobean Church, the *Constitutions and Canons Ecclesiastical* of 1603. The focus of this essay, therefore, is to ask on what grounds Donne distinguishes between pre- and post-Reformation canon law; and whether such distinctions might shed further light on broader questions of Donne's churchmanship, such as his attitude to ecclesiastical discipline and religious conformity.[3]

---

[1] That is, the *jus canonicum*, or sum of the laws made by the Christian church(es) in order to deal with legal matters within their competence. This must be distinguished from 'ecclesiastical law', a broader concept that also includes secular legislation and unwritten laws as well as canon law. See *The Anglican Canons 1529–1947*, ed. by Gerald Bray (Woodbridge: Boydell, 1998), p. xxi.

[2] John Boys, *An Exposition of the Dominicall Epistles and Gospels used in our English Liturgies*, in *The Workes of Iohn Boys* (London: [n. pub.], 1629), p. 277. Cited in R. C. Bald, *John Donne, A Life* (Oxford: Clarendon Press, 1970), p. 226.

[3] Jeanne Shami observes that claims for Donne's religious identity range across the theological, political, and ecclesiastical spectrum, from 'Donne of the Puritan imagination', to Donne the

In recent years the significance of canon law to Donne's thought and writing has received little attention.[4] One reason may be, as Jeremy Maule has observed, that it is simply no easy matter to hold together the whole picture of law in early modern England: including legal practice, legal theory, prerogative justice, emerging international, canon, criminal, civil, statute, and judge-made law.[5] And while scholarly interest in connections between early modern civil and common law and literature continues to grow,[6] this renewed interest has not yet extended to canon law. Yet questions of ecclesiastical discipline reach to the heart of religious divisions in Jacobean England. It is to Romanist canon law and its ad hoc nature that Donne objects when he declares: 'the Additionall things exceed the Fundamentall; the Occasionall, the Originall; the Collaterall, the Direct; And the Traditions of men, the Commandements of God.'[7]

What, then, is the canon law context in which Donne's disparaging remarks may be understood? Scriptural origins for the Christian Church's legal tradition lie in New Testament passages such as Acts 15. 20, when St Paul speaks of keeping the 'necessary things', including abstaining from blood sacrifice, things strangled,

---

'conformist Calvinist' and 'Donne the Arminian' (*John Donne and Conformity in Crisis in the Late Jacobean Pulpit* (Cambridge: Brewer, 2003), p. 19).

[4] The fullest work on the subject is a 1949 unpublished PhD thesis by Robert Louis Hickey, 'John Donne's Legal Knowledge' (Duke University), to which I am indebted. For an overview of recent scholarship on Donne's training in the related areas of common and civil law and casuistry, see H. Adlington, 'The Preacher's Plea: Juridical Influence in John Donne's Sermons, 1618–1623', *Prose Studies*, 26 (2003), 344–56, especially pp. 344–45.

[5] Jeremy Maule, 'Donne and the Words of the Law', in *John Donne's Professional Lives*, ed. by David Colclough (Cambridge: Brewer, 2003), pp. 22–23.

[6] See *Shakespeare's Legal Language: A Dictionary*, ed. by B. J. Sokol and Mary Sokol (London: Athlone, 2000); Paul Raffield, *Images and Cultures of Law in Early Modern England: Justice and Political Power, 1558–1660* (Cambridge: Cambridge University Press, 2004); *Rhetoric and Law in Early Modern Europe*, ed. by Lorna Hutson and Victoria Khan (New Haven: Yale University Press, 2001); Bradin Cormack, *A Power to Do Justice: Jurisdiction, English Literature, and the Rise of Common Law, 1509–1625* (Chicago: Chicago University Press, 2008); Gregory Kneidel, 'Coscus, Queen Elizabeth, and Law in John Donne's "Satyre II"', *Renaissance Quarterly*, 61 (2008), 92–121; Subha Mukherji, *Law and Representation in Early Modern Drama* (Cambridge: Cambridge University Press, 2006); Andrew Zurcher, *Spenser's Legal Language: Law and Poetry in Early Modern England* (Cambridge: Brewer, 2007).

[7] In an undated sermon preached at St Paul's on Psalms 90. 14. First published in *LXXX Sermons Preached by that Learned and Reverend Divine, Iohn Donne* (London: [n. pub.], 1640). See *The Sermons of John Donne*, ed. by George R. Potter and Evelyn Simpson, 10 vols (Berkeley and Los Angeles: University of California Press, 1953–62), V, 294. Subsequent references are cited as parenthetically in the text, by volume and page number.

and fornication.[8] However, canonical jurisprudence in the sense of enacted legislation did not originate until the fourth-century regional and ecumenical councils held in Asia Minor.[9] Early Latin canonical collections, such as that of Dionysius Exiguus in the sixth century, were then taken into Roman law by Christian emperors. As Donne states in *Biathanatos* (1607): 'It is evident that the primitive Church had *Codicem canonum* which was inserted into the body of the *Roman Law* [...]. From this *Codex canonum*, the Emperors determin'd and decreed in many Ecclesiastique Causes.'[10]

Following the disintegration of the Roman Empire, canon law developed independently in the different kingdoms, leading to an assortment of variant texts.[11] Consequently, at the end of the eleventh century Ivo of Chartres prepared a set of principles for the interpretation and harmonization of these texts; the actual work of harmonization, however, was completed fifty years later (*c.* 1140) by the Camaldolese monk Gratian in his *Decretum*, or *Concordance of Discordant Canons*.[12] The final landmark in the development of pre-Reformation canon law was the publication in 1503, by the legist Jean Chappuis, of the *Corpus iuris canonici*, containing Gratian's *Decretum* and three official and two private collections of papal decretals. The *Corpus*, along with the decrees of the Council of Trent (1545–63), then remained the fundamental law of the Catholic Church until the *Codex iuris canonici* appeared in 1917.

In pre-Reformation England the ecclesiastical law was an amalgam: it comprised both the papal canon law (the *Corpus iuris canonici*) and the so-called domestic canon law (made up of legatine and provincial constitutions).[13] After the break with Rome, plans were made for a complete revision of canon law but were thwarted by political disagreements during the reigns of Henry VIII and

---

[8] Also, in I Corinthians 11 St Paul refers to keeping the 'ordinances'.

[9] In many sermons Donne displays his familiarity with the proceedings of these councils. See *Sermons*, III, 91 (Nicaea); VI, 138 (Antioch); IX, 71 (Chalcedon). These enactments dealt with the structure of the church (its provincial and patriarchal organization), the dignity of the clergy, the process of reconciling sinners, and Christian life in general (see *Anglican Canons*, p. xxv).

[10] John Donne, *Biathanatos*, ed. by Ernest W. Sullivan, II (Newark: University of Delaware Press, 1984), pp. 67–68 (pt 2, dist. 2, sec. 1).

[11] Collections made at the time of Charlemagne (*c.* 800) and the Gregorian reform (*c.* 1050) reflected the attempt to restore traditional discipline.

[12] See Gratian, *Decretum Gratiani*, in *Patrologiae cursus completus [...] Series Latina*, ed. by J.-P. Migne (Paris: Garnier, 1861), vol. CLXXXVII. Gratian's *Decretum* contained all the canon law from the earliest popes and councils up to the Second Lateran Council (1139).

[13] Collected by William Lyndwood and published in 1433 as the *Constitutiones provinciales*.

Edward VI, and were only partially revived under Elizabeth.[14] Thus, by the time of James's accession in 1603 the English Church's *Code of Canons* continued to presuppose the pre-Reformation canon law, except where it had been affected by contrary statute or English custom, or was deemed to abrogate the royal prerogative, or had fallen into desuetude.[15] Key aspects of pre-Reformation canon law that had been dropped included certain titles of the papal code relating to liturgical matters,[16] contract and criminal law, matrimony, defamation, and church appointments.[17] Areas of continuity included laws of testamentary succession and the holding of pluralities, laws governing the relation between the clergy and the laity, and laws relating to such matters as ordination, confirmation, and the dedication of churches and churchyards.[18] In essence, the medieval canon law, both papal and domestic, had been modified by post-Reformation legislation in England, yet in such a manner as to preserve its continuity.[19]

Regarding Donne's education in canon law, his first knowledge of the 'Th' immense vast volumes' would have been privately acquired, as canon law study had been prohibited at Oxford University since 1535.[20] At Lincoln's Inn, by his own admission, Donne read widely outside of the prescribed common law texts, but according to Izaak Walton and R. C. Bald it was during the early years

[14] See *Tudor Church Reform: The Henrician Canons of 1535 and the Reformatio Legum Ecclesiasticarum*, ed. by Gerald Bray, Church of England Record Society, 8 (Woodbridge: Boydell, 2000), especially the introduction.

[15] Other sources included the Thirty-Nine Articles, and Matthew Parker's 'Book of Advertisements'. This caused the *Code of Canons* to be repugnant to more reform-minded Puritans. See *Anglican Canons*, pp. 258–453, and *Moore's Introduction to English Canon Law*, ed. by T. Briden and Brian Hanson, 3rd edn (London: Mowbray, 1992), pp. 4–5.

[16] Including the title of the Mass, the title of the relics, and the worship of saints. See *The Canon Law of the Church of England: Being the Report of the Archbishops' Commission on Canon Law* (London: SPCK, 1947), pp. 47–48.

[17] Richard Helmholz, 'The Canons of 1603: The Contemporary Understanding', in *English Canon Law: Essays in Honour of Bishop Eric Kemp*, ed. by Norman Doe, Mark Hill and Robert Ombres (Cardiff: University of Wales Press, 1998), pp. 22–35 (p. 32).

[18] Also, a great deal of the English ecclesiastical law in testamentary cases, and to a lesser extent in matrimonial ones, was taken from the *Corpus iuris civilis*. See *The Canon Law of the Church of England*, pp. 48–49.

[19] *The Canon Law of the Church of England*, p. 50. After 1535, no official definition was ever made of which parts of the ecclesiastical law were still in force and which parts were no longer binding. Indeed, the whole of canon law rested for its authority in England upon received usage: it was not binding *proprio vigore*.

[20] J. H. Baker, *Introduction to English Legal History*, 4th edn (London: Butterworths & Tolley, 2002), p. 170.

of married life at the Wolley estate at Pyrford that Donne devoted 'himself in the main to an intensive study of the civil and canon law'.[21] This study provided the necessary preparation for *Biathanatos*, on the evidence of which Walton declared Donne to be 'perfect in the Civil and Canon law'.[22] It was also in this period that Donne's legal expertise grew sufficiently for him to assist the Dean of Gloucester, Thomas Morton, in works of theological controversy (1606–07) against the Jesuits Robert Persons and Cardinal Bellarmine.[23]

Bald also draws attention to Donne's required understanding of the civil and canon law when acting in a judicial capacity as Dean of St Paul's. As one of his decanal duties Donne was appointed on fifteen occasions to the Court of Delegates to hear appeals from lower ecclesiastical courts, as well as being a member of the Court of High Commission.[24] In two sermons in 1627 Donne refers to his experience of such duties in the higher church courts: 'Many times I have seene a suitor that comes *in forma pauperis*, more trouble a Court, and more importune a Judge, then greater causes, or greater persons' (VII, 175); 'Thou maist have a *Commission* too; In that of the Peace, in that for Ecclesiasticall causes, thou maist have part' (VII, 443).[25]

Books relating to canon law in Donne's extant library include both the 1604 quarto edition of the English *Constitutions and Canons Ecclesiasticall* and an octavo edition of the *Codex canonum vetus ecclesiae Romanae* (Lutetiae Parisorum, 1609).[26] Also included are works by canonists such as Andreas Dudith, Joannes de Gallemart, Antonius Sylvius, and Gulielmus Durandus.[27] Evidence in Donne's

---

[21] Bald, *John Donne*, p. 141.

[22] Izaak Walton, *Life of Dr John Donne* (1640, later revised), in Izaak Walton, *The Lives of Dr John Donne, Sir Henry Wotton, Mr Richard Hooker, Mr George Herbert* (London: printed by T. Roycroft for R. Marriot, 1675), p. 8.

[23] Alison Shell has also suggested that Donne may have collaborated with Sir Edward Hoby on polemical religious works. See 'Donne and Sir Edward Hoby: Evidence for an Unrecorded Collaboration', in *John Donne's Professional Lives* (see n. 5, above), pp. 121–32.

[24] Bald, *John Donne*, pp. 414–23. See records of the Court of Delegates in the Public Record Office (PRO), London, Del. 4/9, 4/11, 4/12, 5/7, 8/70.

[25] First sermon preached at St Paul's, 21 May 1626, on I Corinthians 15. 29; second sermon preached at St. Paul's, upon Whitsunday 1627, on John 14. 26. Both first published in *LXXX Sermons*.

[26] Now in the University of Cambridge Library (Syn.7.60.26.[1]), and in private ownership respectively. See Sir Geoffrey Keynes, *A Bibliography of Dr John Donne*, 4th edn (Oxford: Clarendon Press, 1973), pp. 266–67, 279.

[27] Dudith, *Orationes in Concil. Trident. habitae* (Offenbach: Typis Conradi Nebenii, 1610), 4°; Gallemart, *Decisiones et declarationes illustrissimorum cardinalium sacri Concilii Tridentini*

writing of his reading of canon law derives from his scholarly habit of citing his sources when he quotes or paraphrases. In *Biathanatos*, Gratian's *Decretum* is the source of the majority of Donne's citations of canon law, although Donne is at pains to disparage Gratian as little more than a 'borrower', merely one of the many compilers of church canons:

> For, of Gratians Decret, that learned and ingenuous Bishop of Tarracon, hath taught us what we should thinke, when he says, That he is scarse worth so much reprehension; who having nothing that is proffitable or of use, exept [*sic*] he borrows it, is admir'd of the Ignorant and laugh'd at of the Learned.[28]

Perhaps not surprisingly, Donne held the papal decretal compilations, which appeared after Gratian in the late thirteenth and early fourteenth centuries, in even lower regard. These compilations held high authority in the *Corpus iuris canonici*. Donne refers to these papal decrees when he observes, 'I speake here of the Canon Law, to which the Canonists will stand: which are the decretall Letters, and all the extravagants.'[29] Donne is also careful to indicate, in his numerous citations of Gratian in *Biathanatos*, whether he is citing a true canon law, one of the Fathers, or one of the councils of the church.[30] Donne's caustic view of the more abstruse parts of the *Decretum* is exemplified in *Biathanatos* by his reference to the canon law concerning hunting by clergymen: 'But there is perchance some mistique interpretation, belonging to that Canon which allowes Cleargy Men to hunt. For they may do it by nets, and snares, but not by Dogges. For clamor and biting are forbidden them.'[31]

---

interpretum (Douay: Baltazis Belleri, 1615), 8°; *De Summi Pontificis auctoritate [...] grauissimorum auctorum complurium opuscula ad Apostolicæ Sedis dignitatem maiestatemque tuendam spectantia*, ed. by Remigio Nannini (Venice: [n. pub.], 1562), 4°; Sylvius, *Commentarius ad leges [...] Romani iuris antiqui* (Paris: [n. pub.], 1603),4°; and Durandus, *Rationale divinorum officiorum. Tomus primus* (Lyon: [n. pub.], 1605), 8°.

[28] *Biathanatos*, pp. 69–70 (pt 2, dist. 2, sec. 2). The 'Bishop of *Tarracon*' refers to Antonius Augustinus (1517–86), a Spanish jurist and Dominican reformer of Gratian's *Decretum*. In *Pseudo-Martyr*, Donne uses Augustinus's *De emendatione Gratiani* (Paris: P. Cheualier, 1607) to attack the Roman Catholic system of decretals.

[29] *Biathanatos*, p. 69.

[30] Specific canon laws to which Donne refers include those pertaining to bigamy, burial, and *felo de se*. For bigamy, see *Biathanatos*, p. 119, marginal ref. to Distinctio 34 lector glossa, *Decretum*, I.34.5. For burial, see *Bia.*, pp. 71–72, referring to *Decret.* II.13.2.22. For *felo de se*, see *Bia.*, p. 72, considering *Decret.* II.23.5.12; *Decret.* II.24.3.3; *Decretal Gregor.* IX.5.13; and *De Torneamentis*.c.1.2.

[31] *Biathanatos*, p. 111 (pt 3, dist. 2, sec. 1). Donne probably derived this gloss from the 1584 Lyon edition of Gratian's *Decretum*. His mockery of canon laws constraining sporting clergymen

Seventeenth-century Roman Catholic histories of canon law to which Donne refers in *Biathanatos* are the *Concilia generalia* (1606) by the German Counter-Reformation canonist Severinus Binius, and the *Annales ecclesiastici* (1588–1608) by the Oratorian Caesar Baronius. Both works record the events of Christian history, church council by council, from the earliest synods after the apostle Peter. Both also, like Bellarmine's *De controversiis Christianae fidei* (1590–93), refer themselves to Judaic history from the creation of Adam onward to explain the correctness of their procedures.[32] Thus an important aspect of post-Tridentine commentary on canon law was the attempt to authenticate ecclesiastical governance on the basis of historical continuity. Such a method, of course, was not exclusive to the Romanist side of the debate. Continuity of tradition was also a governing principle of John Jewel's linking of the sixteenth-century Church of England with its origins in the 'Primitive Church of the ancient Fathers and Apostles'.[33] Donne, in turn, deftly draws on ecclesiastical historians on both sides of the confessional debate to justify forms of English Church ceremony, such as the use of candles, the maintaining of the Sabbath, and making the sign of the cross at baptism.[34]

In *Pseudo-Martyr* (1610) Donne extends his critique of papal interference in pre-Reformation canon law, analysing how it has led to 'the deformity and corruption of the *Canons*'.[35] Decretals, breves, and bulls are distinguished and controverted, though Donne is once again careful to remind his Roman Catholic readers that his complaint is against papal innovation, not against the authentic 'body of the *Canon law*, which was called *Codex canonum*, which contained the Decrees of certaine auncient Councels'.[36] Coming to the crux of his thesis in

might have been tempered had he foreseen the accidental killing, in 1621, of a huntsman by a misdirected arrow shot by George Abbot, Archbishop of Canterbury. See Bald, *John Donne*, p. 372.

[32] See Anthony Raspa, 'Donne's *Pseudo-Martyr* and *Essayes in Divinity* as Companion Pieces', *John Donne Journal*, 18 (1999), 2–3.

[33] John Jewel, *The Apology of the Church of England* (London: printed by T. H. for Richard Chiswell, 1685), p. 139.

[34] See, respectively, *Sermons*, X, 90; IV, 316; VIII, 197–98.

[35] John Donne, *Pseudo-Martyr*, ed. by Anthony Raspa (Montreal: McGill-Queen's University Press, 1993), chap. 10.29, p. 200.

[36] Donne, *Pseudo-Martyr*, chap. 10.2–3, p. 190. See also Geoffrey Bullough, 'Donne the Man of Law', in *Just So Much Honor*, ed. by Peter A. Fiore (University Park: Pennsylvania State University Press, 1972), pp. 57–94 (p. 71).

Pseudo-Martyr, Donne claims that the papacy usurps the proper use of canon law in defending its claim to temporal jurisdiction. Close study of canon law, Donne observes, actually reveals that the popes 'have abstained [...] from giving any binding resolution, in the question, *how farre the civill lawes of Princes doe binde the subjects conscience*'.[37] This protest echoes a more general objection, made in *Biathanatos*, to the sprawling, ill-defined sphere of the authority of canon law: '[I]t is so vast, and undetermin'd, as we know not in what Bookes to seeke the Limits thereof, nor by what rules to set the Land-marks of her Jurisdiction.'[38] Such 'undetermination' notwithstanding, Donne remained vigilant in warning against the perilous consequences of the notion of papal *plenitudo potestatis*, erroneously sanctioned by canon law. Thus in a sermon preached at St Paul's in 1622 in the midst of the Bohemia-Palatinate war, Donne cites the Neapolitan bishop and doctor of canon law Alfonso Alvarez Guerrero, on the canonists' 'generall Tenent, that into what place so ever the Pope may send *Priests*, he may send *Armies* for the security of those Priests' (IV, 157).[39]

Donne's effort throughout *Pseudo-Martyr* is to undermine unquestioning Catholic assent to the canon law. First, Donne demonstrates the tension in the writings of many medieval canonists, between a theory of supreme papal authority and those specific situations that appear to restrict the exercise of that power. Second, Donne inverts the argument from papal canon law for jurisdiction over both spiritual and temporal affairs. If the legal domains of civil and canon law are deemed to overlap, Donne argues, then must not civil law also hold in ec-clesiastical affairs? In attacking the arguments for papal supremacy made by Bellarmine and others, Donne's *quid pro quo* between temporal and ecclesiastical jurisdictions also reflects a broader strand of contemporary legal thought: in 1602 the English civilian William Fulbecke noted that the civil, canon, and customary law 'should not be opposed like the two faces of Janus, but rather joined like the three graces'.[40]

---

[37] Donne, *Pseudo-Martyr*, chap. 11.3, p. 227.

[38] Donne, *Biathanatos*, p. 67 (pt II, dist. 2, sec. 1).

[39] Concerning canon law, Guerrero († 1577) was the author of *Thesaurus Christianae religionis et speculum sacrorum summorum Romanorum pontificum, imperatorum ac regum et sanctissimorum episcoporum* (Venice: Apud Cominum de Tridino, 1559).

[40] William Fulbecke, *The Second Part of the Parallele; or, Conference of the Civill Law, the Canon Law, and the Common Law of England* (London: printed by Adam Islip for Thomas Wight, 1602), preface.

Two further points drawn from the *Corpus iuris canonici* furnish Donne's argument in *Pseudo-Martyr*. First, the canon law states that the pope cannot command a man to do an impossible thing. This being so, Donne shows how the canonists extend the word *impossible* to mean anything that cannot conveniently be done, such as swearing the Oath of Allegiance.[41] Second, Donne points out that the canon law itself recognizes that iniquity in the church springs largely from the priesthood.[42] On this basis, therefore, Donne concludes that the canon law itself calls into question the moral authority of pope and priests in forbidding English Catholics from recognizing the supremacy of the king in temporal matters.[43]

In his later prose works Donne's knowledge of canon law is applied to other related questions of legal jurisdiction. In *Essays in Divinity* (1614), Donne turns his attention, via numerous references to canon law, to the question of the relation between divine and human law.[44] The topic of overlapping legal authority also serves as the focus of a number of Donne's sermons,[45] including the tangled roots of canon law and English common law in the larger *jus commune*. Evidence of this complicated legal inheritance can be found in a baptismal address preached by Donne on Ephesians 5. 25–27.[46] Showing how Pontius Pilate fails to judge Jesus according to the evidence, Donne remarks:

> A good Judge does nothing, sayes he [Pilate], *Domesticae proposito voluntatis*, according to a resolution taken at home; *Nihil meditatum domo defert*, he brings not his judgement from his *chamber* to the *bench*, but he takes it there according to the Evidence. (V, 121)

The comparable passage from Gratian's *Decretum* on the necessity for judgement by evidence reads:

---

[41] Donne, *Pseudo-Martyr*, p. 23, referring to *Decretum* (Lyon, 1584), dist. 61, chap. 17, col. 310.

[42] *Decretum*, I.50.15 and II.24.3.

[43] '[Y]et out of them, [the *Canons* of the old Councels], you can find nothing to assure your consciences, that you may incurre these dangers for refusall of the Oath' (*Pseudo-Martyr*, chap. 10.52, pp. 224–25.

[44] As well as to specific aspects of canon law such as *Purgatio Canonica*: that is, a man clearing himself of an alleged crime by swearing an oath, with other compurgators swearing to the truth of the man's oath. See *Essays in Divinity*, ed. by E. M. Simpson (Oxford: Clarendon Press, 1952), pp. 141–42. Donne also refers to *Purgatio Canonica* in five sermons: IV, 8, on John 1. 8; V, 6, on 1 John 5. 7–8; VIII, 16, on Job 4. 18; IX, 4, on Matt. 11. 6; and I, 5, on Prov. 8. 17.

[45] E.g., *Sermons*, II.15 and VI.12.

[46] Undated. First published as no. 5 in *Fifty Sermons, Preached by that Learned and Reverend Divine, John Donne* (London: J. Flesher, 1649).

Bonus judex nihil ex arbitrio suo facit et domesticae proposito voluntatis, sed juxta leges et jura pronunciat, statutis juris obtemperat, non indulget propriae voluntati, nihil paratum et meditatum domo defert.

(A good judge does nothing from his own opinion, nor by the resolution of his private wishes, but he pronounces in accordance with laws and judgements, he complies with statutory judgement, and he does not yield to his own wishes, nor does he bring with him anything prepared and thought about at home.)[47]

Sir Edward Coke, in his common law *Reports* (1600–1616), uses the same Latin phrasing: 'Iudex bonus nihil ex arbitrio suo faciat nec proposito domesticæ voluntatis sed iuxta leges & iura pronuntiet' (A good judge does nothing by his own whim, nor by the suggestion of his own will, but pronounces according to statutes and laws).[48] It seems clear, therefore, that Donne's comments pertaining to Pilate's basis for judgement, and Coke's remarks on a point of common law, both refer to the same law in Gratian. However, it is probable that Donne is quoting from Gratian rather than from Coke, as shown by his inclusion of the phrase *nihil meditatum domo refert*. This phrase is not contained in Coke. The larger point remains, however, which is the continuing significance of canon law, even after 1615, in the broader field of both secular and ecclesiastical legal thought.

Perhaps Donne's central objection to pre-Reformation canon law is its elevation of noncanonical writings to a position of equal authority with the Bible. In a sermon preached before Charles I in 1627 Donne cites the fourteenth-century canonist Baldus de Bartholinis[49] to show that

they make their decretall Epistles of their Popes and of their *Extravagants*, [...] and their occasionall *Bulls*, nay their *Bull-baitings*, their Buls fighting, and crossing and contradicting one another, equall to Canonicall Scripture. (VII, 402)

Donne argues further, in a sermon preached on Easter Day 1629,[50] that the papal canon law uses patristic sources to endorse papal authority in a retrospective manner, *a posteriori*: 'when any sentence of a Father is cited, and inserted into a Decretall Epistle of a Pope, or any part of the Canon Law, that sentence is thereby

---

[47] *Decretum*, II.3.7.4; my translation.

[48] Sir Edward Coke, *La Sept part des reports Sr. Edw. Coke* (London: printed by Adam Islip for the Societie of Stationers, 1608), pt 7, p. 27; *The Selected Writings and Speeches of Sir Edward Coke*, ed. by Steve Sheppard (Indianapolis: Liberty Fund, 2005), p. 229 n. 244.

[49] Baldus (1327–1400) was an Italian professor of law at Perugia and Bologna.

[50] Preached at St Paul's on Job 4. 18, 'Behold, he put no trust in his servants; and his angels he charged with folly'; first published in *LXXX Sermons*.

made authenticall, and canonicall' (VIII, 366). Importantly, Donne's objection is
not to the canonical status of papal decrees per se (the earliest canonical collection
in the Western Church, that of Dionysius Exiguus, included thirty-nine papal
decretals added to the canons of the Eastern councils).[51] Rather, his objection is to
the misuse of the Fathers after the fact, merely to endorse a current papal decree.

The same complaint against papal legislative expediency can be heard in an
earlier sermon preached by Donne to King Charles in 1627. Here Donne speaks
of the seemingly endless legal embroidery of Romanist canonists: they 'that first
compiled the *Decretals*, and the *Extravagants*, and they who have since recompiled
more *Decretals*, and more *Extravagants*, the *Clementins*, and the *Sextins*, and of
late yeares the *Septims*, with those of *John the* 22' (VII, 402). In exasperation,
Donne asks, how long will such decrees persist in being 'our Rule what to beleeve'?

> Till they fall out with some State, with whom they are friends yet, or grown friends with
> some State, that they are fallen out with now; and then upon a new *Decretall*, a new
> *Extravagant*, I must contract a new, or enlarge, or restrain my old beleef. (VII, 402)

Thus Donne censures the canon law for being, like all positive laws, subject to
alteration according to time and place. However, Donne's criticism is one of
degree, not of kind. For the temporal nature of ecclesiastical legislation was central
to governance of the English Church itself, exemplified in Richard Hooker's *Of
the Laws of Ecclesiastical Polity* (1594–1662). While recognizing that the natural
law is unchangeable and eternal (bk I, chap. 3), Hooker's *Lawes* also acknowledged
that the positive law of the State, including law affecting the form of church
government, is mutable, and may be altered when change is necessary or expedient
(bk I, chap. 15).[52]

The occasional, flexible nature of certain pre-Reformation canonist writings
also informs Donne's treatment in his sermons of topics of significant public
interest. In the first sermon preached to King Charles, on 3 April 1625, Donne
acknowledges widespread concern over the future direction of the church in his
choice of text, Psalms 11. 3: 'If the Foundations be destroyed, what can the
righteous doe?'[53] In his exposition, Donne attempts to allay popular hostility to

---

[51] See Rhidian Jones's introduction to his *The Canon Law of the Roman Catholic Church and
the Church of England: A Handbook* (Edinburgh: T&T Clark, 2000).

[52] Bk. I, chap. 3: 'The Law which natural agents observe, and their necessary manner of
keeping it'. Chap. 15: 'Laws positive contained in Scripture, [and] the mutability of certain of
them'. For Hooker's view of the mutability of canon law, see Helmholz, 'The Canons of 1603',
pp. 28–31.

[53] Published in quarto in 1625. See Shami, *John Donne and Conformity in Crisis*, pp. 269–70.

royal tolerance of recusant English Catholics, arguing that such religious dispensations conduce to the *'Generall good'*. To support his appeal to the *spirit* rather than to the *letter* of ecclesiastical law, Donne cites the twelfth-century canonist St Ivo of Chartres:[54]

> For, when such things as these are done, *Non astu Mentientis, sed affectu compatientis*, not upon colourable disguises, nor private respects, but truly for the *Generall good*, all these *Pardons*, and *Dispensations* conduce and concurre to the *Office*, and contract the *Nature* of the *Foundation* it selfe, which is, that the whole Bodie may bee the better supported. (VI, 254)

Also for illustrative purposes, but in a more sardonic vein, Donne cites the thirteenth-century canonist Gulielmus Durandus in a 1628 Whitehall sermon.[55] In this case, Donne's sermon came at a time when Laudian innovations in church ceremony and liberal theology were placing increasing strain on the formerly moderate Calvinist consensus of the Jacobean Church. To distract from such internal strife, Donne uses Durandus to illustrate internecine squabbles in the Roman Church over the status of church officials. He considers the heated dispute between canon lawyers — as to whether the office and function of deacons 'be so *è sacris*, a part of holy Orders, as that it is a Sacrament, or any part of the Sacrament of Orders' (VIII, 183)[56] — and thus deflects attention from divisions in the English Church. At the same time, Donne also uses his reading in canon law and commentary to support positive arguments for a Reformed posture in doctrinal, historical, or ecclesiastical matters. In a sermon preached at St Paul's on the Penitential Psalms, for instance, Donne refers to the Dominican canonist and

---

[54] Bishop of Chartres (*c.* 1040–1116), who because of his forthright critique of what he saw as the errors of the papacy was often later quoted as a patron of Gallican Liberties.

[55] Durandus (1230–96) was Bishop of Mende from 1285, and one of the chief medieval canonists. His principal works include *Rationale divinorum officiorum* (first edn by Fust and Schoeffer at Mainz, 1459), an account of the laws, ceremonies, customs, and mystical interpretation of the Roman Rite; and *Speculum iudiciale* (first edn at Strasbourg in 1473), a treatise on the canonical rights of legates and forms of canonical procedure. Donne's 1628 Whitehall sermon was preached on 29 February 1628, and was devoted to Acts 7. 60: 'And he kneeled down and cried with a loud voice, Lord, lay not this sin to their charge. And when he had said this, he fell asleep.' First published in *XXVI Sermons Preached by that Learned and Reverend Divine John Donne* (London: printed by T. N. for James Magnes, 1661).

[56] Similarly, in a 1625 sermon, Donne cites Baldus de Bartholinis to show how confused and self-contradictory the canon and civil law may be in relation to abstruse legal distinctions such as that between, *'Bonorum possessio*, and *possessio bonorum*, that one should amount to a right and propriety in the goods, and the other but to a sequestration of such goods' (VI, 234).

theologian, Cardinal Turrecremata,[57] to argue that there was no moment in the history of the church, even from its earliest inception, when there weren't reformers and opposition to the Roman Church's 'tyrannie and her Idolatry', 'men that have opposed those points that we oppose' (IX, 338).

In conclusion, the grounds on which Donne distinguishes between the canon law of Rome and the *Code of Canons* of the English Church seem clear. For what Donne rejects in the Roman canon law are papal and Tridentine interpolations, which are seen as 'problematicall' rather than dogmatical, man-made rather than divinely inspired. In controversy with the Roman Church Donne's most frequent tactic is to use canon law against itself. As Anthony Raspa puts it regarding *Pseudo-Martyr*, 'Donne writes as a canonist in order not to be a canonist.' Rather, Donne attempts to shift the basis of law out of the canonical range into the realm of the Protestant 'dictate of conscience' and its associated law of nature.[58] In this respect, Donne's antipathy toward papal canon law reflects the curiously ambiguous position occupied within Christianity itself by that law. For while Christ directs the apostles to 'bind' and to 'loose' their congregations, both Jesus and St Paul seem to take up almost anti-legal positions in the New Testament: regarding contravention of Pharisaic law about the Sabbath in Matthew 12. 1–8, and in the early church's rejection of the demand to keep Mosaic law in Acts 15. 5. Paul goes even further in Romans 7. 4–6, asserting that Christians are 'dead to the law' by the body of Christ, because in Jesus they have entered a new kind of morality predicated on the Golden Rule. Thus the angle of Donne's enquiry is not to reject ecclesiastical law in itself, but rather to rediscover from church history the authentic tradition of canon law — a tradition that provides for conciliarism, and which might be variously interpreted in cases that are *sui generis*. On a logical and philological plane, the attraction for Donne of the study of canon law, as with scriptural exegesis itself, appears to lie in the attempt to bring harmony to inherent contradiction. As has been noted, the name given to the *Decretum* in the Middle Ages was the *Concordia discordantium canonum*. This suggests at least a passing symmetry with Samuel Johnson's infamous reference to the *discordia concors* of Donne's conceited, dialectical approach, not only to the images of his poetry and prose, but also to the religious and political contradictions of his, and England's, present and past.

---

[57] Or Juan Torquemada (1388–1468), whose works include *Commentarii in Decretum Gratiani* (1519) on canon law, and *Summa de ecclesia* (1489).

[58] Donne, *Pseudo-Martyr*, p. xxxi.

In Thy Passion Slain: Donne, Herbert, and the Theology of Pain

Jan Frans van Dijkhuizen

Modern Western culture customarily conceives of pain as a purely physical phenomenon. We have become used to seeing pain as a matter of tissue damage only; a meaningless, strictly medical problem. In addition, we think of pain as something to be avoided, or at least minimized. The idea that pain can be experienced as positive, meaningful, or enlightening, and could even be actively sought rather than shunned, would strike many of us as deluded and irrational, even pathological. As historians of pain have pointed out, this clinical view of pain is to a large extent the product of nineteenth-century developments in medical science.[1] For example, the first surgical use of ether in 1846, often seen as one of the defining moments in medical history, changed not only the art of surgery but also our cultural attitudes toward pain. Before 1846, intense agony was a virtually unavoidable part of virtually all surgical procedures — from pulling teeth to limb amputation. After 1846, something like pain-free surgery seemed a feasible medical ideal. This also meant that post-1846 (medical) culture quickly forgot about the very different, frequently religious, conceptions of pain that existed before the medical breakthroughs of the nineteenth century. As a result, pain came to be isolated from other realms of experience and was stripped of the cultural meanings which it had possessed for centuries.

---

[1] See for example David B. Morris, *The Culture of Pain* (Berkeley and Los Angeles: University of California Press, 1991), pp. 60–65, and Ariel Glucklich, *Sacred Pain: Hurting the Body for the Sake of the Soul* (Oxford: Oxford University Press, 2001), pp. 179–206.

Pain and Christianity:
From the Late Middle Ages to the Reformation

The nineteenth century was not the only watershed moment in the history of pain. Indeed, nineteenth-century views on pain, in which physical suffering was no longer seen as productive, were in some ways the culmination of a process that began with the Protestant Reformation. Some of the impact of the Reformation on cultural assumptions about pain becomes clear, for example, from Mitchell Merback's fascinating study *The Thief, the Cross and the Wheel.*[2] Merback's book opens with an analysis of woodcuts by the famous German painter and print-maker Lucas Cranach the Elder (1472–1553) in which the Crucifixion of Christ is depicted (Figs 1 and 2).[3] Among other things, Merback notes the important role in these images of the Two Thieves who were crucified together with Christ. In Cranach's 1510–12 *Calvary* woodcut, the emphasis is on the extreme pain experienced by the thieves, rather than on Christ's bodily suffering. They are crucified in more clearly uncomfortable postures than Christ himself, and their anguish is more apparent. The thief to Christ's left struggles against the weight of his own body, and his feet, placed awkwardly at different heights, almost slide off the cross, kept in place only by the nails. The thief to Christ's right is most clearly in agony: his body is broken backwards over the crossbar rather than crucified in the usual upright position.

In depicting the Two Thieves in this manner, Cranach was participating in a well-established late-medieval artistic tradition. In numerous artistic representations of the Crucifixion, the suffering of the thieves is emphasized, and differentiated from that of Christ himself. In Merback's words, 'whereas Christ so often hangs placid and impassive, asleep in death, the Thieves kick, pull, strain and some-times thrash in painful torpor against the ropes which bind them'.[4] An early, and striking example of this tradition is an altarpiece by an anonymous Bohemian Master, dating from around 1360, in which the thieves' bodies are twisted around their respective crosses, creating a suggestion of maximum physical discomfort (Fig. 3).

[2] Mitchell B. Merback, *The Thief, the Cross and the Wheel: Pain and the Spectacle of Punishment in Medieval and Renaissance Europe* (London: Reaktion, 1999).

[3] I made efforts to contact all copyright holders and should any have been missed, I and the publisher will be happy to rectify this on the occasion of a reprint.

[4] Merback, *The Thief, the Cross and the Wheel*, p. 72.

Fig. 1. Lucas Cranach the Elder, *Calvary*, 1502. Department
of Prints and Drawings — Metropolitan Museum, New York.

Fig. 2. Lucas Cranach the Elder, *Calvary*, *c.* 1500–04. Berlin, Kupferstichkabinett. Reproduced with the permission of the Bildportal der Kunstmuseen/Kupferstichkabinett — Staatliche Museen zu Berlin.

Fig. 3. Bohemian Master, *Calvary*, c. 1360. Berlin, Gemäldegalerie. Reproduced with the permission of the Bildportal der Kunstmuseen/Gemäldegalerie — Staatliche Museen zu Berlin.

Why would late-medieval artists have stressed in such detail the pain suffered by the crucified thieves? What attitude toward physical pain does this imply? On one level, images such as Cranach's *Calvary* woodcuts present not only the pain suffered by Christ, but also pain suffered by non-divine humans as theologically meaningful and productive, and invite the viewer to see human physical suffering as an integral aspect of the Crucifixion. This becomes manifest in the opposition between the Two Thieves, which finds its biblical source in Luke 23. In Luke's account, one thief mocks Christ's apparent inability to do anything about his own and the thieves' suffering. The other repents and acknowledges Christ's divinity in a last-minute conversion: 'And Jesus said unto him, Verily I say unto thee, Today shalt thou be with me in paradise' (Luke 23. 43).[5] On the 1360 altarpiece, the thief to Christ's left averts his face, while the other, whom we are to see as the Penitent Thief, turns his face to Christ's bleeding hand, receiving Christ's blood in his mouth in a kind of combined Eucharist-baptism. In this way, the Penitent Thief (who is generally positioned to Christ's right) serves as a mediator between the crucified Christ and the viewer. Through his suffering, the Passion is extended to include humans and becomes an event not merely to be witnessed but to be shared and participated in. This participation occurs on the level of empathy and compassion; the viewer is encouraged to identify with the suffering, penitent human being whom he watches. Yet there is also a more literal side to this; late-medieval visual representations of the Two Thieves stressed the *inherent* usefulness of pain as an instrument for salvation. It was by suffering bodily agony that the Penitent Thief attained salvation. As Merback writes, the Good Thief's 'worthiness also sprang directly from his fleshly pains. As both spectacle and image, the demolished body of the Penitent Thief constituted a sign of this soul's lightning progress through purgation and towards redemption.'[6]

The idea that pain can be a useful spiritual tool, and a source of mystical insight and self-transformation, is part of a long tradition of Christian conceptions of pain. The idea that the suffering of Christ can be shared and re-enacted, on a lesser plane, by humans, plays a crucial role especially in medieval Christianity. As a result, pain, for the Christian mystic, was not something to be avoided, but to be actively sought, and even self-inflicted, in an attempt to become one with Christ. We should resist the temptation to see self-inflicted religious pain as mere 'mortification of the flesh', rooted in a contempt of the body, a chastising of the body for the sake of the soul. Rather than merely despising the

---

[5] All Bible quotations are taken from the Authorized Version.

[6] Merback, *The Thief, the Cross and the Wheel*, p. 221.

flesh, the pain-seeking mystic actively *employs* his or her body as a spiritual instrument and operates on the assumption that the body is a legitimate, even crucial, site of religious experience.[7]

The Christian tradition of seeing pain as positive reached a heightened intensity in late-medieval culture. Diarmaid MacCulloch has described how late-medieval Christianity was characterized by a new 'emphasis on the suffering Christ' who 'endured the worst possible physical and emotional pains to atone for human sin'.[8] This focus on Christ's suffering was 'part of a new exploration of his true humanity' that played an especially powerful role in Franciscan Christology:

> From the time of its foundation in the thirteenth century, the Franciscan Order of Friars emphasized this humanness of Jesus when they preached about him. St Bonaventure, one of their most celebrated early theologians, preachers and mystics, wrote passionately about his vision of sleeping beside the crucified Christ: the image of divine empathy with human suffering much comforted the generation traumatized by the Black Death and left a lasting impression on late medieval spirituality.[9]

Similarly, Esther Cohen has argued that late-medieval religious culture was characterized by what she describes as an attitude of 'philopassianism' — a valorization, as well as an active seeking, of pain as spiritually meaningful and productive.[10] Physical anguish could serve as a source of spiritual enlightenment partly because it was a form of *imitatio Christi*, and so offer an avenue to salvation: 'By the end of the Middle Ages, the love of Christ's passion and the search for individual purification through pain merged in a perception of the human body as the one and only medium for salvation and identification with Christ.'[11] While the most extreme manifestations of philopassianism may have been confined to a small group of mystics, its underlying attitude toward pain was 'was clearly grounded in a widespread popular form of piety'.[12]

---

[7] Elaine Scarry has voiced a similar idea in her *The Body in Pain: The Making and Unmaking of the World* (New York: Oxford University Press, 1985), p. 34.

[8] Diarmaid MacCulloch, *Reformation: Europe's House Divided, 1490–1700* (London: Allen Lane, 2003), p. 20.

[9] MacCulloch, *Reformation*, p. 20.

[10] Esther Cohen, 'Towards a History of European Physical Sensibility: Pain in the Later Middle Ages', in *Science in Context*, 8 (1995), 47–74.

[11] Cohen, 'Towards a History of European Physical Sensibility', p. 61.

[12] Cohen, 'Towards a History of European Physical Sensibility', p. 59. For suffering as *imitatio Christi* in late-medieval culture, see also Caroline Walker Bynum, *Holy Feast and Holy Fast: The Religious Significance of Food to Medieval Women* (Berkeley and Los Angeles: University of California Press, 1987). Walker writes that late-medieval fasting female mystics strove 'to merge

Reformation theologians voiced strikingly different attitudes toward the spiritual meaning of pain. In the *Institutes of the Christian Religion* (1536), John Calvin specifically attacks the idea that physical suffering can in itself contribute to salvation. One of his targets is the notion that, in the words of Thomas Norton's 1561 translation, 'martyrs have by their death done more to God, and deserved more, than was nedefull for themselves: and that they had remaining so great a plentie of deservinges, as did also overflowe unto other: and that therfore [...] their bloud is mingled with the bloud of Christ.'[13] For Calvin, the idea that physical suffering can contribute to salvation — of oneself as well as others — is an intolerable impingement on Christ's unique role as Saviour and on his unique bodily suffering: 'what is this els but to leave Christ only his name, otherwise to make him but a common pet[t]y saint [...]? He only, only should have bene preached, he only set fourth, he only named, he only ben loked unto, when the obteining of forgivenesse of sinnes, satisfaction, and sanctification are entreated of.'[14] Calvin approvingly quotes St Augustine, who claims in the *Enarrationes in Psalmos* that 'the suffringes of Christ [...] are in Christ only', and therefore not extendable to human beings.[15] Pain, in other words, cannot serve as a sign of one's

their own humiliating and painful flesh with that flesh whose agony, espoused by choice, was salvation' (p. 246). The notion that physical suffering can be a re-enactment of Christ's passion and contribute to personal salvation also plays a role in modern Catholicism, as becomes clear from an Apostolic Letter from 1994 by John Paul II, entitled *Salvifici Doloris*. Here, John Paul II writes that through physical suffering, human beings are called to 'share in that suffering through which all human suffering has also been redeemed. In bringing about the redemption through suffering, Christ has also raised human suffering to the level of redemption'; see John Paul II, Apostolic Letter *Salvifici Doloris*, 11 February [World Day of the Sick] 1994, p. 19, quoted in David J. Melling, 'Suffering and Sanctification in Christiany', in *Religion, Health and Suffering*, ed. by John R. Hinnells and Roy Porter (London: Kegan Paul, 1999), pp. 46–64 (p. 54).

[13] John Calvin, *The Institution of Christian Religion*, trans. by Thomas Norton (London: Arnold Hatfield for Bonham Norton, 1599), III.5, fol. 153ᵛ.

[14] Calvin, *Institution*, III.5, fol. 153ᵛ.

[15] Calvin, *Institution*, III.5, fol. 154. The quotation from the *Enarrationes in Psalmos* is taken from St Augustine's exposition of Psalm 61: 'Si enim passiones Christi in solo Christo, immo in solo capite, unde dicit quoddam membrum eius Paulus apostolus: *Ut suppleam quae desunt pressurarum Christi in carne mea*? Si ergo in membris Christi es, quicumque homo, quisquis haec audis, quisquis haec nunc non audis (sed tamen audis, si in membris Christi es); quidquid pateris ab eis qui non sunt in membris Christi, deerat passionibus Christi' (If the sufferings of Christ are in Christ only, then they are indeed only in the head; why did the apostle Paul, being a member, say: 'So that I can fill up in my flesh what is lacking in the distresses of Christ?' If therefore you are one of the members of Christ, whoever you are, whoever hears this, whoever does not hear this now (but you do hear it if you are among the members of Christ); whatever you suffer from those who are not among the

own salvation, or as a way of influencing the fate of one's soul. In this passage, Calvin also comments on St Paul's words in Colossians 1. 23–24 (a text that appears time and again in early modern discussions of martyrdom): 'I Paul am made a minister, who now rejoice in my sufferings for you, and fill up that which is behind of the afflictions of Christ in my flesh for his body's sake, which is the church.'[16] He argues that St Paul does not mean to say that physical suffering can in itself contribute to salvation (which would suggest that Christ's suffering was incomplete). Rather, Paul's 'sufferings' refer to 'those afflictions wherwith all the memb[er]s of Christ [...] must be exercised, so long as they shall be in this fleshe'.[17] These afflictions are not simply physical; nor can they lead to salvation, but only to 'the edifying and profit of the churche'.[18] In negating the spiritual use of pain, Calvin implicitly formulates an idea of Christian martyrdom in which physical pain is not relevant or productive *in itself*, as it was in late-medieval conceptions of martyrdom. Instead, the essence of martyrdom lies in Christian steadfastness in the face of persecution; martyrs 'by their stedfastnesse [...] strengthen the faith of the churche, and overcome the stubbornes of the enemies'.[19] In Calvin's definition of martyrdom, pain is only secondary.

A similar shift in attitudes toward pain can be seen in later representations of the Crucifixion by Lucas Cranach. A particularly pertinent example is the lime-wood panel *Crucifixion with Centurion* (1539), in which the physical agony of the Two Thieves has disappeared, as well as the visual exuberance of Cranach's earlier depictions of the Crucifixion (Fig. 4). Both thieves hang on their crosses as placidly as Christ himself, and the difference between the Good and the Bad Thief is registered only in the Bad Thief's averted face. There is a deliberate theological rationale to this. By 1539, Cranach had become involved in the Protestant movement of his friend Luther, and, as Merback argues, in the *Crucifixion with Centurion*:

members of Christ, was lacking in the sufferings of Christ'); Aurelius Augustinus, *Enarrationes in Psalmos LI–C*, ed. by Eligius Jan Dekkers, Corpus Christianorum Series Latina, 39 (Turnhout: Brepols, 1956), p. 774. I am grateful to Arnoud Visser for providing an English translation.

[16] The phrase 'that which is *behind* of the afflictions of Christ' seems deliberately vague about the relationship between Paul's suffering and that of Christ. The Douay-Rheims version, by contrast, suggests more openly that Christ's sacrifice was incomplete, and can be re-enacted by humans who 'fill up those things that are *wanting* of the sufferings of Christ'.

[17] Calvin, *Institution*, III.5, fol. 154. Calvin's reading draws heavily on St Augustine; see also n. 11, above.

[18] Calvin, *Institution*, III.5, fol. 154.

[19] Calvin, *Institution*, III.5, fol. 154.

Fig. 4. Lucas Cranach the Elder, *Crufixion with Centurion*, 1539. Staatsgalerie Aschaffenburg.

Cranach has [...] blocked the popular expectation that redemption was achievable, in large part, through an earthly purgatory of pain.[...] Pain does not 'work' to save [the Penitent Thief], and so its visualization becomes worse than superfluous — it now threatens to create the illusion that sin can be overcome at will [...], rather than by Grace alone.[20]

In spite of — or perhaps precisely because of — Protestant challenges, Catholic views of pain continued to stress the spiritual 'productivity' of pain. In St Ignatius Loyola's *Spiritual Exercises* (1548), pain is advertised as spiritually desirable: 'I should keep myself intent on experiencing sorrow and pain.'[21] The reader of the *Exercises* is encouraged 'to chastise the body, that is, to inflict pain on it, by wearing hairshirts, cords, or iron chains; by scourging or wounding oneself; and by similar austerities'.[22] Although 'chastising the body' is here presented as one of the aims of self-inflicted pain, pain also has an intrinsic meaning, since it forms an incentive to shed 'abundant tears because of [...] the pains and sufferings which Christ our Lord underwent in his Passion'.[23] Self-inflicted pain, in other words, offers a technique for contemplating the sufferings of Christ.

John Donne and the Theology of Pain

The issues that I have outlined held a fascination for John Donne, who repeatedly addressed questions of pain and salvation in his sermons, prose works, and poetry. He devoted his 'Lent-Sermon Preached at White-Hall, February 20.1617' to the Penitent Thief's admonition to the Bad Thief: 'Dost not thou fear God, seeing thou art in the same condemnation' (Luke 23. 40).[24] The question of the theological meaning of suffering comes to the fore early in this sermon, when Donne, in an allusion to Colossians 1. 23–24, tells his audience that '[he] would be loath to think that you never fulfill the sufferings of Christ Jesus in your flesh, but upon Goodfriday, never meditate upon the passion, but

[20] Merback, *The Thief, the Cross and the Wheel*, pp. 290–91.

[21] St Ignatius Loyola, *Spiritual Exercises and Selected Works*, ed. and trans. by George E. Ganss (New York: Paulist, 1991), p. 143.

[22] St Ignatius Loyola, *Spiritual Exercises*, p. 144.

[23] St Ignatius Loyola, *Spiritual Exercises*, p. 144.

[24] John Donne, 'Sermon No. 6: Preached at Whitehall, February 20, 1617/1618, on Luke 23.40', in *The Sermons of John Donne*, ed. by George R. Potter and Evelyn M. Simpson, 10 vols (Berkeley and Los Angeles: University of California Press, 1953), I, 252. All quotations from Donne's sermons are taken from this edition.

upon that day'.[25] Donne's 'Lent-Sermon' is clearly informed by Calvin's reading of I Colossians according to one recent commentator, Calvin was 'Donne's favourite Reformation theologian').[26] Christ's suffering is vividly imagined in the sermon, but it is a unique event that can only be meditated on, not imitated, by humans; this is what it means to 'fulfill the sufferings of Christ Jesus in your flesh'. Moreover, Donne adopts a Calvinist perspective on the story of the Two Thieves. The conversion of the Penitent Thief, he claims early in the sermon, reveals

> the infallibility, and the dispatch of the grace of God upon them, whom his gracious purpose hath ordained to salvation: how powerfully he works; how instantly they obey. This condemned person who had been a thief, execrable amongst men, and a blasphemer, execrating God, was suddainly a Convertite, suddainly a Confessor.[27]

The Penitent Thief is presented only as a sign of Christ's irresistible grace. The initiative lies wholly with Christ; the thief himself is utterly passive, and his physical suffering is so spiritually insignificant that Donne does not even mention it. Or at least only fleetingly. As Donne writes later in the sermon, the Good Thief 'came to know those Wounds which were in Christ's Body' and 'began to love him perfectly, when he found his own wounds in the body of his Saviour'.[28] Donne here suggests that Christ's suffering *does* have a vicarious property, that there *is* an analogy between Christ's wounds and those of the thief. This brief remark does not undermine the dominance, in this sermon, of a 'non-participatory' model of sacred pain. Yet it does alert us to an ambivalence in Donne's attitudes toward the matter that is also to be found in other texts.

In a sermon on Matthew 4. 18–20, for example, Donne shows his Calvinist credentials in his disparaging comments on the belief that 'the martyrs in the Primitive Church [...] suffered so much more then was necessary for their owne salvation'.[29] The 'treasure of the blood of Christ Jesus' is self-sufficient and cannot be complemented by human suffering. Yet in the same sermon Donne suggests that the following of Christ, to which the disciples are called in Matthew 4, entails an intensely physical identification with his passion. Alluding once again to Colossians 1, he presents this as an almost literal re-enactment of the Crucifixion:

[25] Donne, 'Sermon No. 6', p. 253.

[26] P. M. Oliver, *Donne's Religious Writing: A Discourse of Feigned Devotion* (London: Longman, 1997), p. vii.

[27] Donne, 'Sermon No. 6', p. 254.

[28] Donne, 'Sermon No. 6', p. 259.

[29] John Donne, 'Sermon No. 14', in *The Sermons of John Donne*, II, 300.

[W]hen I am come to that conformity with my Saviour, as to *fulfill his suffering in my flesh*, (as I am, when I glorifie him in a Christian constancy and cheerfulnesse in my afflictions) then I am crucified with him, carried up to his Crosse: [...] I put my hand into his hands and hang upon his nailes, [...] I put my mouth upon his mouth, and it is I that say *My God, my God, why hast thou forsaken me?*[30]

In a sermon devoted specifically to Colossians 1. 24, Donne again dismisses the 'supererogation' of martyrs, but also defines the 'filling up' of 'that which is behind of the afflictions of Christ' as much more than a mere meditation on Christ's suffering.[31] He emphasizes that the phrase '*in Carne*' implies that Christians should suffer for Christ 'not onely in spirit and disposition, but really in [their] flesh', and even claims that it not only contributes to but effectively 'makes sure [...] mine own salvation'.[32] As a result, it takes some verbal agility on Donne's part to avoid the awkward implication that Christ's own passion is somehow incomplete: '[T]he suffering of Christ being yet, not unperfect, but unperfected, Christ having not yet suffered all, I fill up that which remaines undone.'[33]

The *Devotions upon Emergent Occasions* (1623), Donne's most extensive exploration of physical anguish, written when he was recovering from a bout of relapsing fever, is concerned more with the moral significance of illness than with its effects on his own salvation.[34] Donne construes his illness as a sign of his own sinfulness, and turns to Christ to be cured of both his sickness and the sins to which it points. That physical suffering could serve as an incitement to spiritual self-examination was also recognized by Calvinist theology, yet Donne goes against the grain of Reformed thinking when, in the ninth Expostulation, he likens his own suffering to that of Christ: '[T]hou carriest me thine own private way, the way by which thou carryedst thy *Sonne* who first lay upon the *earth*, & praid, and then had his *Exaltation*, as himselfe calls his *Crucifying*, and first

---

[30] Donne, 'Sermon No. 14', p. 301.

[31] John Donne, 'Sermon No. 11', in *The Sermons of John Donne*, X, 333. The *OED* defines *supererogation* as 'the performance of good works beyond what God commands or requires, which are held to constitute a store of merit which the Church may dispense to others to make up for their deficiencies' (*OED*, s.v. 'supererogation', 1a).

[32] Donne, 'Sermon No. 11', p. 334.

[33] Donne, 'Sermon No. 11', p. 334.

[34] For a thoughtful analysis of Donne's 'reading' of his illness in the *Devotions*, see Stephen Pender, 'Essaying the Body: Donne, Affliction, and Medicine', in *John Donne's Professional Lives*, ed. by David Colclough (Cambridge: Brewer, 2003), pp. 215–47.

descended into hell, and then had his *Ascension*.'[35] In the same section, Donne equates himself with Christ in what Jonathan Goldberg has called a 'calculated stylistic ambiguity': 'Doe this, *O Lord*, for his sake, who did, and suffered so much, that thou mightest, as well in thy Justice, as well as in thy Mercy, doe it for me, thy *Sonne*, our *Saviour*, *Christ Jesus*.'[36] Donne here asks to be made anew by God through his sufferings but also suggests that in this process of self-transformation he is not only comparable to, but effectively becomes Christ. Moments such as these certainly do not dominate the *Devotions*, but they do illustrate that Donne could not altogether banish non-Reformed views of physical anguish from his religious sensibility.

Perhaps the only prose text in which Donne unambiguously rejects the spiritual efficacy of physical suffering is *Pseudo-Martyr* (1610). In a thoroughly Calvinist spirit, he fulminates against the notion that 'because many martyres have but fewe sinnes of their owne, and their passion is of a large and rich satisfaction, a mightie heape of Satisfaction superabounds from martyrs'.[37] Martyrs are incapable of effecting their own salvation, or that of others. Actively sought martyrdom, therefore, is both foolish and pointless, and Donne expresses his contempt for the fourth-century Spanish martyr St Eulalia of Barcelona who — in her 'over-vehement affectation of Martyredomme' — 'sp[a]t in the Judges faces, and provoked him to execute her'.[38] Anthony Raspa has suggested that the struggle over the meaning of martyrdom — to which *Pseudo-Martyr* was a contribution — revolved in part around the question of the *contemporaneity* of martyrdom: '[C]anonization was no longer the domain of the often legendary figures who had lived and died in a faraway past, but came to be thought of internationally in terms of present martyrs.'[39] Donne's concern, by contrast, is to push martyrdom back into the past and deny its contemporary relevance. Even though martyrdom does not guarantee salvation, the martyrs of the 'primitive Church' at least died because they held on to essential Christian beliefs 'which were the Elements of

---

[35] John Donne, *Devotions upon Emergent Occasions*, ed. by Anthony Raspa (Montreal: McGill-Queen's University Press, 1975), p. 17

[36] Donne, *Devotions*, p. 19; Jonathan Goldberg, 'The Understanding of Sickness in Donne's *Devotions*', in *Renaissance Quarterly*, 24 (1971), 507–17 (p. 515).

[37] John Donne, *Pseudo-Martyr*, ed. by Anthony Raspa (Montreal: McGill-Queen's University Press, 1993), p. 92. Donne ascribes this view specifically to the Jesuit theologian and cardinal St Robert Bellarmine (1542–1621).

[38] Donne, *Pseudo-Martyr*, p. 35.

[39] Donne, *Pseudo-Martyr*, p. xvii.

the Christian Religion, of which it was fram'd and complexioned; and so to shake that, was to ruine and demolish all'.[40] Contemporary Catholic martyrs, by contrast, merely die for the questionable integrity of the 'Romane Church' and the scholastic 'perplexities of Schoolemen' which it teaches, and therefore do not deserve the title of martyr.[41]

In his spiritual poetry, Donne also repeatedly addresses issues of physical anguish and redemption, and explores the same uncertainties that characterize his sermons. However, while, in the sermons Donne does not seem to register the paradox inherent in his stance toward pain, the poems confront different models of pain in a more explicit manner, and with a stronger sense of urgency. This becomes clear if we consider, for example, the opening lines of 'Holy Sonnet 11':

> Spit in my face ye Jewes, and pierce my side,
> Buffet, and scoff, scourge, and crucify me,
> For I have sinned, and sinned, and only he,
> Who could do no iniquity, hath died.[42]

Rather than stressing the inimitable nature of Christ's self-sacrifice, these lines express a wish to *become* Christ and to suffer the physical pain he suffered. Incidentally, the anti-Semitic dimension of this identification with Christ on the Cross is no coincidence (although the speaker claims that his own sins surpass 'the Jews' impiety'; l. 6). As Diarmaid MacCulloch has shown, the late-medieval focus on the suffering Christ, for example in Franciscan Christology, 'often led directly to deep hatred of Jews'.[43] In spite of his initial wish to re-enact the Crucifixion, the speaker subsequently realizes that his sins 'by [his own] death can not be satisfied (l. 5) and the poem goes on to celebrate the uniqueness of Christ's 'strange love' (l. 9). The poem ends by stressing Christ's human, physical vulnerability, his capacity for enduring both mental and physical 'woe' (l. 14), but his passion cannot be shared, or even approximated, by humans. That the poem moves so abruptly from a fervently expressed philopassianism to a Calvinist perspective on the Crucifixion only serves to highlight the unresolved tension between the two.

[40] Donne, *Pseudo-Martyr*, p. 35.

[41] Donne, Pseudo-Martyr, p. 36.

[42] John Donne, 'Holy Sonnet 11', in *The Complete English Poems*, ed. by A. J. Smith (1971; repr. London: Penguin, 1996), p. 313, ll. 1–4. All quotations from Donne's poems are taken from this edition.

[43] MacCulloch, *Reformation*, p. 9.

There is a comparable 'applied' Christology in the second poem of 'The Litany', in which the guilt-conscious speaker longs both to be the instrument of Christ's suffering and to suffer *with* Christ, to be both cross and crucified:

> O be thou nailed unto my heart,
>   And crucified again,
> Part not from it, though it from thee would part,
> But let it be by applying so thy pain,
> Drowned in thy blood, and in thy passion slain.
>
> (ll. 14–18)

The verb *apply* here may suggest that Christ's pain is a medical remedy against damnation for the speaker, echoing Donne's use of the word in the *Devotions*: 'There is no *spirituall health* to be had by *superstition*, nor *bodily* by *witchcraft*; thou Lord, and onely thou art *Lord* of both. Thou in thy selfe art *Lord* of both, and thou in thy *Son* art the *Phisician*, the *applyer* of both.'[44] Yet *apply* also has another theological resonance that is relevant in the light of the poem's concern with suffering and salvation. In the sermon on Matthew 4, Donne dismisses the belief that the 'superabundant crosses and merits' of Christian martyrs 'can *apply* to me'.[45] *Apply* here means 'to possess transferable soteriological efficacy': the abundant sufferings of the martyrs can contribute to the salvation of other Christians. In the poem, it is Christ's anguish that applies to the speaker, yet the syntax of line 17 is ambiguous since both Christ and the speaker's heart ('it' in l. 17) can serve as the subject of 'applying'. In the latter case, the speaker re-enacts Christ's suffering — who is 'crucified again' (l. 15) — and actively applies it to himself. The poem, in other words, is unclear about the agent of the speaker's wished-for salvation. In consequence, it is also undecided about the theological role of physical pain suffered by humans. This sense of uncertainty is underscored in the tenth poem in the 'Litany' sequence, which suggests — in spite of Donne's repeated protestations in the sermons — that the sufferings of martyrs are comparable to Christ's passion:

> Thou [i.e., Christ] in thy scattered mystic body wouldst
> In Abel die, and ever since
> in thine
>
> (ll. 4–6).

---

[44] Donne, *Devotions*, p. 21.

[45] Donne, 'Sermon No. 14', p. 300, my italics.

IN THY PASSION SLAIN

The opposing theological models of pain which I have outlined are confronted with particular intensity in Donne's 'Holy Sonnet 14':

> Batter my heart, three-personed God; for, you
> As yet but knock, breathe, shine, and seek to mend;
> That I may rise, and stand, o'erthrow me, and bend
> Your force to breake, blow, burn and make me new.
> I, like an usurped town, to another due,
> Labour to admit you, but oh, to no end,
> Reason your viceroy in me, me should defend,
> But is captived, and proves weak or untrue,
> Yet dearly'I love you, and would be loved fain,
> But am betrothed unto your enemy,
> Divorce me, untie, or breake that knot again,
> Take me to you, imprison me, for I
> Except you enthral me, never shall be free,
> Nor ever chaste, except you ravish me.[46]

In the first quatrain of this sonnet, Donne evokes late-medieval theological attitudes toward pain, in which physical suffering is seen as a key to salvation. The speaker longs for a spiritual experience that has the immediacy and absoluteness of bodily pain: in a formulation that recalls 'Holy Sonnet 11', he expresses a wish to be 'battered', 'broken', and 'burnt', and to receive violent 'blows'. This pain is presented, moreover, as a way of bringing about an inner transformation in the speaker; a method of dissolving, even destroying, the speaker's self, so that God can forge a new identity for him. Yet it is also Donne's own distance from this view of pain that is registered in the poem. At the heart of this sonnet is precisely the *absence*, even the impossibility, of pain. Sacred pain is presented as a wished-for experience, but it does not become reality; the speaker's obsessive imperatives remain mere imperatives. This unfulfilled longing for pain points to the ambivalent theological attitude toward pain that is explored in this poem. Donne is unable to evoke late-medieval, Catholic concepts of pain as unproblematic, neither can he erase them from his religious sensibility altogether. As a result, the idea that pain is a spiritually useful experience appears in 'Holy Sonnet 14' only as a rhetorical gesture, not as a lived belief. At the same time, however, this idea is reinvigorated by infusing it with a Protestant sensibility. In this poem, pain cannot be actively sought, or self-inflicted, and this is where it departs most clearly

---

[46] Donne, 'Holy Sonnet 14', in *Divine Poems*, p. 11

from pre-Reformation views on pain. The speaker is utterly dependent on God, who is the only potential source of 'good' pain in the poem. As a converted Protestant, Donne knows that to inflict pain on oneself for spiritual ends is to turn Christ into 'a common pettie saint' — to use Calvin's phrase — and he therefore stresses man's passivity in the distribution of pain.

In spite of this theological manoeuvre, 'Holy Sonnet 14' leaves intact the rather unreformed assumption that pain constitutes an absolute, uniquely authoritative spiritual experience. The desire for pain in the poem is rooted in a lack of other powerful signs of God's presence; in an absence of other indications of the speaker's unity with God, and of his salvation, that are as palpable and unambiguous as the experience of physical pain. Paradoxically, God himself, on whose signals the speaker is dependent, remains only a dim, stubbornly silent presence in the poem, registered audio-visually (He 'knocks', 'breathes', and 'shines'), but not as the longed-for, direct bodily sensation. Studies of the role of pain in religion and, more broadly, in ritual have stressed that physical pain confers a sense of reality and immediacy on abstract concepts. Roy Rappaport has argued that in physically injurious initiation rituals, 'the abstract is not only made substantial but immediate: nothing can be experienced more immediately than the sensations of one's own body — and if the mark is indelible, as in the cases of the subincision, the excised canine, the lopped finger, the scarified face, chest or back, it is ever-present.'[47] In Elaine Scarry's words, 'To have pain is to have *certainty*.'[48]

That this is a notion that exercised Donne's mind is also suggested by the *Devotions*, which is preoccupied with the moral epistemology of physical suffering. As Stephen Pender has observed, in the *Devotions* 'physical signs urge spiritual diagnosis'; sickness serves as an index of Donne's spiritual state.[49] The state of Donne's soul is inscribed on his body:

> [T]here is no *Artery* in me, that hath not the *spirit of error, the spirit of lust, the spirit of*
> *giddines* in it; no *bone* in me that is not hardned with the custome of *sin*, and nourished,
> and soupled with the *marrow* of *sinn*; no *sinews*, no *ligaments*, that do not tie, & chain sin
> and sin together.[50]

---

[47] Roy A. Rappaport, *Ritual and Religion in the Making of Humanity* (Cambridge: Cambridge University Press, 1999), p. 149.

[48] Scarry, *The Body in Pain*, p. 13.

[49] Pender, 'Essaying the Body', p. 216. For my observations on the *Devotions*, I am indebted to Pender's reading.

[50] Donne, *Devotions*, p. 48.

Indeed, the symptoms of the body offers the surest route to spiritual self-knowledge: 'why is not my *soule*, as sensible as my *body*?' Donne wonders, 'why is there not alwayes a *pulse* in my *Soule*, to beat at the approch of a tentation to sinne?'[51] God uses the materiality of the body to confer experiential immediacy upon the more abstract realm of the soul: 'I know that in the state of my *body*, which is more *discernible*, than that of my soule, thou dost *effigiate* my *Soule* to me.'[52] In the *Devotions*, to undergo physical suffering is to acquire spiritual certainty, albeit via a tortuous interpretative process. It is precisely a *lack* of spiritual certainty that makes the speaker in 'Holy Sonnet 14' long for the clarity of physical suffering. This lack of certainty, moreover, is Protestant in origin. If, as I have tried to show, Protestantism denied the validity of pain as an inherently meaningful religious experience, and emphasized man's passivity in the face of God's decrees, in Donne's sonnet this results only in a spiritual doubt that borders on despair. The unresolved question at the heart of 'Holy Sonnet 14' is how religious experience can offer certainty if it is stripped of the conclusiveness of bodily sensations.

In his well-known study *John Donne: Life, Mind and Art*, John Carey has posited that Donne's apostasy is the key to his art: '[T]he first thing to remember about Donne is that he was a Catholic; the second, that he betrayed his Faith.'[53] Carey's thesis has come in for a good deal of criticism, yet it seems appropriate in the light of Donne's struggle with the theological meaning of physical suffering. The sermon and poems that I have commented on suggest that Donne felt drawn to both Catholic and Protestant models of pain but was also deeply sensitive to what he saw as the shortcomings of both. Indeed, Donne's writings on the theological meaning of pain illustrate P. M. Oliver's claim that Donne's 'religious thinking was consistently hybrid in nature'.[54] In view of Donne's approach to physical suffering, moreover, this hybridity does not imply a synthesis of Catholic and Reformed attitudes but rather a rehearsing of what Oliver has called 'different, often mutually hostile, religious positions'.[55]

---

[51] Donne, *Devotions*, p. 8.

[52] Donne, *Devotions*, p. 119.

[53] John Carey, *John Donne: Life, Mind and Art* (1981; repr. London: Faber and Faber, 1990), p. 1.

[54] Oliver, *Donne's Religious Writing*, p. 5.

[55] Oliver, *Donne's Religious Writing*, p. 147.

The Theology of Physical Suffering in 'The Temple'

Donne was only one among a range of early modern English spiritual poets who explored the different, conflicting theological models of pain that were available to them. The remainder of this article is devoted to a number of poems from George Herbert's *The Temple* which investigate the same issues and share a number of the theological intuitions of Donne's 'Holy Sonnet 14', yet also offer a way out of the theological deadlock of that poem. Indeed, while Donne, in his spiritual poetry, juxtaposes incompatible religious positions without seeking to reconcile them, Herbert tries to accommodate different perspectives into a genuinely composite model of pain.

That the theological meaning of human pain is a crucial issue in *The Temple* is made clear by a series of poems in the 'Church' section. In 'The Thanksgiving' Christ is addressed as the supreme sufferer — the 'King of grief' and 'King of wounds' — and the speaker ponders the inimitability of Christ's suffering in lines that recall Donne's 'Holy Sonnet 11':

> Shall I be scourged, flouted, boxed, sold?
>   'Tis but to tell the tale is told,
> *My God, my God, why dost thou part from me?*
> Was such a grief as cannot be.
>   [...]
> But how then shall I imitate thee, and
>   Copie thy fair, though bloody hand?[56]

Christ cannot be imitated by copying, and hence actively seeking, the 'grief' which he suffered; the word 'grief' here — as in other poems in *The Temple* that address the Passion — refers not only to Christ's mental pain and sorrow at having been deserted by God, but also to his bodily injuries and physical anguish.[57] The poem imagines various ways of repaying Christ's love, but undergoing pain is not one of them, and the poem ends by asserting yet again the uniqueness of His suffering: 'Then for thy passion — I will do for that — | Alas, my God, I know not what' (ll. 49–50). Similarly, the speaker in 'The Reprisal' stresses the soteriological insignificance of human suffering and the uniqueness of Christ's redemptive work:

---

[56] George Herbert, *The Complete English Poems*, ed. by John Tobin (1991; London: Penguin, 2004), p. 31, ll. 1, 4, 7–10, 15–16. All subsequent quotations from Herbert's poems are taken from this edition.

[57] See *OED*, s.v. 'grief', 5a, 6, 7a. All three meanings listed here were current in Herbert's time.

> I have considered it, and find
> There is no dealing with thy mighty passion:
> For though I die for thee, I am behind;
> My sins deserve the condemnation.
>
> (ll. 1–4)

The phrase 'I am behind' reads like an implicit reversal of Colossians 1. 24. The poem suggests that *nothing* 'is behind of the afflictions of Christ'; rather it is human suffering which will always be inadequate and incomplete in comparison with Christ's overwhelming self-sacrifice.

The gulf between Christ's pain and human pain is underscored most strongly in 'The Sacrifice', spoken by Christ in his sufferings, with its rhetorical question 'was ever grief like mine?' repeated at the end of each stanza. Yet, not unlike Donne's 'Holy Second 7', the poem also presents a poetic *imitatio Christi* — Herbert's attempt to enter imaginatively *into* Christ's experience, rather than to meditate on it from a clearly differentiated human vantage point. Indeed, as Robert Whalen has argued, if 'The Sacrifice' is ostensibly spoken from Christ's point of view, it also fuses the perspectives of the suffering Christ and the penitent Christian, inviting a 'formal identification' between the two.[58] The 'cup' (l. 23) which Christ asks God to let pass refers both to Christ's passion and to the cup of the Eucharist, which holds not only Christ's blood but also the 'sinner's tears' (l. 25) shed by penitent Christians. In addition, the poem repeatedly emphasizes the sacramental effect of Christ's suffering and in doing so, it presents the Passion simultaneously from the perspective of Christ and of the Christian who reaps its benefits: 'how they scourge me! [...] | yet their bitterness | Winds up my grief to a mysteriousness' (ll. 125–27).[59] There is a comparable assimilation between speaker and Christ in the second and third 'Affliction' poems. If, as Helen Vendler notes, these two poems 'seem like one poem twice reworked', the 're-working' is to be located in the revised view of pain in 'Affliction 3'.[60] 'Affliction 2' confirms the disparity between human and divine grief: 'men's tears' (l. 6) only 'discolour [Christ's] most bloody sweat' (l. 10). The gnomic opening line of the

---

[58] Robert Whalen, *The Poetry of Immanence: Sacrament in Donne and Herbert* (Toronto: University of Toronto Press, 2002), p. 152.

[59] The *OED* glosses *mysteriousness* in this line as 'mysterious quality, obscureness' (*OED*, s.v. 'mysteriousness', 1a.), yet meaning 1b is at least equally appropriate to the poem: 'The Eucharist, regarded as a religious mystery'.

[60] Helen Vendler, *The Poetry of George Herbert* (Cambridge, MA: Harvard University Press, 1975), p. 239.

last stanza — 'Thou art my grief alone' (l. 11) — suggests that there is no pain left to undergo for the speaker. Christ has suffered all there is to suffer, even the grief that could theoretically have been undergone by the speaker. 'Affliction 3', by contrast, not only defines Christ as a Man of Sorrows but also, in an allusion to Colossians 1. 24, presents human suffering as a re-enactment of the Passion:

> Thy life on earth was grief, and Thou art still
> Constant unto it, making it to be
> A point of honour, now to grieve in me,
>   And in Thy members suffer ill.
>   They who lament one cross,
> Thou dying daily, praise thee to thy loss.
>
> (ll. 13–18)

The intense concern with the meaning of pain in *The Temple* has led Helen Vendler to claim that 'it would be possible to consider [the] assimilation of Jesus to Herbert unhealthy, a masochistic repose in suffering', yet this ignores the extent to which philopassianism was part of the late-medieval Christian heritage that Herbert attempts to accommodate and reconcile with post-Reformation notions of pain.[61] That this is a problematic effort is suggested by the fact that the rival views of pain in the second and third 'Affliction' poems remain locked in opposition; on a level of doctrine, the two models seem incompatible. The ambivalence of 'The Sacrifice', by contrast, lies not in irreconcilable stated beliefs, but is to a large extent an effect of form. The Christ who speaks in the poem may assert the uniqueness of His suffering, but the formal conceit of 'The Sacrifice' — Herbert's appropriation of Christ's voice — operates on the assumption that humans can share in his pain through imaginative empathy. A similar effort to negotiate Reformed and Catholic models of pain, and to find a *poetic* rather than a doctrinal mediating ground between Christ's suffering and human suffering, is to be found in 'The Agony':

> Philosophers have measured mountains,
> Fathomed the depths of seas, of states, and kings,
> Walked with a staff to heav'n, and traced fountains:
>   But there are two vast, spacious things,
>   The which to measure it doth more behove:
> Yet few there are that sound them; Sin and Love.
>   Who would know Sin, let him repair

---

[61] Vendler, *The Poetry of George Herbert*, p. 238.

Unto mount Olivet; there shall he see
A man so wrung with pains, that all his hair,
    His skin, his garments bloody be.
Sin is that press and vice, which forceth pain
To hunt his cruel food through ev'ry vein.

    Who knows not Love, let him assay
And taste that juice, which on the crosse a pike
Did set again abroach; then let him say
    If ever he did taste the like.
Love is that liquor sweet and most divine,
Which my God feels as blood; but I, as wine.

This poem steers an intriguing middle way between the idea that Christ's pain is unique and that human beings are excluded from it, on the one hand, and the notion that Christ's suffering can somehow be experienced physically by humans on the other. Christ's pain, in this poem, is an object of knowledge: the true nature of sin can be known by seeing and meditating on Christ's pain. If the speaker recognizes his own sinfulness in the pain felt by Christ, there is no suggestion that His sufferings can be re-enacted by humans. Yet the speaker in 'The Agony' does arrive at the spiritual certainty, or knowledge, which seems to elude the speaker in 'Holy Sonnet 14'. He achieves this certainty not by under-going pain himself, but by experiencing Christ's unrepeatable pain in a sensuous, physical manner. As the poem moves from Christ's Agony in the garden of Gethsemane to the Crucifixion, the action that the reader is invited to perform turns from 'see' in the second stanza to the more experiential 'taste and say' in the third. As Helen Vendler writes, 'the involvement in the second emblem [of Mt Calvary] is participatory', and this is underlined by the transition from the generalized 'who' and him' of the second stanza to 'my' and 'I' in the closing line of the poem.[62] In addition, the signs of Christ's suffering are transformed from blood, in the second stanza, to wine in the third stanza; it is as wine that they can be tasted in abundance, and hence known with a serene certainty, by humans. Indeed, if the closing lines of the poem hint at the disparity between the experience of Christ and that of the speaker, there is also a sense of equivalence between them, or at least comparability: 'Love is that liquor sweet and most divine, | Which my God feels as blood; but I, as wine.' Both the speaker and Christ 'feel' at the same time. Both also taste the same 'liquour'; it is only its

[62] Vendler, *The Poetry of George Herbert*, p. 74.

physical manifestation that differs. In this poem, to feel and to know become the
same. Indeed, the material, sensuous knowledge of Christ's love is contrasted with
the more abstract, detached knowledge of philosophers who have only 'measured
mountains', not tasted them, so to speak. 'The Agony' 'renders the Atonement
personal, intimate, and visceral'.[63]

In 'The Agony', then, the Protestant conception of Christ's self-sacrifice as
both radically other and self-sufficient is acknowledged, but also redefined — the
poem turns meditation into a physical act. There is even an extent to which the
poem does re-enact Christ's passion, albeit on a level of form. Julia Guernsey has
persuasively argued that what she terms 'the prosodic subject' of the poem 'enters
into Christ's consciousness':

> The prosodic subject embodies both the psycho-somatic agony of Christ as he struggles
> in the Garden of Gethsemane to accept the coming crucifixion, literally sweating blood,
> and the physical agony of Christ on the cross. The first two lines contort with bodily
> suffering signified by the metric irregularities of scarcely scannable overstressed lines;
> the next two lines throb with the highly regular pulse of pain; the final couplet makes tangible
> [in its diction and enjambment] the shock of pain pressed through the very veins of the
> dying saviour.[64]

It is perhaps paradoxical that a poem which studiously avoids any unqualified
suggestion that humans can take part in Christ's pain should mimic His suffering
in its form. Yet it is precisely because the physical identification with Christ's
suffering is not stated as a matter of doctrine but *performed* in prosody that it can
be accommodated by the poem without jeopardizing the reconciliation between
opposing models of pain for which 'The Agony' strives.

Conclusion

I have investigated how John Donne and George Herbert explored the tensions
between late-medieval Catholic and Reformed notions of pain, and focused especially on the relation between Christ's passion and human pain, and that
between suffering and salvation. The conflict between the two models is evident
in Donne's sermons and in his *Devotions*, and especially in his spiritual poetry.
'Holy Sonnet 11' moves uneasily from philopassianism to Calvinist views of

---

[63] Whalen, *The Poetry of Immanence*, p. 122.

[64] Julia Carolyn Guernsey, *The Pulse of Praise: Form as a Second Self in the Poetry of George
Herbert* (Newark: University of Delaware Press, 1999), p. 97.

suffering, while 'The Litany' offers incompatible conceptions of the soteriological relevance of human physical anguish. The speaker in 'Holy Sonnet 14' longs to undergo physical suffering as a sign of his own salvation but is also aware that this is impossible within a Calvinist theology. In *The Temple*, Herbert addresses the question of pain in a similarly ambivalent manner, yet also attempts to formulate a hybrid understanding of suffering in which Catholic and Reformed models co-exist. He does so in part by accommodating Catholic attitudes on a level of poetic form, rather than as overtly stated doctrines.

The double-edged approach of both Herbert and Donne to the meaning of physical anguish is perhaps indicative of the ambivalent attitude toward pain which characterized English Protestant culture after the Elizabethan Settlement. This is suggested, for example, by John Foxe's *Acts and Monuments* (1563). Foxe offers a clearly Calvinist notion of martyrdom; in spite of his preoccupation with the physical suffering undergone by Protestant martyrs, he carefully avoids any suggestion that human pain is comparable to Christ's pain, or that it has soteriological efficacy. Rather, he presents the martyrs of the Church of England as exemplars of 'Christian fortitude': 'we behold in them strength, so constant above mans reach, such rediness to aunswere, such patience in imprisonment, such godlines in forgeving, cherefulness so couragious in suffering'.[65] Yet the *Acts and Monuments* is also informed by the tensions that I have sketched. In his account of the martyrdom of the Protestant clergyman and martyr George Marsh (c. 1515–55), Foxe includes the 'godly letters' that Marsh wrote during his imprisonment.[66] In one of these letters, Marsh offers a reading of Colossians 1. 24:

> S. Paul does not here meane that there wanteth any thyng in the passion of Christ which may be supplyed by man, for the passion of Christ (as touching his own person) is that most perfect, as many as are sanctified in his bloud: but these his wordes ought to be understand [sic] of the elect & chosen, in whom Christ is & shal be persecuted unto the worldes end. The passion of Christ then, as touching his misticall body, which is the churche, shal not be perfect till al have suffered, whom God hath appointed to suffer for his sonnes sake.[67]

[65] John Foxe, *The Ecclesiastical History, contayning the Actes and Monumentes of things passed in every kinges time in this Realme, especially in the Churche of England principally to be noted, with a full discourse of such persecutions, horrible troubles, the suffring of martirs*, 2 vols (London: John Day, 1576), I, sig. ¶.ii^r.

[66] Foxe, *Ecclesiastical History*, II, 1478. For Marsh, see Thomas S. Freeman, 'Marsh, George (ca 1515–1555)', in *Oxford Dictionary of National Biography* (Oxford: Oxford University Press, 2004), <www.oxforddnb.com/view/article/18109> [accessed 2 August 2005].

[67] Foxe, *Ecclesiastical History*, II, 1489.

While this passage echoes Calvin's reading of Colossians 1 in the *Institutes*, it is ambivalent about the relation between Christ's passion and the suffering of martyrs. Exactly in what sense does Christ's suffering 'touch' that of his 'misticall body', the church? Marsh's diction at least allows for the suggestion that martyrdom is on a par with Christ's anguish.

More overt echoes of pre-Reformation models of pain can be found in the Book of Common Prayer. The 'Order for the Visitation of the Sicke' strikes a Calvinist note in defining illness as 'Goddes visitation' aimed at 'correct[ing]' and 'amending' in the sufferer 'whatsoever dothe offende the eies of our heavenly father'.[68] Yet post-1559 editions also continued to include a statement on illness and physical suffering that recalls late-medieval Catholic attitudes toward the matter, even though Calvinist theology had a nearly hegemonic status in England until the 1620s.[69] The order allows ministers to address 'very sick' persons as follows:

> [T]here should be no greater comfort to Christian persons, then to be made like unto Christ, by suffering patiently adversities, troubles, and sickenesses. For he himselfe went not up to joy, but first hee suffered paine, he entred not into his glory, before hee was crucified: So truely our way to eternall joy is to suffer here with Christ, and our doore to enter into eternall life, is gladly to die with Christ, that wee may rise againe from death, and dwell with him in everlasting life. Now therefore taking your sicknesse, which is thus profitable for you, patiently, I exhort you in the name of God, to remember the profession which you made unto God in your baptisme.[70]

Physical pain is presented here both as a route to salvation and as a way of taking part in the sufferings of Christ. It is worth noting that in the 1549 Prayer Book this passage was still included in the standard exhortation to the ill, while in the 1552 version it had become optional and reserved for the gravely ill. However, the passage itself, in essentially unaltered form, remained part of the Book of Common Prayer Book until the definitive edition of 1662. If, as Peter Lake has written, the English religious landscape of the late sixteenth and early seventeenth centuries was characterized by a 'wreckage of partially disrupted belief systems', English views on pain and physical anguish seem to confirm his point.[71]

---

[68] *The Booke of Common Prayer and Administration of the Sacraments, and Other Rites and Ceremonies in the Church of England* (London: Robert Barker, 1615), sig. C6.

[69] Oliver, *Donne's Religious Writing*, pp. 30–31.

[70] *The Booke of Common Prayer*, sig. C6.

[71] Peter Lake, 'Religious Identities in Shakespeare's England', in *A Companion to Shakespeare*, ed. by David Scott Kastan (Oxford: Blackwell, 1999), p. 78.

EXORCIZING RADICALS:
JOHN OF LEYDEN CARNIVALIZED

Claudia Richter

P ost-Reformation culture is full of continuities with what had gone on before, as Eamon Duffy has emphasized.[1] If this is true, then such culture is not only full of Catholic survivals, but probably of more ancient practices and imaginations, too. This essay will focus on literary representations of John of Leyden and the Münster Anabaptists in the context of pagan cultural practices of shaming, cursing, and derision. R. C. Elliott reminds us of the roots of satire in the magical belief that words uttered in a particular ritual context have the power to harm others: ritual formulae are speech acts which have an imminent power to them, the power to bring about changes in the physical world. If magic is a 'constitutive element in the function of satire',[2] we may wonder about the renaissance of satire in the Elizabethan and Jacobean age, which at the same time witnessed the decline of a magical conception of language. Although satire remained forbidden by episcopal decree until at least 1599, it had achieved prominence by the last decade of the sixteenth century.[3] In fact, the Elizabethan age produced a flood of satirical and polemical pamphlets.

In the light of Elliot's remark, it appears justified to see a connection between the heightened interest in the genre in the post-Reformation era and the Protestant

---

[1] Eamon Duffy, *The Stripping of the Altars: Traditional Religion in England c.1400–c.1580* (New Haven: Yale University Press, 1992).

[2] Robert C. Elliott, *The Power of Satire: Magic, Ritual, Art* (Princeton: Princeton University Press, 1960), p. 276.

[3] Andreas Mahler, *Moderne Satireforschung und elisabethanische Verssatire. Texttheorie — Epistemologie — Gattungspoetik* (Munich: Fink, 1992), p. 15.

contempt for ritual and magical speech acts. This essay argues that religious satire, especially, replaces the magical speech acts of cursing and ritual derision, while implicitly perpetuating the idea of binding the forces that threaten the social order by way of speaking and writing. I understand satire here as a performative textual genre related to magical-ritual speech acts.[4] What follows argues that literary representations of John of Leyden and the Münster Anabaptists in the modes of satire, polemic, parody, curse, and sermon substitute a ritual of exorcism to drive out the demons of doubt and dissidence infesting British society. After the Reformation, heresy became a complex concept. After all, God seemed to allow diverging opinions on religion, in the sense that the enemies of the 'right faith' were not immediately struck down by a thunderbolt for their sacrilegious views. From a sacred-magical perspective, however, sacrilege demands a curse or a related ritual speech act as a means of purgation. Hence it appears justified to read satirical representations of John of Leyden as attempts to 'exorcize' religious radicals. Exorcism as a magical speech act which aims at the expulsion of 'harmful spirits [to] restore the "psychic equilibrium" to whole communities as well as individuals' was persistently campaigned against by religious authorities. In effect, exorcism became illegal in 1604, and was rejected as fraudulent and superstitious.[5] However, as Stephen Greenblatt maintains, exorcism never fully lost its power. Since the English Church failed to replace exorcism with new rituals, it only moved to the periphery.[6] My argument relies on the notion that satire occupies the space vacated by the marginalization of exorcism.

According to contemporary etymology, the word *satire* derived from 'satyr', which reminds us of its relationship to carnival and the dionysiac. 'Satirical speech', Andreas Mahler points out, opens language to 'eruptive-liberating aggression'[7]

---

[4] I am indebted to the *Sonderforschungsbereich 'Kulturen des Performativen'* of the Free University in Berlin for crucial insights into the performativity of texts. Cf. *Theorien des Performativen*, ed. by Erika Fischer-Lichte and Christoph Wulf (Berlin: Akademie Verlag, 2001).

[5] Stephen Greenblatt, 'Shakespeare and the Exorcists', in *After Strange Texts: The Role of Theory in the Study of Literature*, ed. by David L. Miller Gregory S. Jay (Tuscaloosa: University of Alabama Press, 1985), pp. 101–23 (pp. 106–07). Quotation from S. M. Shirokogorov, *The Psycho-Mental Complex of the Tungus* (London: Routledge and Kegan Paul, 1935), p. 265. See also Jan Frans van Dijkhuizen, *Devil Theatre: Demonic Possession and Exorcism in English Renaissance Drama, 1558–1642* (Cambridge: Brewer, 2007).

[6] Greenblatt, 'Shakespeare and the Exorcists', pp. 106–07.

[7] Mahler, *Moderne Satireforschung*, p. 212 (my translation).

and is related to ritualized pagan forms of ridiculing, scoffing, and cursing.[8] In archaic cultures such rituals served in part to absorb human aggression, for instance in sacrificial rites, or in the more playful rituals of carnival, where the anti-king functioned as a scapegoat. According to René Girard, rituals of this kind generally function proleptically as safety valves to absorb and release tension and violent energies before they turn against society.[9]

Like tragedy, then, satire could be described as art cut loose from its ritual origins. As Elliott argues with the Cambridge Ritualists, '[T]he performance has been cut loose from its roots as a ritual act, and has started on its free career as a work of art.'[10] To a significant extent, Elizabethan religious satire had its roots in the late-sixteenth-century Martin Marprelate controversy. This essay therefore reads satirical representations of John of Leyden and the Münster Anabaptists in their function of harming, binding, and exorcizing the demons of dissidence that were threatening the stability of the English Church in the post-Reformation period. The prominence of satire in this particular age could then be understood as a continuation of the ritual contexts of spells and exorcist formulae, as well as a compensation for their loss.

The attempt to expel forces represented as satanic informs the representations of the Münster episode in Thomas Nashe's *Unfortunate Traveller* (1594) and in a lesser-known long poem attributed to Samuel Rowlands, published as *Hell's Broke Loose* (1605).[11] Both texts propagate politico-religious stability by carnivalizing the Münster episode. Carnival, it may be noted, is more than the celebration of life and rebirth emphasized by Bakhtin: it is also about cauterizing those forces that are inimical to society. In this process, the Lord of Misrule, or anti-king, takes on the function of a scapegoat:

---

[8] I am neglecting here the scholarly tradition that derives Elizabethan satire from its Roman predecessors, e.g., Juvenal, and am favouring an anthropological interpretation.

[9] My understanding of the carnivalesque is indebted to the sacrificial theory developed by René Girard, *Violence and the Sacred*, trans. by Patrick Gregory (London: Continuum, 2005).

[10] Gilbert Murray, 'Excursus on the Ritual Forms Preserved in Greek Tragedy', in *Themis*, ed. by Jane Ellen Harrison (Cambridge: Cambridge University Press, 1912), pp. 341–63 (p. 341); quoted in Elliott, *The Power of Satire*, p. 89.

[11] Thomas Nashe, *The Unfortunate Traveller and other Works*, ed. by J. B. Steane (Harmondsworth: Penguin, 1971); Samuel Rowlands, *Hell's Broke Loose* (London: [n. pub.], 1605). I have used the text reproduced in the *English Poetry Full-Text Database*, Software Version 4.0., published by Chadwyck-Healey, 1995.

those mock kings who are crowned at carnival time, when everything is set topsy-turvy and social hierarchies turned upside down; when sexual prohibitions are lifted, and theft permitted; when servants take the place of their masters [...]; when, in short, the throne is yielded only to the basest, ugliest, most ridiculous and criminal of beings. But once the carnival is over the anti-king is expelled from the community or put to death, and his disappearance puts an end to all the disorder that his person served to symbolize for the community and also to purge for it.[12]

Both Nashe and Rowlands represent the Anabaptists in a carnivalesque setting, drawing on traditional topoi of medieval carnival: violent gaming and grotesque buffoonery, excessive indulgence in carnal pleasures and, most significantly, the temporary reversal of social hierarchy. This literary strategy proceeds to open a seemingly paradoxical perspective: on the one hand, it suggests that the Anabaptists and their politico-religious agenda are *not* to be taken seriously, because they are infantile and grotesque in their vain, unrealistic dreams. On the other hand, support is also lent to the view that the case of the Münster Anabaptists *must* be taken seriously as a warning, because radicals do not intend to limit their transgressions to a certain period of time. The danger about this carnival, they imply, is that it will *permanently* turn the world upside down if radicals are not prevented from realizing their plans.

The theological basis for the perceived parallel between radical Protestantism and carnival is to be found in the Apocalypse of St John, the blueprint for millenarian movements, which promises to punish the wicked who are ruling the present corrupted world. The biblical imagination of a 'world turned upside down' goes back to Isaiah:

The Lord maketh the earth [...] waste, and turneth it upside down [...]. And it shall be, as with the people, so with the priest; as with the servant, so with his master; as with the maid, so with her mistress [...]. The earth shall reel to and fro like a drunkard, and shall be removed like a cottage [...]. The Lord shall punish the host of the high ones [...] and the kings of the earth upon the earth.[13]

---

[12] Jean-Paul Vernant, 'Ambiguïté et renversement: sur la structure énigmatique d'Oedipe Roi', in *Echanges et communications*, ed. by Pierre Maronda Jean Pouillon (The Hague: Mouton, 1970), pp. 1253–79 (p. 1271–72); quoted in Girard, *Violence and the Sacred*, p. 124 n. 15.

[13] Isaiah 24. 1–2, 20–21. For the theme of the world turned upside down in radical Protestantism, see Christopher Hill, *The World Turned Upside Down: Radical Ideas during the English Revolution* (Harmondsworth: Penguin, 1975) and Manfred Pfister, 'Gottesreich und Endzeit: Utopisches Denken und utopische Praxis im Puritanismus', in *Alternative Welten*, ed. by Manfred Pfister (Munich: Fink, 1982), pp. 135–50.

Both in *The Unfortunate Traveller* and in *Hell's Broke Loose*, the carnivalesque ritual reversal of order therefore coincides with, and serves as a comment on, the apocalyptic theme of the *mundus inversus*. Moreover, the narrative presentation structurally imitates ritual expurgation by naming and invoking the demons, as it were, so as to expel them in the end.

Nashe

The work of Thomas Nashe is characteristic of what Neil Rhodes has termed the 'Elizabethan grotesque'. Its idiosyncratic style 'is the product of an uneasy relationship between sermon and festive comedy, priest and clown'.[14] Rhodes's observation is confirmed by Nashe's own view that his writing is 'Duncified twixt divinity and poetry' (p. 286). Rhodes's remark is particularly germane to literary representations of the Münster Anabaptists, in which derision and sermonizing are fused into a polemical satire of the Münster insurrection.

Nashe has his narrator Jack Wilton arrive at Münster on the eve of the battle between the inhabitants of Leyden's *New Jerusalem* and the Duke of Saxony. The course of events on the day in question is closely modelled on the ritual clothing and undressing of the Lord of Misrule played by the protagonist, John of Leyden, who leads a mock-procession of 'very devout asses' (p. 278). The narrator creates a visual image of the characters by focusing on dress and armour. The soldiers are dressed up as fools, while the peasants are armed with rusty farming tools and bills, 'bravely fringed with cobwebs' (p. 278). Their costumes are only surpassed in extravagance and absurdity by their king's own attire, 'John the botcher', who enters the field

> with a scarf made of lists like a bow-case, a cross on his breast like a thread-bottom, a round-twilted tailor's cushion buckled like a tankard-bearer's device to his shoulders for a target, the pyke thereof was a pack-needle, a tough prentice's club for his spear, a great brewer's cow on his back for a corslet, and on his head for a helmet a huge high shoe with the bottom turned upwards, embossed as full of hobnails as ever it might stick. (p. 277)

The messianic leader himself is the Lord of Misrule here: the narrator equips him with a fool's cap, along with all the tools befitting his trade but utterly inappropriate for a king, let alone for a soldier hoping to win a battle. The Lord of Misrule's dress vividly illustrates the grotesque forms which threaten to emerge if the divine order is reversed, that is, when a tailor fashions himself as a king. Everything is turned upside down and appears in places where it has little purpose,

---

[14] Neil Rhodes, *Elizabethan Grotesque* (London: Routledge and Kegan Paul, 1980), p. 4.

or simply does not belong: it is not enough that a shoe is worn as a hat; it is inverted so that its dirty sole is pointing upward, as though in mockery of God. Moreover it is embossed with an exaggerated number of hobnails, which would normally be expected to be found on horses' hooves. If John of Leyden's headgear is supposed to be the external reflection of his mind, it can only mean that that his mind is full of nonsense. The resemblance to Rabelais's *Gargantua and Pantagruel* is no coincidence: Nashe, participating in the Marprelate pamphlet war, developed his style in imitation of Rabelais, as a weapon against the Puritan enemy.[15] The saturnalian cycle is completed when Wilton reports how the peasant army is defeated by the Duke of Saxony, and the Anabaptist leaders stripped of their power. Their dethronement is celebrated with a degree of condescending pity when the narrator comments how the

> [e]mperials themselves that were their executioners, like a father that weeps when he beats a child, yet still weeps and still beats, not without much ruth and sorrow prosecuted that lamentable massacre.(p. 285)

Drawing on the structure of saturnalian festivities, the episode ends with the ritual physical abuse [bashing] of the Lord of Misrule in order to restore a safer world.

While the episode exploits the comic potential of the Anabaptist revolt by employing some of the familiar topoi of the carnivalesque, it is interspersed with religious polemic. A preacher's voice announces that 'the sermon begins' (p. 279), interrupting the narrative of Jack Wilton. It is worth noting that the sermonizing and moralizing comment in this episode, which is marked by a highly aggressive tone, has no parallel in the rest of the *Unfortunate Traveller*. As the theological issues addressed demonstrate, the concern clearly is with the millenarianism of radical reformed sects, captured in an apocalyptic scenario of violence:

> And the moon shall be turned into blood [Rev. 6. 12]: those that shine fairest, make the simplest show, seem most to favour religion, shall rent out the bowels of the Church, be turned into blood, and all this shall come to pass before the notable day of the Lord, whereof this age is the eve? (p. 280)

The reference to the bloody moon in *Revelation* and the allusion to Judgement Day point to a millenarian subtext, associated here with the Anabaptist enterprise, which Nashe equates with that of the Puritans: 'Hear what it is to be Anabaptists, to be Puritans, to be villains' (p. 286).

---

[15] Kristen Poole, 'Facing Puritanism: Falstaff, Martin Marprelate and the Grotesque Puritan', in *Shakespeare and Carnival: After Bakhtin*, ed. by Ronald Knowles (Basingstoke: Macmillan, 1998), pp. 97–122 (p. 102). See also Werner von Koppenfels, 'Thomas Nashe und Rabelais', *Archiv für das Studium der Neueren Sprachen und Literaturen*, 207 (1970), 277–91.

The issue of millenarianism is again addressed in Nashe's indignant observation that Puritans and Anabaptists 'snatch the Kingdom of Heaven to themselves with greediness, when we with all our learning sink into hell' (p. 280). His angry sermon is directed at the transgressors themselves, whose aspirations are ridiculed as immature and childish:

> The fault of faults is this: that your dead-born faith is begotten by too-too infant fathers.
> [...] None can be a perfect father of faith and beget men aright unto God, but those that
> are aged in experience, have many years imprinted in their mild conversations, and have,
> with Zachaeus, sold all their possessions of vanities to enjoy the sweet fellowship, not of
> the human, but the spiritual Messias. (p. 282)

Millenarianism is very much at the centre of Nashe's concern and constitutes the core of what he sees as the egregious heresies of all radical reformed sects. The virtue, he seems to imply, is to wait patiently for the Messiah. Continuing a theological tradition that goes back as far as Origen and Augustine, Nashe takes an anti-millenarian position by insisting that the Kingdom of Heaven is *not* of this world. The anti-millenarian stance is also strongly visible in Nashe's repeated censure of radical religious innovation, which favours the 'false glittering glass of innovation' over the 'ancient gold of the gospel' (p. 282).

Nashe makes clear that Münster Anabaptism is to be understood as a form of sacrilege, rooted in worldly ambitions that engender false interpretations of the Scriptures, disrespect for clerical authorities, and even for God himself. As he emphasizes, '[T]he name of religion [...] never suffers unrevenged.' In other words, society must be purged of the maledictory powers set free by blasphemy before harmony can be restored:

> The house of God a number of Church-robbers in these days have made a den of thieves.
> Thieves spend loosely what they have gotten lightly: sacrilege is no such inheritance;
> Dionys[i]us was ne'er the richer for robbing of Jupiter of his golden coat — he was driven
> in the end to play the schoolmaster at Corinth. The name of religion, be it good or bad,
> never suffers unrevenged. (p. 283)

Although Dionysius is known, first of all, for his tyrannical reign at Syracuse, Nashe selects only those two moments of his story which are central to (spi-)ritual purgation: sacrilege and its punishment. The blasphemous seizure of Zeus's golden robe is presented as the key moment provoking a curse, and his expulsion is linked directly to this sacrilegious act. In constructing a parallel to the Greek example, Nashe implies that religious radicals should be similarly expelled from Christ's figurative body, which they desecrate by 'rent[ing] out the bowels of the Church'.

Rowlands

The early and later years of the lesser known satirist Samuel Rowlands (fl. 1598–1628) remain obscure. Most of his work consists of pamphlets on satiric themes. His early satires were considered 'unfytt to be published' by bishops Whitgift and Bancroft, and were burnt on 26 October 1600. Rowlands seems to have borrowed extensively from the works of Nashe and Greene.[16] However, *Hell's Broke Loose* contains elements that must be derived from sources other than these. The most grotesque elements of the story appear as early as 1535 in a German pamphlet.[17] The poem narrates the course of the Münster events as a series that follows the structure of a cathartic ritual: evil spirits are called upon and encountered, and finally expelled in order to purge the affected person or community. The opening passage is reminiscent of a ritual incantation which identifies the dwellings of the harmful demons identified as 'murder', 'sedition', 'heresie', and 'false disloyall plots' (*The Argument*, ll. 7–8):

> From Darke Damnations vault where Horrours dwell,
> Infernal Furies, forth the lake of Hell
> Ariv'd on earth, and with their damned evils
> Fill'd the whole world of Incarnat Devils.
>
> (*The Argument*, ll. 1–4)

Calling on the furies of hell to appear on earth, the poem metaphorically resurrects the spectres of history: the ghost of Jack Straw speaks the prologue to the poem, inviting the reader to draw parallels between the English peasant rising of 1381 and the story of John of Leyden. As Norman Cohn reminds us, the peasant revolt had a strong millenarian subtext.[18] John Ball, who is mentioned as Straw's 'consort' (*Prologue*, l. 11), had preached against social inequality and the exploitation of peasants by feudal lords, who were seen as enjoying a life of luxury and ease at their expense. Ball's revolutionary theology encouraged his audiences to bring about the Day of Judgement, in order to put the ideals of equality and

---

[16] Reavley Gair, 'Rowlands, Samuel', in *Oxford Dictionary of National Biography* (Oxford University Press, 2004), <http://www.oxforddnb.com/view/article/24218> [accessed 10 May 2007].

[17] *Der gantze handel und geschicht/ von der stat Münster in Westphalen gelegen/wie es ergangen ist in einer kurtzen Summa begriffen*, printed by Hans von Guldenmundt in 1535.

[18] Norman Cohn, *The Pursuit of the Millennium: Revolutionary Millenarians and Mystical Anarchists of the Middle Ages* (London: Temple Smith, 1970), pp. 198–204. On Anabaptism and Münster, see pp. 252–80.

justice into practice. But the millenarian *New Jerusalem*, as Rowlands is at pains to point out, is to be understood rather as a 'Campe of Hell' (*The Argument*, l. 20): all evils hitherto safely confined to the netherworld will be unleashed. The prologue is followed by the nocturnal vision of John of Leyden's corpse, foreshadowing his miserable end:

> When nights blacke mantle over th'earth was laide,
> And *Cinthias* face all curtaine-drawne with clouds:
> And nights sweet rest, dayes care in quiet shrowds;
> About the hour of twelve in the dead of night,
> A mangled corpse appeared to my sight
> Skin torne, Flesh wounded, ugly to behold:
> A tottered Body peece-meale pull'd in sunder.
>
> (*The Life and Death of John Leyden*, ll. 1–8)

Both John of Leyden and Jack Straw are 'accursed in the sight of God' (*Prologue*, l. 20). This points to the magical belief that a transgression against the sacred laws of a community will attract God's curse and affect the wider community; the curse has therefore to be directed toward the transgressors. The curse, and the insistence on the demonic nature of the Münster rebels, are repeated ('behold a cursed crue, Such as *Hells-mouth* into the World did spue'; *The Argument*, ll. 11–12) so as to ensure that the Anabaptist ideas invoked in the verses to follow are understood as satanic.

The re-enactment of the Anabaptist regime in *Hell's Broke Loose* goes far beyond Nashe's concentration on the spectacle of the soldier-fools. After the demons are invoked, they are given the opportunity to speak. The famous Reformation slogan coined by John Ball — 'for when old Adam delved and Evah span, where was my silken velvet gentleman' (*Life and Death*, ll. 41–42) — captures the political convictions of Knipperdollinck and 'Tom Mynter' (Thomas Müntzer). Yet to question inequality and protest against economic exploitation is presented as satanic: as the introduction and the concluding line emphasize, Leyden and his crew were seduced by the devil into tempting ignorant citizens.

After John of Leyden has installed himself as the King of Münster, he declares all property to belong to everyone, and that punishment is to be abolished. He tells his counsellor to search the town for

> some lustie wenches of the German breede,
> For to the flesh I feele my selfe inclinde:
> Some halfe a dosen wives for me provid
> and stocke me with some Concubines beside.
>
> (*Life and Death*, ll. 435–38)

Moreover, he commands that gold and jewels be brought to him from the gold-
smith, declaring that he 'neither mean[s] to pay', nor 'go on score' (l. 444); and
further demands piles of luxury materials such as silk, velvet, and taffeta in which
to clothe his soldiers. The banquet to seal the new order is held under the motto
'bee merry, eate, and drinke, and call for more' (l. 462). All trades, from butcher
to brewer, are 'greatly want[ed]' to provide for the feast, including the baker and
his 'mealy-worship' (l. 458). The new dispensation is worded as follows:

> All is our owne that is within the Towne,
> And wee are men that have the world at will:
> Fill Bowles of Wine, carowse a High-Dutch round,
> For Cares lye conquerd, and our Ioyes are croun'd.
>   (*Life and Death*, ll. 465–68)

The reversal of sin and virtue signals the antinomian spirit prevalent in millenarian movements. At the same time, it corresponds to the carnivalesque order of
a Land of Cockaigne, where earthly suffering has disappeared and everlasting joy
has finally been realized.

Rowlands's spectacle of merry laughter in *New Jerusalem*, however, will soon
be over for the Münsterites, while it has only just begun for the reader. The period
of excess is immediately followed by the fasting and abstinence of Lent, and the
Lords of Misrule are stripped of their glory. Besieged by the Duke of Saxony,
'Ambitions wheele' (l. 469) turns to the disadvantage of the rebels, who now
suffer famine. The new Lords are utterly helpless, and their despair drives them
to eat mice and rats and boil old shoes for soup:

> Horses and Dogges they lickt their lips upon,
> Then Rats and Mise grew daintie meate at last,
> Olde shooes they boyld, which made good broth beside,
> Buffe-lether Ierkins cut in Steakes they fride.
>   (ll. 489–92)

When all the boots and leather in town have been consumed, the inhabitants start
to raid the shops of scribes, to still their hunger with parchment. Although debts
had already been cancelled when the new order was established, the narrator adds
that not even the stock accounts are spared:

> When they had eaten up the Chaundlers trade,
> As likewise all the ware Shoomakers had,
> The Scriveners shops for parchment they invade,
> And seize upon it even hunger mad,

> Cancelling with their teeth both bond and bill,
> Looke after debts and pay them he that will.
>
> (ll. 506–11)

Weakened by hunger so that 'such leane Anatomies they seemed all, | Like those dry bones in the Chirurgeons hall' (ll. 570–71), the transgressors are defeated by the Duke and are 'restored to their first degree' (l. 576). This is the end of the anti-king and his host of fools, whose dethronement restores the familiar hierarchy, and whose defeat secures the banishment of evil from society. The poem ends with a warning to 'like offenders' (l. 590): recalling the forces of evil which are now overcome, the final lines form a spell to ward off any further sacrilege, which in *Hell's Broke Loose* is mainly understood to be treason. Treason, however, is not only a violation of political rules; there are repeated reminders that treason comes from the devil and is therefore an act of sacrilege against the sacred order. This, of course, calls for a curse, which in post-Reformation culture takes the form of the supposedly secular genre of satire.

Conclusion

If satire is linked to the cultural practices known as carnival, *saturnalia* or Shrovetide, as well as to the confrontational religious climate of the late sixteenth century, the curses uttered in religious satire seem to fill a ritual vacuum left behind by the Reformation of the English Church. As Kristen Poole has argued, portrayals of Puritans as ridiculous and grotesque characters in Elizabethan drama and literature began with the Marprelate affair:

> [I]n a climate of undefined, transitional, ambiguous and metamorphosizing religious identities, the grotesque, with its incessant ambiguity and mergence of bodies, best articulated the emergence of popular Protestantism.[19]

As my examples suggest, however, grotesque representations of the religious 'Other' do not only emerge from religious uncertainty. They might also have a deeper connection to pagan and Catholic practices than is generally recognized. The carnivalesque presents a particularly suitable conduit for the expression of political anxieties. In Nashe and Rowlands, the temporary reversal of order in carnival merges with the idea of the *mundus inversus* of apocalypticism, the world turned upside down. This correlates directly with the reformers' own view of their

---

[19] Poole, 'Facing Puritanism', p. 116.

agenda, as the temporal kingdom of the millenarian reign is conceived of as a return, and therefore a reversal of the present world, which sets the perverted world right again.

However, the narratives not only represent carnival and transgression but structurally imitate cathartic ritual: they invoke the demons, dress them as fools, ridicule them, and punish them in the end. In doing so, the texts display a performative ritual potential which has hitherto mainly been ascribed to theatre.[20] The narratives in effect re-enact a past catastrophe, celebrating the punishment of the transgressors. The sermonizing additions that comment on and complement the stories then function as curses and spells against future transgressors; Rowlands explicitly refers to them as 'demons'. The offences of radicals go far beyond the precisianism for which Puritans are often mocked in Elizabethan literature. The iconoclastic tendencies of radicals are presented in Nashe and Rowlands as violations of a sacred order. Understood in this way, these satirical texts indeed substantiate Elliott's contention that the 'stuff of which satire is born is a primitive, incantatory invective', a view that may lead us to reconsider the role of religious satire in the ritual vacuum of a post-Reformation context.[21]

---

[20] I am grateful to Tobias Döring for his helpful remarks here.

[21] Elliott, *The Power of Satire*, p. 283.

Part II
The Theology of Word and Image

THE SPEAKING PICTURE:
VISIONS AND IMAGES IN THE POETRY OF
JOHN DONNE AND GEORGE HERBERT

Frances Cruickshank

Western Christianity has a long history of the importance of vision. Visions of glory or prophecy were vouchsafed to chosen individuals in the New Testament era and in the early church. Though St Augustine condemned *concupiscentia oculorum*, he gave credence to spiritual visions, found in dreams or cultivated in meditation, and interpreted allegorically as pictures of abstract truth; the Bible itself was understood by the Fathers in part as a 'picture-book' of moral, spiritual, and eschatological lessons. The medieval cult of images involved the prizing of relics, the contemplation and worship of saints' statues, and the colourful pageantry of Mystery Plays and Corpus Christi masses. In the thirteenth century, Thomas Aquinas argued that the correct veneration of images acted as an aid to devotion for the illiterate believer.[1] In the fourteenth century, mystics such as Julian of Norwich and Margery Kempe recorded visions of Christ in which he spoke with them and gave them instruction. In the European Renaissance Bonaventure, Ignatius Loyola, Teresa of Avila, Luis de la Puente, and François de Sales produced manuals of meditation in which the practitioner was encouraged to visualize and embellish scenes from the life of Christ in minute detail as an aid to increased virtue and devotion. In addition to spiritual vision, the physical vision of the faithful has long been channelled toward the key images and signs of religious history.

[1] Martin Jay, *Downcast Eyes: The Denigration of Vision in Twentieth-Century French Thought* (Berkeley and Los Angeles: University of California Press, 1993), p. 41.

During the English Reformation, however, the long tradition of religious vision and the veneration of images gave way to a Protestant emphasis on reading and hearing the written and spoken word. Ramie Targoff has noted the shift in the period from a visual to an auditory orientation: at literal and figurative levels, pictures were replaced by texts in public Christian spaces. The pulpit gained in prominence throughout the sixteenth and seventeenth centuries, particularly at the Puritan end of the spectrum but also in the English Church (an exception is offered by the archbishopric of William Laud). Catholic architecture, with its lavish renderings in glass, plaster, and canvas of the lives of the saints began to seem unnecessary to the real business of Christian faith: understanding the Word. The dread of images was so great in some quarters that even books were suspect since they were only, in Brownist defector John Smythe's words, 'signs and pictures'.[2] In abstract theology too, there was a change of focus from universal to personal salvation history: the emergence of the 'individual' in early modern culture meant that the spiritual eyes were turned inward to the private conscience rather than outward to the images of redemption held up before a homogeneous congregation. To borrow J. B. Broadbent's useful summary,

> [T]he Catholic scheme of salvation centred on the supernal drama of Incarnation, Passion, and Resurrection [was] replaced by the Protestant scheme centred on the individual and more naturalist drama of human depravity, effectual calling and imputed righteousness — involving a shift of emphasis from the crucified and risen Christ to the fallen and regenerate Adam.[3]

As a result of these changes, the spectacle of the Crucifixion no longer occupied the central place in theology or in practice.

It did, however, occupy a central place in the imaginations of John Donne and George Herbert. Each poet's work registers a strongly visual apprehension of the doctrines of Christianity and a desire to explore the religious landscape through the conceit of the eyes of faith. In the *Holy Sonnets* and in other poems like 'The Crosse', 'The Annuntiation and Passion', and 'Goodfriday, 1613. Riding Westward', Donne vividly revisits the Crucifixion, and the idea of the spectacle underpins his devotional poetics. Herbert reconstructs equally vivid portraits of Christ in the garden ('The Agony') and on the Cross ('The Sacrifice'), as well as celebrating the visual remembrance of the emblems in his Eucharistic poems.

---

[2] Ernest B. Gilman, *Iconoclasm and Poetry in the English Reformation: Down Went Dagon* (Chicago: University of Chicago Press, 1986), p. 42.

[3] J. B. Broadbent, *Some Graver Subject: An Essay on Paradise Lost* (London: Chatto and Windus, 1960), p. 17.

Herbert's poetry is based more on the religious countryside than on the central exhibition of the Passion, but he nevertheless relies overwhelmingly on images and on the conceit of spiritual sight.

Both poets' use of meditative structures and patterns has been well documented by Louis L. Martz and Rosemund Tuve, but to current legatees of Barbara Lewalski's *Protestant Poetics*, their visions of the Cross and of spiritual history pose a difficulty.[4] Why are these Protestant poets so fascinated by the spectacle of the Crucifixion — a spectacle all but erased from public Protestant consciousness — and why do their poems expend so much energy in vividly describing it? There have been various critical responses to this challenge. R. V. Young continues Martz's labour to establish medieval, Catholic, and Continental influences on the poetry; Anthony Low and Arthur Clements similarly find links between the devotional poetry and its medieval ancestors.[5] Others, like Michael Schoenfeldt and Catherine Creswell, have produced theological readings that manage to psychologize, and thereby 'Protestantize', the obvious visuality of the poetry. Schoenfeldt argues cogently that the Passion poems of these Protestant poets are

> not so much vivid dramatizations of the sacrifice as they are performances of the enormous difficulty of apprehending what is, in Donne's words, 'a spectacle of too much weight' [...]. What becomes for these poets the central subject of the Passion, then, is not the tortured body of Jesus, but rather the ethical, intellectual, and finally emotional difficulty of accepting unequivocally the extravagant mercy achieved by the extravagant agony at the centre of the Christian dispensation.[6]

Catherine Creswell argues further that what looks like visuality in Donne is in fact a 'movement away from vision' to intellectual interpretation of verbal revelation.[7] These are insightful readings of the poetry, and they have uncovered

---

[4] Louis L. Martz, *The Poetry of Meditation* (New Haven: Yale University Press, 1954); Rosemund Tuve, *Elizabethan and Metaphysical Imagery* (London: Cambridge University Press, 1947); Barbara Keifer Lewalski, *Protestant Poetics and the Seventeenth-Century Religious Lyric* (Princeton: Princeton University Press, 1979).

[5] R. V. Young, *Doctrine and Devotion in Seventeenth-Century Poetry: Studies in Donne, Herbert, Crashaw and Vaughan* (Cambridge: Brewer, 2000); Anthony Low, *Love's Architecture: Devotional Modes in Seventeenth-Century English Poetry* (New York: New York University Press, 1978); Arthur Clements, *The Poetry of Contemplation* (New York: New York University Press, 1990).

[6] Michael Schoenfeldt, '"That Spectacle of Too Much Weight": The Poetics of Sacrifice in Donne, Herbert, and Milton', *Journal of Medieval and Early Modern Studies*, 31 (2001), 561–84 (p. 562).

[7] Catherine Creswell, 'Turning to See the Sound: Reading the Face of God in Donne's Holy Sonnets', in *John Donne's Religious Imagination*, ed. by Raymond-Jean Frontain and Frances M. Malpezzi (Conway, AR: UCA Press, 1995), pp. 181–201 (p. 184).

valuable connections and associations, but they exhibit a timidity about the way Donne and Herbert negotiate the boundaries between image and word. To those determined to preserve the Protestant sensibility of this poetry, physicality, visuality, and dramatization become metaphors for a psychology of salvation that is both word-oriented and intellectualized. The Catholic cult of the visual is reinterpreted as the imagery of a Protestant metaphysic.

Yet these elaborate theological contortions, however interesting or probable in themselves, tend to occlude the importance, in the adoption of the visual style, of the poetic forms. There is no need to produce theological explanations of problems which the poets themselves did not experience. If we pay attention to the self-conscious voice of the poet in the structures of the poetry, it becomes clear that their visions of the Passion were in the imaginative and devotional power of poetry involved, rather than in any politico-religious debates. In Donne and Herbert and their contemporaries, the techniques of meditation and the cultivation of spiritual vision are literary devices rather than devotional practices. They are symptoms of a literary sensitivity to the power of images rather than of a devotional nostalgia for the vanished splendours of Catholic visuality. The consistency of the theme of visuality in both poets points to their eclecticism, not as religious men, but as poetic makers, and to the privileged position of poetry as a mode of religious discourse operating outside the partisan world of contemporary religious politics. As Debora Shuger has recently pointed out, both poets exhibit a conscious turning away from the 'curious questions and divisions' of fractious theology toward a consensus of the Christian faith as expressed in symbols, stories, and images.[8] Both attribute to poetry the power of escape from abstract doctrine into the realm of true faith, and even true vision, since poetry, like the metaphorical language of the Bible, joins the image and the word, and contrives to do so without inviting quibbling analyses or etymological controversies.

Fundamental to the relationship between word and image in Renaissance literary culture is the Horatian dictum *ut pictura poesis*. This becomes clear, for example, from the idea that pictures contain a readable message, and that, conversely, texts can function as a form of pictogram. Apart from the visual shapes of poems (such as Herbert's 'The Altar' and 'Easter Wings'), poetry as a 'speaking picture' was thought to harness the mind's image-making power. In Sidney's words, the poet 'yieldeth to the powers of the mind an image of that whereof the Philosopher bestoweth but a wordish description: which doth neither strike,

---

[8] Debora Kuller Shuger, 'Literature and the Church', in *The Cambridge History of Early Modern English Literature*, ed. by David Loewenstein and Janel Mueller (Cambridge: Cambridge University Press, 2002), pp. 512–43 (p. 513).

pierce, nor possess the sight of the soul so much as that other doth'.[9] Poetry could invoke the visual without courting, like its sister arts of painting and sculpture, charges of idolatry. Its verbal basis could preserve poetry from iconoclasm, yet its power as an art medium was more dependent on images than on discursive sequences. As Ernest B. Gilman comments in relation to the seventeenth-century lyric,

> [T]he power to move and delight is not carried by the flow of words moment to moment but by their cumulative potential to project or release a richly compacted spatial 'image' of which language itself is only the signifier.[10]

Any approach to the poetry of Donne and Herbert, therefore, should show awareness that they understood it not primarily as a discursive expression of doctrines or ideas, but as a 'speaking picture' of their own devotions and of the images that inspired them.

In Donne's *Holy Sonnets* and other religious poems, the consistent assumption is that vision is an essential part of the relationship with an invisible God. The *La Corona* sequence is based on a series of visions culminating in Christ's death and resurrection. In 'Holy Sonnet I', the 'dimme-eyed' speaker is restored to spiritual health by 'look[ing]' toward God; in IV, the speaker looks forward to seeing God's face after death; in VII, the 'numberlesse infinities of soules' will behold God with their eyes; in XVIII, the plea is 'Show me, deare Christ, thy spouse, so bright and clear'.[11] Interesting as Creswell's reading of the *Sonnets* is, her suggestion that they reflect an iconoclastic mistrust of images is unconvincing. Donne frequently employs visions of the Cross or of the glorified Christ as key mediators between prevenient grace and subjective anxiety, and often it is precisely the 'specular' or physical aspects of the vision which prove most efficacious for Donne. Far from harbouring 'an iconoclastic skepticism about the truth of images', Donne finds in images of Christ's Passion a truth all the more reassuring because it is visual.[12] Perhaps the most striking of the visual conceits is in 'Sonnet XIII', where the vision of Christ crucified is permanently engraved in the speaker's heart. It is the physical

---

[9] Philip Sidney, *An Apology for Poetry*, ed. by Geoffrey Shepherd (Manchester: Manchester University Press, 2002), p. 90.

[10] Ernest B. Gilman, *Iconoclasm and Poetry in the English Reformation: Down Went Dagon* (Chicago: University of Chicago Press, 1986), p. 23.

[11] John Donne, *Poetical Works*, ed. by Herbert J. C. Grierson (London: Oxford University Press, 1971), pp. 293, 294, 296, 301. All quotations from Donne's poems are taken from this edition.

[12] Creswell, 'Turning to See the Sound', p. 184

spectacle of Christ, which R. V. Young likens to a 'Spanish baroque crucifix',[13]
that reassures the troubled conscience:

> What if this present were the worlds last night?
> Marke in my heart, O Soule, where thou dost dwell,
> The picture of Christ crucified, and tell
> Whether that countenance can thee affright,
> Teares in his eyes quench the amasing light,
> Blood fills his frownes, which from his pierc'd head fell.
> And can that tongue adjudge thee unto hell,
> Which pray'd forgivenesse for his foes fierce spight?
> No, no; but as in my idolatrie
> I said to all my profane mistresses,
> Beauty, of pitty, foulnesse onely is
> A signe of rigour: so I say to thee,
> To wicked spirits are horrid shapes assign'd,
> This beauteous forme assures a pitious minde.

Meditating on his own death, Donne turns to an image of the dying Christ, bloody and lachrymose yet strangely beautiful. It is precisely this physical representation of Christ that prepares him for the final confrontation with God: 'This beauteous forme assures a pitious minde.' This sonnet is reminiscent of Laud's famous statement in a speech to the Star Chamber that there is 'greater reverence due to the Body than to the Word of our Lord'; yet here the body is emblematic and heavily coded.[14] Although Creswell reads the 'amasing light' as 'a glare that both blinds and is blinded', the 'light' of Christ's divine spiritual nature is surely quenched, for humanity's sake, by the tears that spring from his physical nature. The Incarnation protects our eyes from a direct and thus fatal vision of divinity, while at the same time giving us a palpable manifestation of that divinity. Thus in the poem, tears are a visual reassurance of the mercy of God, and blood is a physical representation of Christ's atonement. Such tokens are easier to grasp than verbal promises, and the sonnet illustrates the poetics of the Incarnation, where Christ's physical body is the seal of the covenant between God and humanity.

[13] R. V. Young, 'Donne's *Holy Sonnets* and the Theology of Grace', in *Bright Shootes of Everlastingnesse: The Seventeenth-Century Lyric*, ed. by Claude J. Summers and Ted-Larry Pebworth (Columbia: Missouri University Press, 1987), pp. 20–39 (p. 35).

[14] Quoted in Achsah Guibbory, *Ceremony and Community from Herbert to Milton* (Cambridge: Cambridge University Press, 1998), p. 22.

However, the poem takes place not in the speaker's heart but in the textual space marked out by the poetic form. The material out of which the reassuring image of Christ is constructed is neither the transparent haze of pure imagination nor opaque blocks of wood or stone, but poetic words that direct the gaze of the reader toward the central image. This image is not idolatrous, but rather one of the 'pictures' which poetry alone has the capacity to represent legitimately. The instruction is to 'mark the picture', but the reader is not left to look in silence. The speaker builds the picture piece by piece ('look at the tears, see the blood, notice the pierced head') and it takes shape even as the reader follows the speaker's pointing finger. Although the poem is presented as an intensely private meditation, it is in fact an exhibition of the picture, and indeed of its felt implications, by the poet as artist. This sonnet enacts Donne's conviction that the imaginative power of poetry offers a refuge from the unambiguously doctrinal by embodying doctrine in images, just as God was embodied in Christ, and the ideas of love and wrath in blood and tears.

This idea is developed further in lines 11–18 of '*Goodfriday, 1613. Riding Westward*':

> There I should see a Sunne, by rising set,
> And by that setting endlesse day beget;
> But that Christ on this Crosse, did rise and fall,
> Sinne had eternally benighted all.
> Yet dare I'almost be glad, I do not see
> That spectacle of too much weight for mee.
> Who sees Gods face, that is selfe life, must dye;
> What a death were it then to see God dye?

The 'spectacle of too much weight' has drawn some discussion in its own right. P. M. Oliver sees the speaker's reluctance to behold the scene simply as a conceit, an 'endeavour to wrench personal meaning from one of the scenes most frequently depicted by artists and devotional writers by approaching it from an oblique angle'.[15] Michael Schoenfeldt, by contrast, reads that reluctance as pointing to a diffidence about the very construction of poetry around suffering itself. According to Schoenfeldt, Donne asks 'how the immense suffering of the Christian sacrifice can be represented in poetry, free of the inevitable anesthesia of memory and the distorting fictions of the imagination'.[16] Yet despite these qualms, the

---

[15] P. M. Oliver, *Donne's Religious Writing: A Discourse of Feigned Devotion* (London: Longman, 1997), p. 107.

[16] Schoenfeldt, '"That Spectacle of Too Much Weight"', p. 562.

poem is a picture of Christ's death, and one that turns the problems inherent in representation to its own advantage.

Within the structure of the poem, the speaker's reluctance to 'see' derives directly from the double nature of the vision. The historical spectators at Christ's death suffered no similar reserve; they jeered or mourned, but none of them are portrayed as finding the spectacle as intellectually 'weighty' as Donne seems to. His vision of the Cross incorporates both the historical episode and its theological implications, and the combination is overpowering:

> Could I behold those hands which span the Poles,
> And turn all spheares at once, pierc'd with those holes?
> Could I behold that endlesse height which is
> Zenith to us, and our Antipodes,
> Humbled below us? or that blood which is
> The seat of all our Soules, if not of his,
> Made durt of dust, or that flesh which was worne
> By God for his apparell, rag'd and torne?
>
> (ll. 21–28)

In short, can he behold an incarnate Almighty God subject to a very painful, physical death? The real application of this vision does not lie in a reconciliation of the spectacle with the speaker's theological knowledge or his religious affections. Rather, the stunning paradoxes are an end in themselves. When vividly displayed before the soul's theologically informed gaze, the Crucifixion is astounding in its effect, and propositions accepted readily enough by the intellect become precisely 'spectacle[s] of too much weight' for the eyes of faith. Hence the construction of a poem that has this drama as its subject is a 'distorting fiction' only insofar as it renders our perceptions appropriate to the Crucifixion. Without the fiction of the weighty spectacle, our memory of the event would be inadequate. With its powers of vivid representation and articulation of powerful feeling as well as abstract thought, poetry can visualize such spectacles in a way that no other art form can.

If Donne's poems concentrate on the Crucifixion as the central object of imaginative vision, Herbert's 'inner biblical landscape' is more concerned with a typological assimilation of biblical history as one of the marks of the Protestant engagement with Scripture.[17] The liturgical calendar of *The Temple* opens, however, in Passion Week, with the Complaint of Christ in 'The Sacrifice', and, a few pages on, with 'The Agony'. In this poem, Herbert makes the metaphysical

---

[17] Low, *Love's Architecture*, p. 37.

concepts of 'Sinne and Love' visible in the blood, sweat, and tears of the anguished Christ. Philosophers may be able to measure mountains and fathom the sea, but they cannot measure the love of God or the depth of sin; these immeasurable qualities can only be grasped through images:

> Who would know Sinne, let him repair
> Unto Mount Olivet; there shall he see
> A man so wrung with pains, that all his hair,
>   His skinne, his garments bloudie be.
> Sinne is that presse and vice, which forceth pain
> To hunt his cruell food through ev'ry vein.
>
> Who knows not Love, let him assay
> And taste that juice, which on the crosse a pike
> Did set again abroach; then let him say
>   If ever he did taste the like.
> Love is that liquour sweet and most divine,
> Which my God feels as bloude; but I, as wine.[18]

Sin and love are directly expressed in the graphically represented sufferings of Christ. Herbert renders these sufferings so acutely that they cannot fail to affect the reader with the gravity of sin and the extraordinary cost of love. His skin, hair, and clothes are bloodied by the sheer physical stress of his agony, and pain invades his 'ev'ry vein'. His whole body is 'wrung with pains' by the burden of humanity's guilt. The concept of sin is juxtaposed with the physicality of Christ's body, making the doctrines of Incarnation and Atonement painfully real. In the final stanza, love has *become* blood. Love can be felt on the taste buds and in the oesophagus, not just in the 'heart'. God 'feels' the shedding of blood on the Cross as physical rather than emotional. Herbert is deliberately reversing the shift from physical to spiritual interpretations of the Passion: he is not psychologizing vision, but visualizing psychology.

In his Eucharistic poems, Herbert brings to life the sacramental elements and transforms them into the simulacra of achieved spiritual vision. In 'The Banquet', the physical enactment of the Eucharist provides a vision of God:

> Having rais'd me to look up,
>   In a cup
> Sweetly he doth meet my taste.

---

[18] George Herbert, *The English Poems of George Herbert*, ed. by C. A. Patrides (London: Dent, 1974), p. 58, ll. 7–18. All quotations from Herbert's poems are taken from this edition.

> But I still being low and short,
>   Farre from court,
> Wine becomes a wing at last.
>
> For with it alone I flie
>   To the skie:
> Where I wipe mine eyes, and see
> What I seek, for what I sue;
>   Him I view,
> Who hath done so much for me.
>   (ll. 37–48)

For Protestants, the Eucharist was not primarily a visual encounter. The Elevation of the Host was tantamount to idolatry, and the real purpose of the sacrament was an introspective and spiritual communion with God, facilitated by the outward signs. For Herbert in this poem, the signs are not carried into his introspective meditation; rather they carry him out of himself to an encounter that is primarily visual. In this way, his worshipful gaze can be seen as similar to the idolatry of the onlookers at Corpus Christi masses. However, the spectacle he views is God himself and not a man-made representation. Notwithstanding the very strong emphasis placed on the relation of word and sacrament by Protestant theology and Anglican ceremony, no word passes between Herbert and God in this communion, and no word is spoken over the feast apart from Herbert's own rhapsodic 'Welcome' (l. 1). Indeed, the sweetness of the banquet 'passeth tongue to taste or tell'. With wine 'alone' he flies to heaven and views God in silent wonder and gratitude. His gaze is not returned: this engagement with God is not a colloquy but a rapt contemplation. Yet the visual impact of God's 'pitie' inspires not only religious affection, but also the making of poetry. Though it '[p]asseth tongue to taste or tell' (l. 6), the whole poem is Herbert's own 'telling' of his experience, and it ends in a commitment to a life of praise:

> Let the wonder of this pitie
>   Be my dittie,
> And take up my lines and life:
> Hearken under pain of death,
>   Hands and breath;
> Strive in this, and love the strife.
>   (ll. 49–54)

A vision of God's glory might be expressed (however inadequately) in a nonverbal art form, but a vision of God which takes in his character, his actions, and his intentions toward the viewer requires the greater dimensions of poetry. In poetry, Herbert can combine the verbal with the imagistic and can paint the overlap of theology with history in the layered vocabulary of devotional poetry. In painting or sculpture, the imaginative apprehension of biblical or theological scenes is framed by the very occupation of space by the materials of canvas and marble. The nature of such works is to set limits of colour, shape, texture, and movement on the imaginative vision, to fix in time and space a visible representation of an imagined spectacle. By implication, they fix the viewer's apprehension on their own physical dimensions. The more limitless nature of poetic words provides a passage linking textual physicality, imaginative realization, and metaphysical vision. Poetry is a theatre of vision which sets up image after image while precluding idolatry, and which draws the reader's gaze by suggestion, evocation, and predication, not toward its own nature as a made object occupying time and space, but toward a clearer and clearer vision of its supreme subject, God himself. As we saw in Sidney's account, the poet paints a 'perfect picture' and yields to 'the powers of the mind an image' which can 'strike, pierce, [and] possess the sight of the soul'.[19]

Poetry also provides another kind of vision, suggested in 'The Foil':

> If we could see below
> The sphere of vertue, and each shining grace
> As plainly as that above doth show;
> This were the better skie, the brighter place.
>
> God hath made the starres the foil
> To set off vertues; griefs to set off sinning:
> Yet in this wretched world we toil,
> As if grief were not foul, nor vertue winning.

The poem echoes a sentiment from Plato's *Phaedrus* that Francis Bacon paraphrases in *The Advancement of Learning*: '[V]irtue, if she could be seen, would move great love and affection.'[20] If spiritual qualities and realities were visible, they would outshine earthly lights, and humans would live, most properly, 'as if virtue were ultimately more rewarding and worth pursuing than worldly activities. If only we could *see* the spiritual world as clearly as we see the physical, we would no doubt be more enamoured of virtue than we are. This desire is part of the

[19] Sidney, *An Apology for Poetry*, p. 90.

[20] Francis Bacon, '*Imitatio* and its Excesses; Poetry, Rhetoric and the Imagination', in *English Renaissance Literary Criticism*, ed. by Brian Vickers (Oxford: Clarendon Press, 1999), pp. 457–68 (p. 466).

privileging of vision that originated in classical Greece, was emphasized in the Middle Ages, and flourished in the emerging empiricism of the early modern period.[21] It assumes the power of images over words or thoughts to express truth and to inspire virtue. Having cited Plato, Bacon goes on to say that since virtue 'cannot be shewed to the sense by corporal shape, the next degree is to shew her to the imagination in lively representation'.[22] In this account, creative or mimetic arts become a window onto the ideal world, providing both vision and inspiration. Poetry is a way of 'seeing' things inaccessible to the physical eye, as well as a mode of persuasive speech that invites readers to step through the window into the ideal world.

Milton also attributed to poetry the ability to inspire virtue. In *The Reason of Church-Government*, he explains that God has endowed the poets with the power 'to inbreed and cherish in a great people the seeds of vertu'.[23] Sidney's *Apology* claims a similar role for poetry, asserting that the philosopher's definitions of virtue

> lie dark before the imaginative and judging power, if they be not illuminated or figured forth by the speaking picture of poesy [that] ever setteth virtue so out in her best colours [...] that one must needs be enamoured of her.[24]

Herbert likewise credits poetry with powers of edification: his avowed aim in allowing his poems to be published was that the 'picture of [his] many spiritual conflicts' might glorify God and 'turn to the advantage' of poor dejected souls.[25] His evocative pictures of virtue (or of his failure to reach it) are designed to open that window between the real and the ideal, and to bridge the gaps between the intellect and the imagination on the one hand, and on the other, between mortal and immortal vision. Religious poetry, combining the faculties of wit and imagination, and the qualities of the human and the divine, is aptly fitted to perform that dual function, as Herbert's 'Perirrhanterium' suggests:

> Thou, whose sweet youth and early hopes inhance
> Thy rate and price, and mark thee for a treasure;
> Hearken unto a Verser, who may chance

[21] Jay, *Downcast Eyes*, p. 32.

[22] Bacon, '*Imitatio* and its Excesses', pp. 466–67.

[23] John Milton, *The Reason of Church-Government*, in *Selected Prose*, ed. C. A. Patrides (Columbia: University of Missouri Press, 1985), p. 57.

[24] Sidney, *An Apology for Poetry*, pp. 90, 93.

[25] Izaak Walton, *The Lives of John Donne and George Herbert*, ed. by Charles W. Eliot (New York: Collier, 1937), p. 414.

> Ryme thee to good, and make a bait of pleasure.
> A verse may finde him, who a sermon flies,
> And turn delight into a sacrifice.
>
> (ll. 1–6)

Herbert confounds the traditional functions of poetry by suggesting, along Horatian lines, that, in devotional poetry at least, profit is pleasurable, and pleasure becomes profit. Where a sermon might fall wide (or short), a verse may 'pierce the sight of the soul', and bring the reader into direct communion with the beauty of truth. Joseph Summers wrote of the poems that

> as acts of worship they were to symbolize in their elaborate forms the beauty of the divine creation. As acts of edification they were to communicate to others the rational fitness of the symbolic forms, and to inflame them with the desire to follow the 'beauty of holiness'.[26]

As such, poetry was not a picture on the wall, but a window *through* the wall; not an object to contemplate but itself a way of seeing. Donne and Herbert, along with Sidney, Bacon, and Milton, regarded poetry as a 'speaking picture' whose voice was more powerful than homilies. It could dramatically reveal the truths hidden in the words of the Gospel message and heighten the emotional response (and hence the devotional response) to those truths through the legitimate 'distortion' of fiction.

There has been a trend in early modern studies to talk about poems only as the culturally determined artifacts of a previous age, in whose 'textual traces' we can discover biography, history, theology, and politics.[27] Yet, however sceptical we might be, with Stephen Greenblatt, of the notion of the artwork as a 'pure flame that lies at the source of our speculations', some degree of structural integrity remains in any given text — usually the theoretical scaffolding of the poetics operative in its creation. Interpretation depends as much on a knowledge of the poem's environment as on its felt purpose and nature.[28] Although the devotional poems of Donne and Herbert refer to the theological controversies surrounding them, and to the religious politics in which their own careers as churchmen were

---

[26] Joseph Summers, *George Herbert his Religion and Art* (London: Chatto and Windus, 1954), p. 84.

[27] Louis Montrose, 'Professing the Renaissance: The Poetics and Politics of Culture', in *The New Historicism*, ed. by H. Aram Veeser (London: Routledge, 1989), pp. 15–36 (p. 20).

[28] Stephen Greenblatt, 'Towards a Poetics of Culture', in *The New Historicism*, pp. 1–14 (p. 12).

involved, they also register a resistance to political currents and a desire to fence
poetry off from other modes of religious discourse. In her essay on the *Devotions
Upon Emergent Occasions*, Elena Levy-Navarro argues that Donne 'takes an anti-
polemicist position in order to renew and revitalize *"true Religion* in England"'.[29]
As Debora Shuger points out, Donne's and Herbert's lyrics 'do not stake out a
position in contemporary ecclesio-political debates. Like most early Stuart sacred
poetry, these are devotional lyrics, closer to prayer than polemic.'[30]

Within these perimeters, the poetry of Donne and Herbert exemplifies an
alternative religious practice onto which the Protestant prohibition of images
does not impinge. The poetic persona, rather than being a committed member
of the English Church or a closet Catholic, is more like the 'Christian every-
man' whom Anthony Low finds in Donne's *La Corona* sonnets.[31] In their reas-
sessments of Donne's politics Jonathan Goldberg, Arthur Marotti, and David
Norbrook are all concerned, in Norbrook's words, to 'banish simplistic notions
of poetry as serenely transcending its society and political structures', but such
classifications are themselves simplistic.[32] Frances M. Malpezzi's notion of 'sacred
reality', by contrast, articulates a context within which the categories of Catholic
and Protestant, medieval and contemporary, give way to the eternity of Christian
history, and the universality of spiritual experience.[33] As Herbert wrote in 'The
Quidditie', poetry was not 'a crown, | No point of honour [...] no office, art, or
news' (ll. 1–2); it was separate from the public space and the political economy.
It was, for Herbert, 'that which while I use | I am with thee, and *Most take all*'
(ll. 11–12).

This might seem a difficult case to make out for an age in which religion and
politics were so irretrievably entwined, but the poems, for all their theological

---

[29] Elena Levy-Navarro, 'Breaking Down the Walls That Divide: Anti-Polemicism in the
Devotions Upon Emergent Occasions', in *John Donne and the Protestant Reformation: New Perspectives*, ed. by Mary Arshagouni Papazian (Detroit: Wayne State University Press, 2003), pp. 273–
92 (p. 273).

[30] Shuger, 'Literature and the Church', p. 513.

[31] Low, *Love's Architecture*, p. 50.

[32] David Norbrook, 'The Monarchy of Wit and the Republic of Letters: Donne's Politics',
in *Soliciting Interpretation: Literary Theory and Seventeenth-Century English Poetry*, ed. by
Elizabeth D. Harvey and Katherine Eisaman Maus (Chicago: University of Chicago Press, 1990),
pp. 3–36 (p. 5).

[33] Frances M. Malpezzi, 'Donne's Transcendent Imagination: The Divine Poems as Hiero-
phantic Experience', in *John Donne's Religious Imagination* (see n. 7, above), pp. 141–61 (p. 147).

substance, do not necessarily participate in the ongoing public spectacle of religious controversy. For both Donne and Herbert, it was not their poetry that furthered or inhibited their worldly advancement. Whether or not either poet was part of a coterie, recent scholarship suggests a strong tension between a desire to keep the poetry to oneself and the inevitability of its wide dissemination.[34] By conceiving of themselves as purveyors of private praise rather than of public policy, poets could roam with licence through a variety of religious experience. In the preface to *The Glorious Feast of the Gospel*, Richard Sibbes complained that Christians had 'lost much of their Communion with Christ and his Saints [...] they have woefully disputed away, and dispirited the life of Religion and the power of Godlinesse into dry and sapeless Controversies about Government of Church and State'.[35] Donne's and Herbert's poetry was an attempt to animate the 'life of Religion' and to turn away from matters whose bearing on the spiritual life was slight. The 'speaking pictures' they conjured were not declarations of doctrine, nor statements of allegiance, but glimpses of the spiritual vision available to the poetic conscience, and images of the stories — or stories of the images — that lay, still fresh and vital, at the heart of Christian history.

[34] See Harold Love, *Scribal Publication in Seventeenth-Century England* (Oxford: Clarendon Press, 1993); Arthur F. Marotti, *Manuscript, Print, and the English Renaissance Lyric* (Ithaca: Cornell University Press, 1995); H. R. Woudhuysen, *Sir Philip Sidney and the Circulation of Manuscripts, 1558–1640* (Oxford: Clarendon Press, 1996).

[35] Quoted in Bryan Ball, *A Great Expectation: Eschatalogical Thought in English Protestantism to 1660* (Leiden: Brill, 1975), p. 237.

'NOT CLOTHED WITH ENGRAVEN PICTURES': EMBLEMS AND THE AUTHORITY OF THE WORD

Bart Westerweel

The emblem tradition can be traced to the publication of a humanist collection of epigrams by the Italian lawyer Andrea Alciato, published in 1531 with woodcut illustration added by Heinrich Steyner, Alciato's Augsburg publisher. In view of the success story of the emblem genre throughout Europe in the sixteenth and seventeenth centuries, it is most remarkable that its most frequent tripartite structure — motto, *pictura*, and *subscriptio* or epigram — arose from what was, in effect, a publisher's whim. Later emblem collections were sometimes published deliberately without pictures, constituting a small subsection of what are usually called *emblemata nuda*. In England Francis Thynne's manuscript collection *Emblemes and Epigrams* (1600) is a case in point. In the preface to the collection, made for Sir Thomas Egerton, Thynne explains the term naked, 'for soe I doe terme them because they are not clothed with engraven pictures'.[1] I shall return to this issue later on.

The emblem book grew into a fully developed genre with offshoots in various directions, one of which was the sacred emblem book. The first endeavours in this area were of Protestant extraction. In France Georgette de Montenay claimed that her *Emblemes, ou devises chrestiennes* (1571) were quite different from the exquisite examples of her predecessor Alciato precisely because of their Christian nature:

---

[1] Quoted in Rosemary Freeman, *English Emblem Books* (London: Chatto and Windus, 1948), p. 67. Thynne's *Emblemes and Epigrames* was edited by F. J. Fumivall for the Early English Text Society in 1867.

> Alciat feit des Emblemes exquis,
>
> Lesquels voyant de plusieurs requis,
>
> Desir me prit de commencer les miens,
>
> Lesquels je croy estre premier chrestiens.[2]

De Montenay wrote in the social context of the Protestant court of Navarre. A few years before de Montenay, Jan van der Noot, the greatest lyrical poet of his day in the Low Countries and a committed Protestant, had published *Het Theatre* in 1568–69 in three versions, in Dutch, French, and English respectively.[3] The English version, *A Theatre for Voluptuous Worldlings*, is frequently anthologized because it contains verse translations made by the young Edmund Spenser. The engraved illustrations were made by the famous Marcus Gheeraerts, who, like van der Noot, had found refuge from religious persecution in England.

Among the intriguing features of the structure of *Het Theatre* is its lack of conformity to the tripartite structure of the emblem form found in Alciato and many of his followers. But this type of argument is now accepted as a twentieth-century invention of the Procrustean variety. Many authors of emblem books in the sixteenth and seventeenth centuries, who had not yet felt the authority of twentieth-century theorists, designated their works as 'emblem' books, notwithstanding the wide range of forms that the term covered (for example, *emblemata nuda*, collections of *imprese* consisting of motto and picture only, collections with lengthy prose tracts replacing or complementing the epigram). It seems more profitable to ask whether it was the author's intention that his given work be taken as an emblem book. However, Werner Waterschoot maintains that in the case of van der Noot the evidence does not support that claim.[4] Waterschoot points out that in the dedication of *A Theatre* to Queen Elizabeth I, she is praised for her graces and virtues. These should not be accompanied by anything less worthy, such as 'fained Emblemes or Poetical fables'.[5] Waterschoot's view is undermined, however, by a failure to recognize that the derogatory reference to emblems may either be an instance of the *modestia* topos common in dedicatory

[2] Quoted in Barbara Lewalski, *Protestant Poetics and the Seventeenth Century* (Princeton: Princeton University Press, 1979), p. 184.

[3] Jan van der Noot, *Het Bosken en Het Theatre*, ed. by W. A. P. Smit (Utrecht: H & S, 1979).

[4] Werner Waterschoot, 'An Author's Strategy: Jan van der Noot's *Het Theatre*', in *Anglo-Dutch Relations in the Field of the Emblem*, ed. by Bart Westerweel (Leiden: Brill, 1997), pp. 35–47, especially p. 43.

[5] Jan van der Noot, *A Theatre for Voluptuous Worldlings*, facs. ed. by Louis S. Friedland (Delmar, NY: Scholars' Facsimiles & Reprints, 1977), fol. A4ᵛ.

epistles and other preliminaries, or it may indicate other types of emblems more frivolous than the religious visions van der Noot intends to offer.

Karel Bostoen, by contrast, urges that *Het Theatre* be categorized as an emblem book.[6] In support of this view, he cites van der Noot's use of the term *emblem* in the preface to the English version of *A Theatre*. Moreover, in *Het Bosken*, another of his works, van der Noot includes four emblems derived from the 1549 French Alciato edition by Aneau. Bostoen makes an ingenious case for a tripartite structure by referring to the sonnets or epigrams as the 'word' or motto of the emblem, while the picture forms the symbolic expression of the word, and the long prose commentary serves as the *explicatio* or exposition of the emblem. To me, however, Bostoen's solution seems to be as Procrustean as that of his opponents. All impose a normative rhetorical model that fails to do justice to the variety of practice of emblematists in the period.

Historically speaking, the structure of *Het Theatre* paved the way for numerous later Catholic — especially Jesuit — and Protestant emblem books in the meditative tradition. Here, the combination of *pictura*, epigram, and prose commentary was to become a standard structural feature. In the meditative religious emblem the *pictura* usually functions as the *compositio loci* of the meditative exercise, a visual scene drawn from memory or the imagination. The explanatory poem constitutes the meditative analysis — the second phase — and a final epigram, the colloquium, the third part.[7] The function of the final epigram was frequently assumed by the prose commentary that elaborated the general ideas of the first two parts. The expository prose in van der Noot clearly serves this purpose. The full meaning of the picture and verse only becomes clear in the prose commentary. The poems and their illustrations in the three sections of the book are all lyrical expressions of visions that are only fully interpreted in the prose passages. It seems likely that van der Noot consciously chose to commission the plates to be made by Gheeraerts for the Dutch and French editions, and by an unknown artist for the English version. The intention would have been to present a number of meditative units in which picture and poem jointly served a mnemonic purpose, and in which the prose completed each meditative exercise. In addition, as a poet, van der Noot used the visual element in Horatian terms of the adagium *utile dulci*:

---

[6] Karel Bostoen, 'Van der Noot's Apocalyptic Visions: Do You "See" What You Read?' in *Anglo-Dutch Relations* (see n. 4, above), pp. 49–61, especially p. 52.

[7] This scheme, derived from Ignatius's *Spiritual Exercises*, was first imported into scholarly discussions of early modern English literature by Louis Martz's *The Poetry of Meditation* (New Haven: Yale University Press, 1954).

Ende om de ydelheyt ende ongheduricheyt der eertscher dinghen beter te betoonen, heb
ick hier voorts ghebracht twintich ghesichten oft visioenen, ende heb de selue doen maken
int copere, op datmen daer oock // oochsienlyck wt mach mercken tghene dat ick
schriftelyck hebbe willen wtdrucken, tot genoechdoeninghe ende ghenuchte beyde der
ooren ende der ooghen, achteruolghende [...] dat Horatius seyt:

Omne tulit punctum qui miscuit vtile dulci.

Dat is:

Die leering' met ghenuchten menckt
De sake t'heuren eynde brenckt.[8]

Perhaps the greatest interest of van der Noot's book for the theme of this
volume lies in the religious thrust of the prose commentary. The poems are translations, of six sonnets from Marot's French version of Petrarch's visions and of
twelve sonnets by du Bellay, followed by four visions created by van der Noot
himself and inspired by scenes from the Apocalypse. The poems confirm van der
Noot's reputation as the greatest Pléiadist of the Low Countries. The overall
theme of the poetry is the vanity of all human endeavours and desires. The prose
commentaries elaborate on this theme, but, much more than the verse, demonstrate a vehemently anti-Catholic attitude. Van der Noot's intentions with respect
to his religious convictions are made unequivocally clear right from the start:

Het sijn nv 18. maenden Eerweerdighe Heere, dat ick verlatende mijns Vaders Lant in
Enghelant gecomen ben om te schouwen de besmettelycke ende verdoemelycke grouwelen
des Ro. Antichrists die in Brabant ende ouer al de Nederlanden nv wederom met groot
gewelt opghericht waren: ende oock om t'ontvlieden de onredelycke, onmenschelycke,
noyt ghehoorde ende onwtsprekelycke moorderijen ende tyrannyen die sijn lidtmaten,
dienaers ende beulen aenrechten ende ghebruycken ouer de ghene die heur tot sijne
schadelycke superstitien, insettinghen ende ordonnantien niet en willen begheven.[9]

---

[8] Van der Noot, *Het Bosken en Het Theatre*, p. 243; 'And in order to demonstrate the vanity
and mortality of earthly matters, I have presented here twenty views or visions, and have had them
made into copper engravings, thus also enabling the reader to find in clear visual form what I have
tried to express in writing, to satisfy and delight both ears and eyes, imitating [...] what Horatius
says *Omne tulit punctum qui miscuit dulci*. That is to say: Who mixes teaching and delight Brings
matters to their proper end' (my translation).

[9] Van der Noot, *Het Bosken en Het Theatre*, p. 190; 'It has now been 18. months Honourable
Sir, since I, leaving my Father's Country, have come to England shunning the contagious and
detestable horrors of the Roman Antichrist erected once again with great violence in Brabant and
all over the Low Countries: and also to flee from the unreasonable, inhuman, unprecedented and
unspeakable atrocities and tyrannies committed and used by its members against those who refuse
to adopt its pernicious superstitions, institutions and proclamations' (my translation).

These first phrases from the dedicatory letter to 'Rogier Martens' (Roger Martin, Lord Mayor of London in 1567–68) are followed by numerous others in similar vein. All human sinfulness and worldliness, van der Noot argues, are rooted in the misdemeanours of the Church of Rome. The first emblematic book printed in England, then, is one of the most rabidly anti-Catholic in the genre. Of course, this is not surprising in view of the terror from which van der Noot, Gheeraerts, and Lucas d'Heere (author of one of the dedicatory poems in *Het Theatre*) had just escaped.

The first sacred emblem book in English and by an Englishman was the collection of 'naked' emblems by Andrew Willet, *Sacrorum emblematum centuria una* (Cambridge, n.d., but probably 1592), with verses in Latin and English. Whereas van der Noot has literary qualities rare in emblem literature, the interest of Willet's collection is purely historical. One example will suffice to make clear that Willet is as tame as van der Noot is spirited, and his verse limp, where van der Noot's is agile. This is from Emblem 84, which bears the motto *Res crescunt Concordia*:

> The Bees by swarmes abroad doe flye,
> And worke together all:
> Refresht they be with pleasant crye
> And thicke on flowers fall.
> So without wrath we should agree.
> Beeing knit faste in one mind:
> If peace among the wicked bee
> Much more it should us binde.[10]

Rosemary Freeman suggests that the reason for the lack of plates in Willet's book of emblems was the much repeated idea that the quality of the visual arts fell so much below the standards set by Continental artists that Englishmen felt inhibited to include illustrations. In the remainder of this article I want to follow a different track to the well-trodden path of the inferiority of English art in the period. I take my starting point from the fact that, whenever English emblem authors wanted pictures in their books, they could and did incorporate them.

---

[10] Quoted in Freeman, *English Emblem Books*, p. 64. Quoting the English is not quite fair to Willet. He composed the verses in the emblem book in quite competent Neolatin, adding, for the sake of convenience, English translations of the kind included here.

When Geoffrey Whitney published the first printed English emblem book in
Leiden in 1586 the texts were his, but the woodcuts were printed from existing
wood blocks of various earlier emblem books. Whitney was, of course, fortunate
to find the wood blocks in stock in the Leiden workshop of Raphelengius,
Plantin's son-in-law, who ran the famous printer's house after Plantin had returned to Antwerp in 1585. The illustrations in Whitney's *A Choice of Emblemes*
(1586) all derive from Plantin editions of emblem books, by Alciato, Sambucus,
Paradin, Junius, and others. Similarly, in the year after Willet published his
emblems, Thomas Combe managed to find an artist to make wood blocks after
the French original by Guillaume de la Perrière (*Le Théâtre des bons engins*, Paris,
1539) for *The Theater of Fine Devices* (1593).[11]

Henry Peacham lived and worked in the entourage of Prince Henry. Peacham,
the son of the author of the well-known rhetorical treatise *The Garden of
Eloquence*, was himself responsible for a handbook for painters, *The Gentleman's
Exercise* (1612), published earlier as *The Art of Drawing with the Pen* (1606) and
of the courtesy book *The Compleat Gentleman* (1622), with sections on heraldry
and painting. In the former work Peacham complains about the deplorable state
of English engraving: 'scarce England can affoorde us a perfect penman or good
cutter'.[12] Peacham had entertained artistic aspirations from an early age. He was
the first English emblem writer to create both the words and the woodcuts in his
Minerva Britanna; or, A Garden of Heroical Devises (1612).

George Wither's *A Collection of Emblemes* (1635) contains the most beautiful
engravings of any emblem book published in England until the nineteenth
century. They were made by Crispyn de Passe for the *Nucleus emblematum
selectissimorum* (Arnhem, 1611/13), an emblem book by the German Gabriel
Rollenhagen. As Wither explains in the preliminaries to his emblem book, he was
so keen on procuring the magnificent plates of de Passe that he was willing to wait
'almost twentie yeares' for them.[13]

It is evident, then, that there was a variety of ways of putting an emblem book
with illustrations — a major selling point, after all — on the market. In the case
of Willet himself we know that he was familiar with French and Italian emblem

[11] Only two copies of Combe's emblem book are still in existence. See Thomas Combe,
Theater of Fine Devices, facs. ed. by Mary V. Silcox (Aldershot: Scolar, 1990), pp. 1–36.

[12] Henry Peacham, *The Art of Drawing with the Pen* (London: printed by R. Braddock for
W. Jones, 1606), sig. A2ᵛ.

[13] George Wither, *A Collection of Emblemes* (London: printed by A. M. for R. Milbourne,
1635), sig. A2.

books. In the dedicatory preface to the *Sacrorum emblematum centuria una* Willet criticizes an earlier emblem writer. He writes that he wants to set his 'sickle at somebody else's harvest'. That person had written in the vernacular rather than in the Anglo-Latin verse of Willet himself, as is mentioned on the title page. There can be no doubt that the earlier author referred to was Whitney. In the dedicatory epistle to his own book of emblems Whitney had frankly admitted that his emblems were 'gleanings out of other mens harvestes'.[14] Willet was known for his learning and profuse writing, producing an average of two theological works every year, a number of elaborate *Hexapla*, sixfold commentaries on books of the Old Testament, among them. He was a committed Protestant and published a number of anti-Catholic tracts, one of them bearing the curious title *Catholicon, that is, a general preservative or remedie against the Pseudocat Ho-like religion, gathered out of the Catholike epistle of S. Jude [...] with a preface seruing as a preparatiue to the Catholicon, and a dyet prescribed after* (1614). In the emblem book, too, the pope is the object of fierce attacks (e.g., in Emblem 22).[15] Willet used the Calvinist version of the Old Testament, the *Testamenti veteris Biblia sacra* of Immanuel Tremellius and Franciscus Junius, as the source of the biblical quotations in the *Sacrorum emblematum*.[16] Each of the emblems in Willet's collection consists of a Latin motto, a scriptural reference, followed by verses in Latin and their translation into English. As Michael Bath indicates,

> The scriptural references are not, like Whitney's headnotes and marginalia, supernumerary listings of authorities for received topoi, but identifications of the biblical location of the emblem Willet is versifying. In some ways it is the most important part of the emblem, and it is quite pointless to read Willet's emblems without looking up their biblical sources.[17]

Even more significant is what Willet has to say about the status of his emblems in the preliminaries of the emblem book. The title page emphasizes that the emblems are 'omnia à purissimis Scripturae fontibus derivata' (all derived from the purest founts of Scripture) and the dedicatory epistle states: 'omnia ex sacris Scripturis collecta & translata huc sunt' ([These emblems] have all been collected

---

[14] Geoffrey Whitney, *A Choice of Emblemes* (Leiden: F. Raphelenqius, 1586), sig. **2ᵛ. See also Michael Bath, *Speaking Pictures: English Emblem Books and Renaissance Culture* (London: Longman, 1994), p. 171; and Freeman, *English Emblem Books*, p. 53.

[15] For a brief introduction and a few samples of Willet's emblems, see Charles Moseley, *A Century of Emblems* (Aldershot: Scolar, 1989), pp. 110–21.

[16] See Freeman, *English Emblem Books*, p. 65. Cf. Irma Tramer, *Studien zu den Anfängen der puritanischen Emblemliteratur in England: Andrew Willet–George Wither* (Berlin: BL-druck, 1934).

[17] Bath, *Speaking Pictures*, p. 172.

and transferred from Holy Scripture).[18] Essential here is the word *translata*, which in humanist Latin has a variety of meanings. Since Latin is the primary language of Willet's collection, *translata* obviously does not mean 'translated' in the modern sense of the word. Rather, it suggests that the essential form of the emblems resides in the text of the Scriptures themselves and has been expressed metaphorically in the text of Willet's emblems. In this sense, the fact that there are no pictures in the *Sacrorum emblematum* is not an artistic defect but an emphatic statement underlining the Protestant nature of the emblem book. The only true illustrations of these naked emblems are to be found in the Scriptures. Instead of the harvest of multiple sources (as in Whitney) Willet presents the only true source of sacred inspiration: the Word of God Himself.

Barbara Lewalski explains how Calvinist sacramental theology avails itself of the emblematic mode

> not only in the general sense in which physical elements are seen as invested with spiritual significance, but also in the rather more specific literary sense of the emblem books, wherein image, motto, and (verse) explication all set forth a theme in their different modes, mutually interpreting and reinforcing each other.[19]

Lewalski quotes the *Institutes*, in which Calvin treats these 'physical elements' as emblem figures:

> [T]hey are seals of God's promises, representing those promises 'as pointed in a picture. [...] portrayed graphically and in the manner of images'. The word of the promises is like the motto — in Calvin's view prior to the sign in importance so that 'the sign serves the word'. [...] The word of the biblical text is clearly the dominant element in the emblem configuration, the medium through which Truth is primarily apprehended.[20]

John Donne transferred ideas such as these to the realm of prayer and personal devotion in his *Devotions upon Emergent Occasions* (1624):

> My *God*, my *God*, Thou art a *direct God*, may I not say a *literall God*. [...] But thou art also [...] a *figurative*, a *metaphoricall* God too: A *God* in whose words is such a height of *figures*, such *voyages*, such *peregrinations* to fetch remote and precious *metaphors*, such *extentions*, such *spreadings*, such *Curtaines of Allegories*, such *third Heavens of Hyperboles*, so *harmonious eloquutions* [...] as all *prophane Authors*, seeme of the seed of the *Serpent*, that *creepes*; thou art the *dove*, that *flies*.[21]

---

[18] Andrew Willet, *Sacrorum emblematum centuria una* (Cambridge: Ex Officina Iohannis Legate, 1592), title page; sig. A3. The English translation is from Bath, *Speaking Pictures*, p. 171.

[19] Lewalski, *Protestant Poetics*, pp. 186–87.

[20] Lewalski, *Protestant Poetics*, pp. 186–87.

[21] Quoted in Lewalski, *Protestant Poetics*, p. 221.

If the conclusions reached so far with regard to Willet's 'naked' emblems make any sense, they have important consequences for the interpretation of Protestant *emblemata nuda* as such. In the final paragraphs of this article I should like to test what has been said in a brief analysis of two case studies: texts that reached a far greater degree of fame than Willet's emblem book. Francis Quarles's *Emblemes* (1635) remains the most popular English emblem book ever published, and George Herbert's *The Temple* (1633) contains some of the finest lyric poetry in the English language. Both collections have substantial roots in specific strands of the tradition of the sacred emblem book. Along with others I have previously argued that Herbert's poetry is emblematic, and the centrality of this argument to Herbert's poetry has been echoed by Richard Todd, who has claimed that the presence of naked emblems in that poetry has become 'something of a critical commonplace'.[22]

Both works go back to Jesuit sources. Quarles's *Emblemes* is divided into five books, the first two derived from the *Typus Mundi* (Antwerp, 1627), made by students of the Jesuit College in Antwerp, while Books III, IV, and V go back to the influential *Pia Desideria* by the Jesuit priest Hermannus Hugo (Antwerp, 1624). Herbert's poetry is clearly influenced by the type of emblem book dealing with the exploits of Divine Amor and Anima, the human soul. Both the *Typus Mundi* and the *Pia Desideria* belong to this category. The type is characterized by its dialogic nature. The dialogue may be either instructive, reprehensive, morally corrective, or of a catechismal nature, Amor invariably performing the role of instructor, tutor, catechist, etc., while Anima is in a subservient position, suffering the lessons of her Divine guide. In my own study on Herbert, especially in the chapter on 'Love (III)', the relationship between Herbert and the Amor/Anima emblem book is dealt with in greater detail.[23]

Another major influence on Herbert's emblematic poetry was that of the *schola cordis*, or School of the Heart type, a parallel or subgenre of the Amor and Anima emblems. Here the human heart is either the object of the lessons, cures, or punishments of Divine Cupid, or is represented as the space, the room in which such activities take place. The state of the human heart is one of the most frequently explored images in Herbert's poetry. 'Love Unknown' is the most elaborate of his *schola cordis* poems. In the poem the heart undergoes all the penitential tortures that are common in this type of emblem. The relationship

---

[22] Richard Todd, *The Opacity of Signs* (Columbia: University of Missouri Press, 1986), p. 122.

[23] Bart Westerweel, *Patterns and Patterning* (Amsterdam: Rodopi, 1984), pp. 211–50.

between Herbert and the School of the Heart tradition has been explored and
analysed by Colie (1973), then by Westerweel (1983) and Todd (1986), among
others.[24]

Both Francis Quarles and George Herbert, then, drew on Catholic sources.
Both were committed members of the English Church, but, if there are anti-
Catholic tendencies in their work, they are not expressed as virulently as in van
der Noot and Willet. But then neither Herbert nor Quarles were on the run for
their religious convictions, as van der Noot was, and neither of them took a
position that made them vulnerable to political and religious persecution. Willet's
dedication of the *Sacrorum emblematum* to Essex in 1592, by contrast, explicitly
favoured the Protestant cause. In fact, Willet was imprisoned for a short period
by King James on account of his attack on the proposed Spanish match for Prince
Charles.[25] Both Herbert and Quarles were moderate Protestants in the sense
expressed best in Herbert's poem 'The British Church':

> She on the hills, which wantonly
> Allureth all in hope to be
> > By her preferr'd,
>
> Hath kiss'd so long her painted shrines,
> That ev'n her face by kissing shines,
> > For her reward.
>
> She in the valley is so shie
> Of dressing, that her hair doth lie
> > About her eares:
>
> While she avoids her neighbours pride,
> She wholly goes on th' other side,
> > And nothing wears.
>
> But dearest Mother, (what those misse)
> The mean thy praise and glorie is,
> > And long may be.

---

[24] Rosalie L. Colie, *The Resources of Kind: Genre-Theory in the Renaissance* (London:
University of California Press), especially pp. 32–75; Westerweel *Patterns and Patterning*, pp.
106–13; Todd, *Opacity of Signs*, pp. 122–48.

[25] Anthony Milton claims that 'he was apparently released after a month'. See Anthony
Milton, 'Willet, Andrew (1561/2–1621)', in *Oxford Dictionary of National Biography* (Oxford
University Press, 2004), <http://www.oxforddnb.com/view/article/29445> [accessed 23 April
2007].

> Blessed be God, whose love it was
> To double-moat thee with his grace,
> And none but thee.[26]

As Helen Wilcox explains at greater length elsewhere in this volume, in Herbert's poem the advantages of the *via media* (the 'mean') are distinguished from the 'pride' and 'painted shrines' of the Roman Church ('she on the hills') on the one hand and the liturgical bareness of Genevan Calvinism ('so shie | Of dressing, that her hair doth lie | About her eares') on the other. Herbert's use of 'naked' emblems rather than emblems with separate illustrations are an appropriate expression of his moderate Protestantism.

The changes Quarles made in adapting the *Pia Desideria* and the *Typus Mundi* to his purposes were all in a Protestant direction. The mottoes that are quoted from the Vulgate in the original are translated into the English of the Authorized Version. The strictly Ignatian meditative pattern of Hugo's emblem book is changed by Quarles into the episodic, more fragmented progress of the Protestant Christian whose life is depicted as a succession of trials, errors, failures, and triumphs until the final reward in the afterlife. As far as the tone and spirit of Quarles's poetry are concerned they are not essentially unlike those in Herbert. The changes toward a more Protestant slant are subtle rather than drastic. Recent scholarship has moved away from Barbara Lewalski's claim that seventeenth-century devotional poetry is governed by an uncompromisingly Protestant poetics and tended to adopt a more sophisticated and irenic position regarding the differences between Protestant and Catholic devotional discourse. As Karl Josef Höltgen rightly points out:

> Devotional books like those by Hugo and Quarles will usually betray their author's creeds by certain terminological conventions; but as they are not concerned with controversial doctrine and ecclesiological questions or special cults (e.g. of the Blessed Virgin or the Infant Jesus), they are Christian rather than specifically either Catholic or Protestant.[27]

Like Willet, Quarles finds the true foundation of his emblems in the visual nature of the Bible and of God's Creation as such:

> An Embleme is but a silent Parable. Let not the tender Eye checke, to see the allusion to our blessed Saviour figured, in these Types. In holy Scripture, He is sometimes called a Sower; sometimes, a Fisher; sometimes a Physitian: And why not presented so, as well to

---

[26] George Herbert, *The English Poems of George Herbert*, ed. by C. A. Patrides (London: Dent, 1974), p. 123 (ll. 13–30).

[27] Francis Quarles, *Emblemes*, facs. ed. by Karl Josef Höltgen (Hildesheim: Olms, 1993), pp. 19–20.

the eye, as to the eare: Before the knowledge of letters, God was knowne by *Hierogliphicks*;
And, indeed, what are the Heavens, the Earth, nay every Creature, but *Hierogliphicks* and
Emblemes of His Glory?[28]

Unlike Willet, however, Quarles does make room for illustrations. These were
produced by William Marshall, William Simpson, and John Pain, all of them
English artists, and modelled after the beautiful engravings, by Boetius à Bolswert,
in Hugo. The plates occasionally deviate from the original and only very rarely
for doctrinal reasons. In one case a tiny rosary, associated by Protestants with
Roman superstition, is removed. A special case is the illustration to Book V, Emblem 14 (corresponding to no. 44 in Hugo), with a motto from Psalm 84, 'How
amiable are thy Tabernacles O Lord of Hosts'. The engraving shows God the
Father enthroned in heaven, surrounded by angels playing musical instruments.
Interestingly enough, Quarles did not find it necessary to change the plate, but
anticipates Protestant objections to images of God, and apologizes 'for shewing
Sense, what Faith alone should see'.[29] In 1635, at the height of the Laudian ascendancy, it is not surprising to find this kind of imagery in an ostensibly Protestant
work. Two editions later, however, the open heaven has been closed and the figure
of God has been replaced by the Tetragrammaton. Höltgen argues convincingly
that it must have been the publisher, Francis Eglefield, who was responsible for
the change, when London and East Anglia had come under Puritan domination
after the onset of the Civil War.

    If we focus on the emblem as a genre rather than on political and religious
circumstances, one intriguing question remains. Why did Quarles choose to
publish an emblem book of the usual tripartite variety, with motto, picture, and
epigram and why did Herbert refrain from doing so? If this is a reasonable
question at all, I think the answer should lie in the fact that Quarles produced his
emblem book carefully and with a clear market strategy in mind. He wanted to
produce an accessible but high-quality emblem book for a large audience. Rather
than appealing only to an intellectual elite, the emblem book serves private devotional purposes as well. The book had something for every member of the family:
pictures both to be enjoyed and to serve as a starting point for the devotional
exercise, easily accessible poems full of metaphysical wit, dialogue, and lively metaphors of daily life, biblical references, quotations from the Church Fathers and
other ecclesiastical authorities for further study.

[28] Francis Quarles, *Emblemes* (London: printed by G. Miller, 1635), sig. A3.

[29] Quarles, *Emblemes*, p. 301.

While for Quarles the pictures formed a main selling point, and were to be used as a focus for private devotion, Herbert, by contrast, composed *emblemata nuda* of the kind produced by Andrew Willet some forty years earlier, in which the ultimate point of reference of the poetic image is not a picture in a book but the truth as unfolded in the only book with true authority, the Holy Scripture. In this way Herbert's naked emblems underline his religious stance with regard to the ultimate primacy of the word.

If we credit Isaac Walton's *Life of George Herbert* (1670), *The Temple*, published posthumously in 1633, was delivered shortly before Herbert's death into the hands of his good friend Nicholas Ferrar by a messenger. In the accompanying message, Herbert characterizes his poetry as 'a picture of the many spiritual Conflicts that have passed betwixt God and my Soul', and continues as follows:

> Desire him to read it and then, if he can think it may turn to the advantage of any dejected poor Soul, let it be made publick: if not, let him burn it; for I, and it, are less than the least of God's mercies.

It would seem, then, that, unlike Quarles, Herbert was unconcerned about the distribution and marketing of his work. Yet Walton adds that by 1670 more than twenty thousand copies of *The Temple* had been sold since the first impression of 1633. Both Quarles's emblems and Herbert's emblematic verse (notwithstanding Herbert's somewhat disingenuous remarks as reported by Walton and attributed to Ferrar a generation later) enjoyed an exceptional popularity in the seventeenth century. Despite the differences between each case, and the irony inherent in that of Herbert, it can be concluded from these two case studies that English Protestant devotion in the seventeenth century was considerably more fluid in nature than much late-twentieth-century critical orthodoxy has allowed.

Part III
Drama and the Politics of Locale

RELIGION AND THE DRAMA
OF CAROLINE IRELAND

John Kerrigan

When Sir Thomas Wentworth, the newly appointed Lord Deputy, went to Ireland in 1633, he found a country outwardly at peace. Though plots by dispossessed Catholics had intermittently troubled Ulster,[1] rebellion had been avoided since the defeat of Hugh O'Neill, and Sir Cahir O'Doherty, three decades before. Yet the seismograph of literature was telling another story. Texts from Caroline Ireland reveal a mass of unresolved tensions around land ownership, social mores, and the extent of the power of the Crown in matters of religion. Since drama is by its nature well-adapted to express conflict, it is not surprising that it should so sharply register the issues that would break out into violence during the rising of 1641. The surprise lies in just how much dramatic writing survives, how resourcefully it explores the interactions between family, sex, and marriage on the one hand and religion, faction, and archipelagic politics on the other — concatenations rather different from those of English drama at the time — and how deeply it can carry us into the underexplored world of Irish Catholicism.

Signs of what Wentworth had to deal with can be found in all four corners of the kingdom. To the south, in county Cork, a group of masquers disguised as kerns burst into the Earl of Barrymore's house during the Christmas festivities of 1632.[2]

A version of this article appears in John Kerrigan, *Archipelagic English: Literature, History, and Politics, 1603–1707* (Oxford: Oxford University Press, 2008).

[1] For example the events traced out in Raymond Gillespie, *Conspiracy: Ulster Plots and Plotters in 1615* (Belfast: Queen's University, Belfast, 1987).

[2] John Clavell, *Introduction to the Sword Dance*, in Alan J. Fletcher, *Drama, Performance, and Polity in Pre-Cromwellian Ireland* (Cork: Cork University Press, 2000), pp. 310–13.

They were only prevented from molesting the white-robed figure of Peace when Mars appeared and forced them to join in a traditional sword dance. Even in long-planted Munster, trouble was just under the surface, and an Old English Protestant landowner felt obliged (perhaps the more assertively because of his family's Catholic connections) to put on show his willingness to curb his mere Irish neighbours.[3] At the other end of the island one finds the playwright Robert Davenport dedicating his 'Dialogue betweene Pollicy and Piety' (*c.* 1634) to Wentworth's favourite cleric, John Bramhall, Bishop of Derry. In this dramatic poem about the condition of Ireland, Hibernia, clad in a green-fringed mantle, calls the banns for a marriage between economic and religious reform.[4] It was a message congenial to Bramhall who worked for Piety not just by pushing (as an Anglican) for Laudian changes to the Church of Ireland but by recovering lands and fees that had been taken from it by laymen.

As it happens, Wentworth's attempt, abetted by the Bishop, who acquired an estate near Omagh, to develop the Londonderry Plantation while creaming off revenues for the Crown, rapidly encountered resistance. And so, looking west, did his grand scheme to plant Connacht. Wentworth's own account of how the city of Limerick greeted him, in 1637, with a pageant in which 'all the seaven Plannetts [...] utter[ed] in harmony severall verses in our praise, telling us thereby upon my knowledge, rather what wee ought to be, then what wee were' shows that the Old English Catholics who dominated the corporation were willing to criticize him publicly.[5] More psychologically revealing is his gibe that 'the son the King of Planetts [...] did insteade of his indulgent heate benignly squirtt of his sweet waters upon us forth of a Seringe, my hopes being all the whilst the instrument was new, and had not been used before'. Wentworth's mock anxiety that the

---

[3] Fynes Moryson's description of early-seventeenth-century sword dancing in the houses of Old Irish lords brings out the element of threat that Barrymore's masque contained (the more scarcely if, as is entirely possible, Old Irish gentlemen showed their loyalty by participating as masquer-kerns): 'and it seemed to me a dangerous sport, to see so many naked swordes so neere the Lord Deputy and cheefe Commanders of the Army, in the handes of the Irish kerne, who had ether lately beene or were not unlike to prove Rebells' (*The Irish Sections of Fynes Moryson's Unpublished Itinerary*, ed. by Graham Kew (Dublin: Irish Manuscripts Commission, 1998), p. 112; cf. Fletcher, *Drama, Performance, and Polity*, p. 216).

[4] The text is edited from manuscript in Albert H. Tricomi, '*A Dialogue betweene Pollicy and Piety* by Robert Davenport', *English Literary Renaissance*, 21 (1991), 190–216.

[5] Letter to Lord Conway and Killultagh, repr. in Fletcher, *Drama, Performance, and Polity*, pp. 308–09. For the event see John Canon Begley, *The Diocese of Limerick in the Sixteenth and Seventeenth Centuries* (Dublin: Browne and Nolan, 1927), p. 303.

syringe had previously been used (as was standard in medical practice) to sluice out someone's bodily orifices displays the personal abrasiveness that would weaken his government, as Catholic potential allies were driven into an unlikely alliance with his enemies among the Irish Protestants.

It is however, from the east, from Dublin, that most Caroline drama hails. And it is there, with James Shirley's *St Patrick for Ireland*, staged in 1639–40 at the recently opened Werburgh Street playhouse, that I want to begin. Given that the Londoner Shirley had been ordained in the Church of England and, despite rumours of a conversion to Rome, that he left the life-records of a Protestant,[6] and that he went to Dublin with Wentworth's encouragement, or at least that of his circle,[7] it might not seem a useful starting point. Is the play not condemned to see Ireland from an English Protestant point of view? The suspicion might seem confirmed when, near the start of the action, the pagan Irish priest Archimagus recites this prophecy:

> *A man shall come into this Land,*
> *With shaven Crowne, and in his hand*
> *A crooked Staffe, he shall command,*
> *And in the East his table stand;*
> *From his warme lips a streame shall flow,*
> *To make rockes melt, and Churches grow,*
> *Where while he sings, our gods shall bow,*
> *And all our kings his law allow.*[8]

Patrick may have a tonsure, but his 'table', which is not an 'altar', does sound Protestant, and its eastward orientation Laudian.[9] With his crooked staff, or crozier, and his law (in rather Erastian terms?) allowed by royal authority, he could be a medieval version of Bishop Bramhall. He tells the King of Ireland,

---

[6] For a review of the evidence, and scepticism, about conversion, see William D. Wolf, 'Some New Facts and Conclusions about James Shirley: Residence and Religion', *Notes & Queries*, n.s. 29 (1982), 133–34, and Ira Clark's article on Shirley in the *Oxford Dictionary of National Biography*.

[7] Allan H. Stevenson, 'Shirley's Years in Ireland', *Review of English Studies*, 20 (1944), 20–22.

[8] James Shirley, *St Patrick for Ireland: The First Part* (London: printed by J. Raworth for J. Whitaker, 1640), sig. A4.

[9] On the moving of Protestant communion tables to the east end of churches, under the 1634 Laudian reforms of the Irish Canons, spearheaded by Bramhall, see John McCafferty, '"God Bless Your Free Church of Ireland": Wentworth, Laud, Bramhall and the Irish Convocation of 1634', in *The Political World of Thomas Wentworth, Earl of Strafford, 1621–1641*, ed. by J. F. Merritt (Cambridge: Cambridge University Press, 1996), p. 201.

Leogarius, 'We are of Britaine, Sir' (sig. B2) — the Britanny of the saints' lives contracted to imply another country.[10] And he declares that he is legate not, as traditionally, of the pope, but of God (sig. B2).

That distinction derives from the researches of James Ussher, Old English Protestant Archbishop of Armagh,[11] who stripped the story of Patrick of medieval accretions to show how closely the beliefs of the early Celtic church resembled (in his view) those of the Church of Ireland after its belated Jacobean reformation.[12] He thus established for Irish Protestantism the sort of Rome-free origins that the Church of England had earlier derived from the ancient British Church. There are good reasons, however, for not fully equating Shirley's Patrick with Ussher's proto-Calvinist saint. The latter represented the independence of the Irish Church from Canterbury as well as Rome, while Patrick in the play seeks to bring pagan Ireland into congruity with the church in 'Britaine'.[13] Shirley's Patrick is an active missionary, who converts Leogarius's queen, his

[10] Cf. sig. E4ᵛ: 'this is the same *Patrick* | That was my slave once, he was a Brittan too.'

[11] His views on St Patrick, scattered through his correspondence with the Counter-Reformation bishop, David Rothe — edited in William O'Sullivan, 'Correspondence of David Rothe and James Ussher, 1619–23', *Collecteana Hibernica*, 36–37 (1994–95), 7–49 — were aired in *An Epistle Written by the Reverend Father in God, James Ussher Bishop of Meath, Concerning the Religion Anciently Professed by the Irish and Scottish*, appended to Sir Christopher Sibthorp, *A Friendly Advertisement to the Pretended Catholickes of Ireland* (Dublin: printed by the Societie of Stationers, 1622), and developed in his *Discourse of the Religion Anciently Professed by the Irish and Brittish* (London: printed by R[obert] Y[oung] for the Partners and the Irish Stocke, 1631).

[12] On Patrick's beliefs, as extrapolated by Ussher — no prayers for the dead, no belief in purgatory, no idolatry or priestly magic, rejection of transubstantiation, marriage no sacrament — see John McCafferty, 'Saint Patrick for the Church of Ireland: James Ussher's *Discourse*', *Bullán*, 3.2 (1997–98), 87–101 (p. 93). Further contexts are provided by Ute Lotz-Heumann, 'The Protestant Interpretation of History in Ireland: The Case of James Ussher's *Discourse*', in *Protestant History and Identity in Sixteenth-Century Europe*, ed. by Bruce Gordon, 2 vols (Aldershot: Scolar, 1996), II, 107–20.

[13] Some English clerics, Bramhall among them (see Alan Ford, 'Dependent or Independent? The Church of Ireland and its Colonial Context, 1536–1649', *Seventeenth Century*, 10 (1995), 176), believed that an ancient British patriarchate had included Ireland and Scotland. On the congruity sought by Laud in the 1630s, see John Morrill, 'A British Patriarchy? Ecclesiastical Imperialism under the Early Stuarts', in *Religion, Culture and Society in Early Modern Britain: Essays in Honour of Patrick Collinson*, ed. by Anthony Fletcher and Peter Roberts (Cambridge: Cambridge University Press, 1994), pp. 209–37; for how this looked from Ireland, see Amanda L. Capern, 'The Caroline Church: James Ussher and the Irish Dimension', *Historical Journal*, 39 (1996), 57–85.

younger son, and others, whereas the commitment of Ussher's church to converting the Irish has often, rightly, been doubted. The economic attractiveness to the New English of expropriation and plantation — stripping land from troublesome Catholics — encouraged them to subscribe to the Calvinistic belief that the stubborn ignorance of the Irish proved them not of the elect and therefore unconvertible.[14] And Patrick, in any case, has an ecclesiastical style at odds with official Calvinism. When he comes onstage, he is accompanied by an angel carrying a banner marked with a cross followed by a procession of 'other Priests' singing a Latin hymn (sig. B1ᵛ). Just acceptable in Bramhall's Derry, this would go down badly in Ussher's Armagh.

How would the pagan Ireland represented in the play strike the religiously mixed audience in the Werburgh Street Theatre? For New English Protestants, at least, Archimagus, whose very name recalls the papistical sorcerer in Book I of *The Faerie Queene* (Archimago), would call to mind stereotypically negative features of Romanist priestcraft. He conjures up devilish spirits, is devious, greedy, has King Leogarius under his thumb, and does nothing to civilize the kerns. The opening phase of the play turns on contrasting miracles. A nobleman who threatens Patrick is frozen rigid by God and brought numbly back to life by the saint. Archimagus matches this by persuading a couple of young men to disguise themselves as statues of Jove and Mars on a candlelit altar. When, in a rudimentary or parodic version of the Mass, staged before the royal family, these idols are offered incense, sung and prayed to, they unbend, instruct the King to act against Patrick, and generally deceive those present — including, initially, the theatre audience, who have not been warned that the actors are impersonating more than statues. A ribald follower of Archimagus calls this 'precious jugling' (sig. D1ᵛ), a term used by hot Protestants to denounce the Mass and the fake miracles (weeping statues of the Virgin and so on) used to stir devotion in Catholic Ireland.

What *sort* of Catholicism would Archimagus evoke for the disapproving in Shirley's audience? To some extent that depends on how the actors exploited the resources of the relatively advanced Werburgh Street playhouse. If the 'jugling'

---

[14] Alan Ford, *The Protestant Reformation in Ireland, 1590–1641*, 2nd edn (Dublin: Four Courts, 1997), pp. 171–78. Some would later argue that the 1641 rising was divine retribution for the Protestants having been (in Davenport's words) Politic rather than Pious in not vigorously pursuing conversion or extirpation. See, e.g., Ford, *Protestant Reformation in Ireland*, on Daniel Harcourt, who declared in 1643 that the English in Ireland now found 'how dearly the Israelites paid for their cruel mercy in not extirpating the idolatrous Canaanites [...] teaching us [...] that policy without piety is a damnable discretion' (p. 221).

scene could remind audiences how much superstitious paganism had gone into the pre-Reformation Catholicism that persisted in many parts of Caroline Ireland, its use of solemn ritual in the presence of royal worshippers could equally well evoke the sort of noble Counter-Reformation chapel that Shirley would have found in the house of his patron, and Charles I's queen, Henrietta Maria. In any case, though this essay will pursue some distinctions, and bring them to bear on a series of plays written by Irish Catholics — Henry Burnell's *Landgartha*, Henry Burkhead's *Cola's Furie*, and the anonymous, Jesuit *Titus* — it is often hard to disentangle the survivalist from the post-Tridentine in a country where the Counter-Reformation was probably not ascendant until the mid-seventeenth century.[15] The success of Catholic reformers in penetrating not just the relatively accessible and educated Old English areas of the Pale, but also, as we are increasingly aware, Gaelic Ireland,[16] was in some measure a product of its willingness to absorb long-standing, often local attachments to shrines, holy wells, and the like.

One strand in Archimagus's character that would certainly connect him for early audiences with negative images of priestcraft is his appetite for plotting. This view of the Catholic clergy ran deep in Protestant prejudice on both sides of the Irish sea;[17] it was reinforced by the secrecy with which persecuted Franciscans and Jesuits had to conduct themselves; and it found an answering paranoia in Irish Catholic imputations of conspiracy among Protestants in all three kingdoms. Plotting in this sense can be peculiarly charged in plays because it instantiates the narrative, character-manipulating drives which create drama in the first place, and it became so self-reinforcingly conspicuous on the Irish stage during the late 1630s and 1640s that it will thread through the remainder of my account. In *St Patrick*,

---

[15] The debate about the chronology is summarized by Ford in *Protestant Reformation in Ireland*, pp. 7–20 (i.e., preface to 2nd edn). On the persistence of popular ignorance beyond the period covered by this essay see Edward Ward, *A Trip to Ireland, Being a Description of the Country, People and Manners* (London: [n. pub.], 1699), p. 10.

[16] Nicholas Canny, *Making Ireland British, 1580–1650* (Oxford: Oxford University Press, 2001), p. 406, and, more extensively, Tadhg Ó hAnnracháin, *Catholic Reformation in Ireland: The Mission of Rinuccini, 1645–1649* (Oxford: Oxford University Press, 2002). For a reinflection of the view that the Counter-Reformation affected Old English and mere Irish communities at different rates and in different ways, see Colm Lennon, 'The Counter-Reformation in Ireland 1542–1641', in *Natives and Newcomers: Essays on the Making of Irish Colonial Society, 1534– 1641*, ed. by Ciarán Brady and Raymond Gillespie (Dublin: Irish Academic Press, 1986), pp. 75–92.

[17] For impressive fulminations by one Englishman settled in Munster see Alan Ford's edition of the long poem (*c.* 1621) by 'Parr Lane, "Newes from the Holy Isle"', *Proceedings of the Royal Irish Academy*, 99 (C) (1999), 115–56.

where Leogarius assumes that the saint is pursuing a 'bold designe' (sig. B1ᵛ), there is a 'plot' to poison Patrick with a goblet of wine. Since he is, even as he drinks, asking Leogarius for permission '[t]o build a little chappell in this place', it is not surprising that he proves invulnerable (sigs. D4ᵛ–E1). At the climax of the play, Shirley stages the best known of Patrick's miracles. Archimagus schemes and conjures, and unleashes against the saint a wriggling, masque-like tableau of 'serpents, vipers, and what ere | Doth carrie killing poyson' (sig. I2ᵛ). Fortunately, Patrick is protected by his guardian angel, Victor, and the false priest is dragged down to hell.

At this point it might seem tempting to revert to an English Protestant vs Irish Catholic polarity and conclude that Shirley was determined to damn Catholicism by whatever means. That would be to underrate, however, not just the commercial and ideological pressures that, as I shall show, encouraged him to produce a multi-purposive play — a work too conflicted and compromized to be fully coherent as drama, and, as recent scholarship shows, open to contradictory interpretations — but the paradoxes of survivalism.[18] For as Wentworth and Laud recognized, with distaste and a certain relish, one locus of old Catholicism was the Church of Ireland itself, whose reformation had been so recent that its purgation was incomplete. From an Anglican point of view, it combined the doctrinal offence of Calvinism with recusant irregularity. In a substantial letter to Laud, dated 31 January 1634, Wentworth set out the problems.[19] The church's buildings were in decay, funds were being diverted to keep 'Popish School-Masters' employed, while the family lives of many ministers ('whose Wives and Children are Recusants') suggested that they were only outwardly conforming. From this perspective, Shirley's Patrick resembles Bramhall because he comes to reform not so much Catholic/pagan Ireland as a state church — Archimagus works closely with his king — which is corrupt, steeped in superstition, short of properly built places of

---

[18] E.g., Raymond Gillespie, 'Political Ideas and their Social Contexts in Seventeenth-Century Ireland', in *Political Thought in Seventeenth-Century Ireland: Kingdom or Colony*, ed. by Jane H. Ohlmeyer (Cambridge: Cambridge University Press, 2000), pp. 120–21 (Patrick as 'a Church of Ireland bishop [with] impeccable Laudian credentials'); Patricia Coughlan, '"Cheap and Common Animals": The English Anatomy of Ireland in the Seventeenth Century', in *Literature and the English Civil War*, ed. by Thomas Healy and Jonathan Sawday (Cambridge: Cambridge University Press, 1990), pp. 208–09 (Shirley was a Catholic but had a 'strictly colonising viewpoint') — cf. Deana Rankin, *Between Spenser and Swift: English Writing in Seventeenth-Century Ireland* (Cambridge: Cambridge University Press, 2005), pp. 99–104 (*St Patrick* 'far from being an "Irish" play').

[19] *The Earl of Strafforde's Letters and Dispatches*, ed. by William Knowler, 2 vols (London, 1739), I, 187–89.

worship, and failing in its duty to instruct ordinary Protestants (who were drawn, like their papist neighbours, to holy wells, everyday miracles, and portents).[20] It would not be too contrary to reverse the *prima facie* interpretation and draw out of the play's tragicomic, multi-plotted, entertaining, unstable fabric a vision of Shirley's Patrick as a (Laudian) Catholic coming to reform Protestant Ireland.

Such a reading can be taken further — to the point, perhaps, of identifying *St Patrick for Ireland* as one source of Shirley's seventeenth-century reputation for being a Romanist convert. For the play relies heavily on the Irish Franciscan Robert Rochford's *Life of the Glorious Bishop S. Patricke*, a Counter-Reformation version of a medieval Latin vita by the Anglo-Norman Jocelyn of Furness.[21] This *Life*, prefaced by an epistle denying that Patrick was any sort of Protestant,[22] circulated widely in Ireland and is heard of in the hands of rebels after 1641.[23] Shirley does not simply echo the Catholicism of his source, making Patrick a miracle worker, giving him that Protestant-sounding 'table' in the East,[24] and having him utter the prediction of a glorious future for Catholic Ireland that Rochford had put in his epistle.[25] The Patrick of the play is several times called a 'pale man', the pun on Palesman identifying him with the Old English Catholics who lived in and around Dublin.[26] And the role ends with a sudden, ardent

---

[20] Raymond Gillespie, *Devoted People: Belief and Religion in Early Modern Ireland* (Manchester: Manchester University Press, 1997), e.g., pp. 94, 109.

[21] Rochford (who identified himself as '*Fr. B. B. one of the Irish Franciscan Friars at Louvain*') cut fifty-four of Jocelyn's 196 chapters to bring Patrick's life into line with post-Tridentine standards of sanctity. Published at Saint-Omer in 1625, along with similarly reformed biographies of St Bridget and St Columba, this *Life* was reissued as an appendix to the Spanish Dominican Alfonso de Villegas' *Lives of the Saints* in its Saint-Omer (1627) and Rouen (1636) editions. Cf. Bernadette Cunningham and Raymond Gillespie, 'The Most Adaptable of Saints: The Cult of St Patrick in the Seventeenth Century', *Archivium Hibernicum*, 49 (1995), 82–104 (p. 90).

[22] The controversion of Ussher's thesis is part of an ongoing Catholic-Protestant contest over Patrick and his legacy, which Shirley's play negotiates. Cf., most forcibly, on the Counter-Reformation side, Philip O'Sullivan Beare, *Archicornigeromastix, sive Vsheri Haeresiarchae confutatio*, in his *Patricinia decas* (Madrid: [n. pub.], 1629).

[23] Richard Burke of Enniskillen reports an 'English book printed in the Low Countries imparting another prophecy of St Patrick' in the possession of rebels near Limerick; cited by Cunningham and Gillespie, 'Most Adaptable of Saints', p. 97.

[24] *Life of the Glorious Bishop S. Patricke*, p. 16 (*contra* Gillespie, 'Political Ideas', pp. 120–21).

[25] *Life of the Glorious Bishop S. Patricke*, pp. iv–vii; *St Patrick for Ireland*, sigs. I1ᵛ–I12.

[26] 'We saw a pale man coming from the sea', 'all that were with me, [...] fled to this pale man', 'This pale thing shall not trouble you' (sig. B1) — nothing of this is in Rochford.

declaration of Counter-Reformation missionary zeal: 'The Blood of Martyrs is the Churches seed'.[27]

All this is consistent with the prominence among Shirley's admirers of such men as Richard Bellings[28] who would become Secretary of the Council of the Confederate Catholics of Kilkenny once the rising of 1641 gave way to civil war. If the Old English gentry warmed to Patrick, however, what did they make of Archimagus? They cannot have relished a play that made it so easy for Protestants to view Catholicism as superstitious. Yet they could hardly object to Shirley giving a dark account of pagan Ireland, since this showed up the light of the faith that Patrick brought to the country and that Catholics claimed still to live by. The saint's mission from Britain could anticipate (as it did for Jocelyn) the twelfth-century invasion of Ireland by the Anglo-Normans. Much as their ancestors, authorized by Adrian IV, supposedly rooted out evil manners and brought papal Catholicism into the country, so the Old English now imported the Counter-Reformation. To that extent, the play flattered their long-standing self-image as culturally superior to their Gaelic neighbours.

Why would Shirley be friendly to aspects of the Counter-Reformation while feeding Protestant hostility toward a superstitious, Gaelic Ireland, represented not just by Archimagus but by (among others) the treacherous Leogarius, an indulgently treated Bard, and a pair of decidedly contemporary, basely motivated kerns? His leading motive was no doubt commercial. Just as *St Patrick* mixes saint's life, romantic intrigue, masque-like spectacle, and chronicle history in a vain attempt (as it turned out) to please all tastes and put a stop to the dramatist's run of failures at the Werburgh Street Theatre,[29] so it tries to square the circle of appealing to both New English Protestants and Old English Catholics (the Gaelic-speaking Old Irish were not part of the potential market).[30] But Shirley

---

[27] This grows out of Rochford's slightly wishful 'a Martyr he was, in regard of the many conflicts he had against Kings, Magitians, Idolaters, and Diuels' (*Life*, pp. 103–04).

[28] Bellings's complimentary verses preface Shirley's *The Royall Master* (London: [n. pub.], 1631).

[29] Most of Shirley's nine extant prologues to Werburgh Street productions — see the 'Prologues and Epilogues' section of *Narcissus; or, The Self-Lover* (London: Humphrey Moseley, 1646), pp. 35–159 — complain about small audiences, and lack of theatrical sophistication.

[30] This analysis has points of contact with Sandra A. Burner, *James Shirley: A Study of Literary Coteries and Patronage in Seventeenth-Century England* (Lanham, MD: University Press of America, 1988), p. 121; Fletcher, *Drama, Performance, and Polity*, pp. 274–75; and Christopher Morash, *A History of Irish Theatre 1601–2000* (Cambridge: Cambridge University Press, 2002), pp. 7–8.

was also responding to the opportunities for religious accommodation generated by an historical moment in which programmes of doctrinal purification,
social regulation, and ecclesiastical consolidation around episcopacy in Counter-
Reformation Catholicism chimed with, even as they rivalled, similar processes
at work within a Laudianising Church of Ireland. It seems clear, moreover, that
he did so within the pragmatics of patronage. For Wentworth and his circle
recognized the limited value of anti-papist propaganda. It must have seemed more
promising to support a playwright rumoured to be a Romanist who might draw
Old English Catholics toward the Laudian policy of the Castle while seeking
to fan their condescension toward their Gaelic co-religionists. The unlikelihood
of such a tactic succeeding, especially in the face of developments within Irish
Catholicism designed to defuse ethnic difference and consolidate a single community,[31] does not make the attempt less implausible, especially, it might be
thought, from the hand of a newcomer to Ireland. The play is compatible with the
Lord Deputy's strategy of dividing and ruling, and coming down hard, when
necessary, on the Castle's natural supporters.

   Shirley's ingenuity failed him. The epilogue to *St Patrick* promised a sequel if
the play were liked. It was not, and Shirley soon returned to England. Nor did
Wentworth's strategems long survive the signing of the covenant in Scotland in
1638 and the spread of unrest to Ulster. Religion was his undoing.[32] If it were not
for the dominance of Laudianism in England, and Wentworth's dutiful attempt
to foster this in the Church of Ireland, his position would have been bolstered by
an alliance among Irish Protestants. As it was, his reputation for manoeuvering
counted against him, in 1640, when Old English Catholics, aggrieved by his

---

[31] The process, which has deep roots, is often traced back to the pressures of the Nine Years
War; see, e.g., Peter Lombard's 1600 arguments for a change in sovereignty in Ireland based on
shared Catholicism, *De regno hiberniae, sanctorum insulâ, commentarius* (Louvain: Apud Viduam
S. Martini, 1632). For early Stuart initatives see, e.g., the life and works of David Rothe: P. J.
Corish, 'David Rothe, Bishop of Ossory, 1618–1650', *Journal of the Butler Society*, 2 (1984),
315–23; Colm Lennon, 'Political Thought of the Irish Counter-Reformation Churchmen: The
Testimony of the "Analecta" of Bishop David Rothe', in *Political Ideology in Ireland, 1541–1641*,
ed. by Hiram Morgan (Dublin: Four Courts, 1999), pp. 181–202; Thomas O'Connor, 'Custom,
Authority, and Tolerance in Irish Political Thought: David Rothe's *Analecta Sacra et Mira*
(1616)', *Irish Theological Quarterly*, 65 (2000), 133–56. Trends within hagiography that would
prevent the figure of St Patrick from dividing Catholics along ethnic lines are brought out in
another article by Thomas O'Connor, 'Towards the Invention of the Irish Catholic *Natio*:
Thomas Messingham's *Florilegium* (1624)', *Irish Theological Quarterly*, 64 (1999), 157–77.

[32] Hugh Kearney, *Strafford in Ireland 1633–41: A Study in Absolutism*, 2nd edn (1959;
Cambridge: Cambridge University Press, 1989), p. 220.

plantation policy and his failure to extend religious toleration, were joined by hostile Protestants in framing a Remonstrance. This led directly to his attainder and execution in England and made the outbreak of the civil wars if not inevitable then a great deal more likely. This is the broader, archipelagic context in which Patrick's 'We are of Britaine' should be understood — and it can be opened up by turning to Henry Burnell's *Landgartha*.

In his letter to Archbishop Laud about the persistence of pre-Reformation practices within the Church of Ireland, Wentworth goes on to denounce 'Polygamies, Incests and Adulteries'.[33] His thinking partly reflects a routine English habit of 'othering' the Irish by regarding them as sexually lax — a prejudice luridly apparent in the subplot of *St Patrick for Ireland*, where Emeria is raped by the brother of her fiancé, disguised as the pagan god, then threatened with further assault by a couple of uncivil kerns.[34] But it also has some basis in the survival into early modern Ireland of medieval or older customs governing cohabitation, illegitimacy, fostering, and the sort of negotiable divorce that could be thought bigamous — conventions attractive enough to tempt the settler English into 'degeneracy'.[35] Dipping his insinuating pen into the acid of his inkpot, Wentworth suggested to Laud that marriage in Caroline Ireland was often little more than post-prandial fornication:

> They are accustomed here to have all their Christnings and Marriages in their private Houses, and which is odd they never marry till after Supper and so to Bed. This breeds a great Mischief in the Commonwealth, which is seen in this, that because these Rites of the Church are not solemnized in the publick and open Assemblies, there is nothing so common as for a Man to deny his Wife and Children, abandon the former and betake himself to a new Task; I conceive it were fit, these Particulars should be reduced to the Custom of *England*, which is not only much better for the Publick, but the more civil and comely. (I, 188)

Legislation against bigamy had failed in the troublesome Irish Parliament of 1613–15, though steps were taken within the Dublin and Armagh dioceses of

---

[33] Knowler, *Strafforde's Letters*, I, 188.

[34] See, e.g., Anne Laurence, 'The Cradle to the Grave: English Observations of Irish Social Customs in the Seventeenth Century', *Seventeenth Century*, 3 (1988), 63–84 (pp. 65–68).

[35] John Bossy, 'The Counter-Reformation and the People of Catholic Ireland, 1596–1641', in *Historical Studies: 8 [9th Conference], Dublin, 27–30 May 1969: Papers Read before the Irish Conference of Historians*, ed. by T. D. Williams (Dublin: Gill and MacMillan, 1971), pp. 155–71 (p. 160) — a pioneering article probably too much influenced by the comments of English observers; also Laurence, 'The Cradle to the Grave', pp. 68–72.

the Catholic Church to regulate marriage in accordance with the Council of Trent.[36] Now, in 1634, Wentworth put another bill before Parliament — hence the topicality of Davenport's allusion to the calling of banns for marriage (the opposite of clandestine) in his 'Dialogue'. He was, however, frustrated. Though resistance to his reforms came from both sides of the religious divide,[37] the Lord Deputy blamed the Catholic clergy for preferring the authority of Rome to that of the Crown in sealing up marriages:

> [T]he Friars and Jesuits fearing that these Laws would conform them here to the Manners of *England*, and in Time be a Means to lead them on to a Conformity in Religion and Faith also, they catholickly oppose and fence up every Path leading to so good a Purpose: And indeed I see plainly, that so long as this Kingdom continues Popish, they are not a People for the Crown of *England* to be confident of. Whereas if they were not still distempered by the Infusion of these Friars and Jesuits, I am of Belief, they would be as good and loyal to their King, as any other Subjects.[38]

Here is the comforting message that Protestants could derive from Shirley: get rid of Archimagus, and Catholic Ireland will be governable. But it is not surprising, given the background, that, when measures to curb bigamy came back to a new parliament, in 1640, they were again resisted. This renewed rejection has been seen as merely tactical, designed to embarrass the Lord Deputy, but it is hard to believe that Catholic MPs were unaware of his anglicizing agenda. Perhaps there was some advantage for Wentworth in losing this battle. He was almost inciting papists to defend the customs that their hierarchy was rejecting along Counter-Reformation lines.

Landgartha was first performed on St Patrick's Day 1640, in the Werbugh Street Theatre, shortly after the opening of the Parliament. Much about the play suggests that it was written to appeal to MPs gathered for the session, and, given its sexual politics, and lighthearted dedicatory address to women, to their wives and daughters. If the Master of the Revels, John Ogilby,[39] took the play's hostility

---

[36] Bossy, 'Counter-Reformation and the People', pp. 161–62. On English measures following the accession of James I, see S. W. Bartholomew, 'The Origin and Development of the Law of Bigamy', *Law Quarterly Review*, 74 (1958), 259–71.

[37] I am grateful to John McCafferty for advice on the workings of the Parliament.

[38] To Sir John Coke (Secretary of State), Knowler, *Strafforde's Letters*, I, 351.

[39] On the Scoto-British Ogilby, whose Dublin-London theatrical career peaked in his management of Charles II's 1661 coronation, who translated Virgil and Homer, and became best known for his road map of England and Wales, *Britannia* (London, 1675), see Katherine S. van Eerde, *John Ogilby and the Taste of his Times* (Folkestone: Dawson, 1976).

to bigamy as a sign of support for Wentworth's larger position, however, he made a serious mistake when he licensed the play.[40] An Old English Catholic, who joined Wentworth's 'New Army' in Ireland — the force whose inclusion of papists made English Parliamentarians so apprehensive about the King's intentions — but who then fought for the Confederate Catholics and is last heard of being transplanted to Connacht, Burnell made few concessions to the Lord Deputy in his play even while he underlined the traditional loyalty of his community to the Crown.

Like *Hamlet*, *Landgartha* reflects on the problems of multiple monarchy by using material derived from Saxo Grammaticus's *Historia Danica* via Belleforest's *Histoires tragiques*.[41] In Burnell's case, however, the Anglo-Scoto/Danish-Scandinavian issues that go into *Hamlet* are applied with independence and ingenuity to all three Stuart kingdoms. The play begins with the godless Swede Frollo, who has invaded and occupied Norway, treating a woman abusively. This sets in train the work's interlocked accounts of religious, sexual, and political issues. Frollo is opposed by the Amazon Landgartha, 'with a mighty troope of women, | Gatherd to her from all the parts of *Norway*'.[42] Reyner, King of Denmark, who has a better claim to Norway than Frollo, brings in his forces, and, although Landgartha is less interested in his rights than in female (even feminist) virtue, she does fight Frollo to his advantage. Reyner, Hubba, and other Danes come onstage just as she is defeating the Swedish tyrant in single combat. Naturally, Reyner is smitten, though Landgartha, reluctant to be wooed, feels obliged to listen to his suit only out of duty and her desire for the public good. When Reyner plays on his status as monarch, she says that, while she is willing to love him, he ought to consider carefully what marriage with her would mean since the infamy of breaking up would be grave.

Between the wooing and the predictable betrayal comes a long wedding celebration, a 'semi-masque' which, in a metadramatic gesture, is said to be underprovided 'For want of fitting Actors here at Court; | The Warre and want of

[40] Fletcher, *Drama, Performance, and Polity*, pp. 275–76, spots the topicality of the issue but gives no account of Burnell's exploration, and use, of it. Catherine M. Shaw, '*Landgartha* and the Irish Dilemma', *Éire-Ireland*, 13 (1978), 26–39, and, more securely, Rankin, *Between Spenser and Swift*, pp. 105–08, also place the play historically.

[41] 'Amours de Regner Roy de Noruege, et comme il espousa Landgerthe, et puis la repudia: et des faits louables d'icelle Princesse', Histoire 80 in François de Belleforest, *Le Quatriesme tome des histoires tragiques, partie extraites des oeuures Italiennes du Bandel, & partie de l'inuention de l'Autheur François* (Turin: [n. pub.], 1571), pp. 838–75.

[42] *Landgartha* (Dublin, 1641), sig. B2ᵛ.

Money' (sig. E2); Wentworth was, at this date, equipping his army to fight the Scots. This restages, or at least recites, with no encouragement from Belleforest, the horrors of the Trojan war and the medieval story of British descent.[43] But an Irish perspective creeps in as Reyner is told that the British will conquer and be conquered by their 'neighbour Nations' (sig. F2). At length, there will arise

> a Prince (one way descended
> Of *Trojan* race: I'th'other side extended
> Up by the Royall bloud of *Danes*, unto
> A warlike King call'd *Reyner*, that shall wooe
> And wed a Lady Amazonian,
> *Landgartha* nam'd).
>
>   (F2ᵛ)

— in other words, Charles I, descended on the one hand from Brut, and on the other, through Anne of Denmark, from Reyner and Landgartha. So long as 'sad dissentions' are kept within bounds, this prince, we are assured, will not just enjoy his own government but conquer and rebuild Troy and, invading Greece, 'there restrayne | Th'impieties of wicked men' (sig. F2). The prediction is as unlikely as any to be found in romance, that a valiant Charles I would defeat the Turks on their own ground.[44]

---

[43] As an exemplar of the ferocity of war, a forerunner of what might consume the Stuart multiple monarchy, the fall of Troy would have been familiar to Dublin theatregoers. The story was widely disseminated (in Gaelic as well as English), and, as it happens, the earliest piece of nongovernment printing in the country was *A Most Pithy and Pleasant History Wherein is the Destruction of Troy Gathered Together of all the Chiefest Authors Turned into English Metre* (Dublin, 1558?); see, e.g., Raymond Gillespie, *Reading Ireland: Print, Reading and Social Change in Early Modern Ireland* (Manchester: Manchester University Press, 2005), p. 161. The legend of British descent from a child of the Trojan diaspora, Brut, was, however, more contentious: it had been rejected on both scholarly and ideological grounds by such Gaelic-aligned humanists as Céitinn; see Brendan Bradshaw, 'Geoffrey Keating: Apologist of Irish Ireland', in *Representing Ireland: Literature and the Origins of Conflict, 1534–1660*, ed. by Brendan Bradshaw, Andrew Hadfield and Willy Maley (Cambridge: Cambridge University Press), pp. 166–90 (p. 171).

[44] Charles was not the last Stuart to be praised as an enemy of the Turks (see Waller's 'Of the late Invasion and Defeat of the Turks, &c'. [Charles II], 'A Presage of the Ruine of the Turkish Empire, Presented to His Majesty on His Birth-Day' [James VII and II]), but Burnell appears to draw on an earlier prophetic tradition, one which cast James VI and Prince Henry as latter-day Constantines, whose retaking of Constantinople — avoiding involvement in anti-Catholic warfare on the continent — would usher in apocalyptic events. See, e.g., Arthur H. Williamson, 'An Empire to End Empire: The Dynamic of Early Modern British Expansion', *Huntington Library Quarterly*, 68 (2005), 227–56 (pp. 243–44).

Reyner does not proceed wisely to bring this prophecy about. By Act IV, he is regretting his marriage to 'A poore gentlewoman, an ordinary | Noble mans daughter' (sigs. F3^{r-v}). On one level an audience would take this reversal as a feature of tragicomic plotting, rather less startling than, for instance, Leontes' falling into jealousy in *The Winters Tale*; but they could hardly miss, in the wake of the semi-masque, its political application. Since it is already obvious that Reyner is shot through with elements of Charles I's conduct that were unattractive to Irish Catholics, while Landgartha represents the Old English gentry, it will not give too much away if I gloss the King's description of his poor but noble wife as implying that the Old English, who are now being treated so badly, are virtuous, gallant, and strategically valuable to the Stuarts, however lacking in resources compared with the magnates of Britain. Despite the urging of a prudent counsellor, Reyner prepares to go back to Denmark, leaving Landgartha pregnant in Norway. This is not just immoral, it is politically imprudent. 'She'll be reveng'd at full for her dishonour', he is warned, 'And snatch the Crownes you weare from of your trech'rous Temples' (sig. F4). How could she overthrow her husband? Pym, as it were, and his fellow MPs in London might join her, much as they helped Old English Catholics and Irish Protestants make their case against Wentworth. We are now told about a faction of Danes, led by one Harold, who wants to oust Reyner.

So virtuous is Landgartha, however, that, when she hears that Reyner is threatened, she musters her Amazons, and, to his astonishment, saves him from Harold and the rebels. It is worth remembering that Catholic as well as Protestant Old and New Englishmen were arming to protect Charles I against the Puritans and their Scottish allies — Burnell, as we have seen, being one of them. *Landgartha* plays out the hope that Old English Catholics, denied religious toleration and threatened by plantation, would rescue Charles I and earn political favours. It would not, though, be easy to draw them into the Royalist camp. In a calculatedly awkward, half-comic sequence, Reyner tries to woo Landgartha back to be his queen, while she confronts and denounces his hapless new partner, Vraca, daughter of Frollo. That the women wrangle about the 'lawfulnesse' of the King's second liaison using technical vocabulary ('clayme'; 'Possession'; 'intrusion'; 'due') connects the sequence the more firmly with the 1640 parliamentary debates about bigamy (sig. I3). In the end Landgartha will only agree to be a faithful wife to Reyner to the extent of preserving her chastity; she will not live with him, at least not yet.

That Burnell experienced the instabilities of 1639–40 as a crisis of multiple monarchy is clear. More ingenious is the way he turned to advantage the topic of bigamy. The play does not just aim to please Old English MPs and their women in the Werburgh Street audience by saying that their community is best depicted as a noble Amazon faithful to her marriage vows, it also repels the charge of laxity by saying that the English are the bigamous ones and proves it at the level of politics. Charles's (Reyner's) relations with the Sweden of Vraca (Scotland)[45] and Landgartha's Norway (Ireland) are scandalously two-timing. When Reyner finds Landgartha victorious against Frollo (i.e., when Old English Catholics have kept down the covenanters in Ulster), he grants the Norwegians power to legislate for themselves — a claim in line with the arguments of such Old English lawyers as Patrick Darcy[46] — and he endorses their long-established right to give the Danish (English) Crown counsel. Landgartha later reminds Reyner that she could have married Frollo but chose not to. The implication is that the Old English do not rely on England's power but are independent agents, with options. They could — at least in playland — find another sovereign (Catholic views about this would harden).

It is worth pausing over the Amazon who represents Gaelic and/or Gaelicized Ireland (a character not found in Belleforest, who derives her name from an Asian warrior-queen in Ariosto's *Orlando furioso*): 'Marfisa in an Irish Gowne tuck'd up to mid-legge, with a broad basket-hilt Sword on, hanging in a great Belt, Broags on her feet, her hayre dishevell'd, and a payre of long neck'd big-rowll'd Spurs on her heels' (sig. E3). This costume was questionably legal in the eyes of Protestant authority,[47] and potentially subversive. There had been a reversion to Irish dress during Tyrone's rebellion and the same thing would happen in some areas during the 1640s.[48] Burnell is being playful when he has Hubba assert that this costume came to Norway from Denmark but originated in Ireland, because Norway, in the allegory, *is* Ireland. Equally striking, however, is the appeal to the applause of the audience when Marfisa says that, whatever its origins,

[45] On Scottish-Swedish co-operation at this date, in support of the covenanters, see, e.g., Steve Murdoch, 'Scotland, Scandinava and the Bishops' Wars, 1638–1640', in *The Stuart Kingdoms in the Seventeenth Century: Awkward Neighbours*, ed. by Allan I. Macinnes and Jane H. Ohlmeyer (Dublin: Four Courts, 2002), pp. 113–34.

[46] See, e.g., Aidan Clarke, 'Patrick Darcy and the Constitutional Relationship between Ireland and Britain', in *Political Thought in Seventeenth-Century Ireland* (see n. 18, above), pp. 35–55.

[47] See, e.g., the 'Act for the English Order, Habite and Language', passed by the Dublin Parliament in 1537 (28 Henry VIII).

[48] Canny, *Making Ireland British*, pp. 487, 523.

> a handsome woman
> Lookes as well in't, as any dresse, or habit
> Whatsoever.

(sig. E3ᵛ)

That this slightly defensive assertion is endorsed by the admiring Hubba makes for a complex theatrical moment, one which overall counters the legacy of Old English condescension toward the Gaelic Irish that Shirley apparently hoped to exploit. Yet the groups remain distinct. After the semi-masque, Hubba and Marfisa 'Dance the whip of Donboyne merrily'. This popular romp[49] is followed by 'the grand Dance in foure Couple' — a more formal, courtly affair, for the Danish and Norwegian nobility, that leaves out Marfisa and her partner (sigs. F2ᵛ–3ʳ). The contrast is partly a cultural one between traditional, country Irishness and those (e.g., the nobility of the Pale) equipped with courtly refinement, but the ethnic inheritance is such that the implication is palpable that the Old Irish and their associates are not integral to the ruling elite, though they are loyal to Landgartha's party. With the 1640 Parliament in session, the play tacitly proposes that the Old English Catholics can deliver their Irish cousins[50] to Charles I so long as he keeps to the terms of their political marriage. And Landgartha does bring Marfisa to fight the rebel Harold. Again, though, the Irish Amazon remains distinct within the Royalist ranks, and has a subsidiary role in the fighting. In Old English fantasy, only months before the 1641 rising flared up in Gaelic Ulster, the Old Irish are colourful, brave, and subordinate.

Running through it all is religion. Frollo, lowest on the scale of spirituality as well as of sexual conduct, starts the play with declarations of stage atheism in the style of Tamburlaine. Reyner, despite his lapses, remains a pious pagan, so there is always the hope, however uncertain, that he will live a better life. As for Landgartha herself, the Christians Harold and Eric are blessed, after their defeat, by the visit of an angel (added to Belleforest), who announces an imminent conversion:

---

[49] Shaw, '*Landgartha*', p. 35, notes that the Burnell family had estates near Dunboyne, Co. Meath, though 'te *Phip-a-Dunboyne*', as the Irish footmen call it in Ben Jonson's *Irish Masque at Court* (1613), was already an established marker of indigenous culture. Cf. Kew, *Irish Sections of Moryson's Itinerary*, p. 112, *The Irish Hudibras; or, The Fingallian Prince* (London: Richard Baldwin, 1689), pp. 27, 35, 101.

[50] See, e.g., Donald Jackson, *Intermarriage in Ireland 1550–1650* (Minneapolis: Cultural and Educational Productions, 1970).

> Norway and *Denmarkes* whole precinct
> Shall be rul'd by *Landgartha's* line,
> And *Reyners*. Her the pow'rs divine
> Will (for her Morall vertues) turne
> A Christian, ere she come to th' Urne.

> (sig. I1)

Landgartha's moral virtues make her ripe for conversion to Christianity. Nothing similar is claimed for Marfisa. In what sense, though, will both Norway and Denmark (in their roles as Ireland and England) be ruled by Landgartha's line and the King's? Through Charles I, descended, as the semi-masque has predicted, from a Trojan-Danish/Norwegian match. More comprehensively, the English people, of whom the Palesmen are one branch, will rule both England/Wales and Ireland.

The play's ending is challengingly open. Not content with refusing a potentially bigamous cohabitation, Landgartha leaves Reyner in Denmark and returns to Norway. After giving the King counsel, on the great Irish theme of plotting ('Be just and vertuous, and you neede not | Feare poyson, poynards, or conspiracie), she adds, boldly though obliquely, that '*Norway* shall be preserv'd for your young sonne' — which is a loyal-sounding way of announcing that the government of her country will fall into the hands of her own child (sig. I4). Can Reyner extract nothing more? When urged to follow Landgartha, the King seems eager to co-operate, but the future remains uncertain. In an afterword to the printed text, Burnell reports: 'Some (but not of best judgements) were offended at the Conclusion of this Play, in regard *Landgartha* tooke not then, what she was persuaded to by so many, the Kings kind night-imbraces.' His reply makes much of genre: 'To which kind of people (that know not what they say) I answer (omitting all other reasons:) that a Tragie-Comedy sho'd neither end Comically or Tragically, but betwixt both: which *Decorum* I did my best to observe' (sig. K1ᵛ). It may be that Burnell really did encounter the sort of ignorance that Shirley took to complaining of in his prologues and epilogues. But Catholics were also divided about what demands should be made of Charles I and 'all other reasons' must have included, at least for Burnell, political doubts. All that became explicit seventeen months later when Landgartha joined Marfisa in rebellion.

Historians have been scouring the archives to establish the causes and dynamics of the 1641 rising.[51] There was a plot by the Old Irish in Ulster — encouraged

---

[51] See, e.g., *Ulster 1641: Aspects of the Rising*, ed. by Brian Mac Cuarta (Belfast: Institute of Irish Studies, Queen's University, 1993); M. Perceval-Maxwell, *The Outbreak of the Irish*

by the success of the Scots in resisting the Laudian prayer book — to relieve the pressure on Catholicism and recover land lost to British planters. A move by Old English Palesmen to seize Dublin Castle (a scheme that possibly enjoyed some backing by the Crown) was abandoned before the rising began, but it did not take long for the Catholics of Leinster to join the rebels once a harsh reaction from the government cut down their options. Both groups feared that they were merely countering a conspiracy among Puritans in Britain and Ireland to destroy the King's power and suppress Catholicism in all three kingdoms. Economic and cultural factors contributed, as did slow-burning resentment against the Ulster Plantation, but religious commitment impelled the rebellion and shaped its violence.

Certainly, if one looks for Landgartha and her Amazons in 1641, they can be found among the 'lewd viragoes', led by an Old Englishwoman, who reportedly abused the bodies of Protestants in Kilkenny. As the rebels warmed to their task, they took the head of a minister called Bingham, gagged it, 'and laying the leaf of a bible before him bade him preach, saying his mouth was open wide enough'.[52] It was a common belief among Protestants that Catholic priests stirred up rebellion. Yet the Roman Church brought some order out of turmoil by encouraging the organization of the Confederation.[53] Clergy administered the Oath of Association, which bound Old English and Old Irish leaders together and helped them mobilize armies. Without the church's incitement, Marfisa would not have gone to war — as we know she did. After the Battle of Ballintober (county Roscommon), in 1642, when the helmet was pulled from the head of one of the Irish soldiers, 'there fell down long Tresses of flaxen hair, who being further search'd, was found a Woman'.[54]

Rebellion of 1641 (Montreal: McGill-Queen's University Press, 1994); Canny, *Making Ireland British*, chap. 8; and, a qualifying perspective, Joseph Cope, 'The Experience of Survival during the Irish Rebellion', *Historical Journal*, 46 (2003), 295–316. For archipelagic angles, see Conrad Russell, 'The British Background to the Irish Rebellion of 1641', *Historical Research*, 61 (1988), 166–82.

[52] Canny, *Making Ireland British*, p. 510.

[53] My account has been informed by J. C. Beckett, 'The Confederation of Kilkenny Reviewed', in *Historical Studies: II*, ed. by Michael Roberts (London: Bowes and Bowes, 1959), pp. 29–41; Donald F. Cregan, 'The Confederation of Kilkenny', in *The Irish Parliamentary Tradition*, ed. by Brian Farrell (Dublin; Gill and Macmillan, 1973), pp. 102–15, and Micheál Ó Siochrú, *Confederate Ireland, 1642–1649: A Constitutional and Political Analysis* (Dublin: Four Courts, 1999).

[54] Edmund Borlase, *The History of the Execrable Irish Rebellion* (London: [n. pub.], 1653), p. 82, cited by Mary O'Dowd, 'Women and War in Ireland in the 1640s', in *Women in Early*

The early history of the Confederation went into a play published, and conceivably performed, in Kilkenny, a town whose theatrical traditions, almost as strong as those of Dublin,[55] would burgeon under the Confederation as diplomatic and military missions called for displays and entertainments.[56] Probably composed in the second half of 1645, and published the following year, Henry Burkhead's *Cola's Furie* gives an Old English Catholic account of events between the rising (almost obscured, for apologetic reasons) and the truce between the Catholic and the Royalist, Protestant forces of 1643.[57] Individuals are identifiable (Cola is the ruthless Governor of Dublin, Sir Charles Coote), but the play has a persuasive grasp of the collective order of events. Plots, real and imputed, are thus flagged from the outset,[58] and this shapes Burkhead's dramaturgy, in which scenes of deliberation — the participant's view of a conspiracy — alternate with sudden shocks as the unforeseen designs of an unscrupulous enemy are put into effect. The play, also from the start, gives a significant role to religion. While Protestants fear that 'A few Romish Recusants | Thinke to subvert the true reformed Gospell', the Catholics fight a 'pious warre' to 'stop | The current of their puritan designe | Intended for our totall ruine'.[59]

Modern Ireland, ed. by Margaret MacCurtain and Mary O'Dowd (Edinburgh: Edinburgh University Press, 1991), p. 94; and Bernadette Whelan, 'Women and Warfare, 1641–1691', in *Conquest and Resistance: War in Seventeenth-Century Ireland*, ed. by Pádraig Lenihan (Leiden: Brill, 2001), p. 332.

[55] See the extensive coverage in Alan J. Fletcher, *Drama and the Performing Arts in Pre-Cromwellian Ireland: A Repertory of Sources and Documents from the Earliest Times until c. 1642* (London: Boydell & Brewer, 2001).

[56] E.g., the anonymous *Aphorismical Discovery of Treasonable Faction*, in *A Contemporary History of Affairs in Ireland from 1641 to 1652*, ed. by J. T. Gilbert, 3 vols in 6 (Dublin: Irish Archaeological and Celtic Society, 1879–80) notes, around the arrival of the Confederate general, Thomas Preston, from the Netherlands, 'dayly invitations, feasts and banquetts with the varietie as well of pallat-inticing dishes, as of gratulatorie poems, civill and martiall representations of comedies and stage playes, with mightie content' (I, 46).

[57] The best account of the play is Patricia Coughlan, '"Enter Revenge": Henry Burkhead and *Cola's Furie*', *Theatre Research International*, 15.1 (1990), 1–17, rev. in *Kingdoms in Crisis: Ireland in the 1640s*, ed. by Micheál Ó Siochrú (Dublin: Four Courts, 2001), pp. 192–211.

[58] They would remain the starting point for full-scale accounts of the rising from the New English Protestant Sir John Temple's *The Irish Rebellion* (London, 1646) to the Old English Catholic Richard Bellings, *History of the Irish Confederation and the War in Ireland, 1641–1643*, ed. by John T. Gilbert, 7 vols (Dublin: Gilbert, 1882–91).

[59] *A Tragedy of Cola's Furie; or, Lirenda's Miserie* (Kilkenny: printed by Thomas Bourke, 1645), pp. 2, 5–6.

War is always fought with words (fortunately for the early modern theatre, which was better at representing speeches than the mass physicality of battle). This was particularly so in Ireland where a defining grievance for Catholics — who formally joined the confederacy by swearing their Oath of Association — was itself the swearing of oaths. The Stuarts had repeatedly sought to split and coerce the Catholics of Ireland by requiring them to commit themselves to oaths of supremacy and allegiance.[60] (The Oath of Allegiance even bound them to counter the sorts of conspiracy that were typically bound by oaths.)[61] The visibility of this issue helps explain why Burnell used marriage to figure archipelagic ties. The vows that should hold lovers and spouses together in *Landgartha* are inter-personal versions of the oaths which regulated relations between leading subjects of the three kingdoms and their monarch. The Confederation offered Catholics the chance of swearing an oath to support the King (as well as their religion and their *patria*) in terms they had chosen for themselves. It created an open conspiracy that demanded to be seen as the opposite of a plot.

Oaths were widely used in mid-seventeenth century Britain to consolidate alliances, and the contradictions they gave rise to, between such undertakings as the Solemn League and Covenant and the Engagement, generated a body of Protestant casuistry and a habit of avoidance.[62] In Ireland, religious difference gave rise to distinctive complications. Compared with the Scottish national covenant, which historians, rightly, regard as an immediate precedent, the Oath of Association is much less legalistic and preoccupied with the errors of other

[60] Alan Ford, '"Firm Catholics" or "Loyal Subjects"? Religious and Political Allegiance in Early Seventeenth-Century Ireland', in *Political Discourse in Seventeenth- and Eighteenth-Century Ireland*, ed. by D. George Boyce, Robert Eccleshall, and Vincent Geoghegan (Basingstoke: Palgrave, 2001), pp. 1–31.

[61] 3 & 4 James I, chap. 4, 1606; this feature was preserved in the softened version of the oath proposed for use in Ireland in the tolerant aftermath of the accession of Charles I (quoted by Ford, '"Firm Catholics"', p. 20).

[62] E.g., Edward Vallance, *Revolutionary England and the National Covenant: State Oaths, Protestantism, and the Political Nation, 1533–1682* (Woodbridge: Boydell & Brewer, 2005), chaps 2–7. My discussion is informed by David Martin Jones, *Conscience and Allegiance in Seventeenth-Century England: The Political Significance of Oaths and Engagements* (Woodbridge: Boydell & Brewer, 1999); John Spurr, 'A Profane History of Early Modern Oaths', *Transactions of the Royal Historical Society*, ser. 6, 11 (2001), 37–63, and '"The Strongest Bond of Conscience": Oaths and the Limits of Tolerance in Early Modern England', in *Contexts of Conscience in Early Modern Europe, 1500–1700*, ed. by Harald E. Braun and Edward Vallance (London: Palgrave, 2004), pp. 151–65; Conal Condren, *Argument and Authority in Early Modern England: The Presupposition of Oaths and Offices* (Cambridge: Cambridge University Press, 2006), chaps 11–14.

religions.[63] The emphasis is on loyalty to the Crown, Parliament, law, and 'the general cause', rather than on individual 'conscience', national 'covenant', and the discourse of federal theology.[64] When it came to politics and warfare, it may be that, as the enemies of the Confederation were quick to contend, Counter-Reformation thinking about equivocation and the acceptability of breaking faith with heretics made Catholic promises tractable to casuistry. Yet oaths in Confederate Ireland retained something of their medieval sacralism because they could underpin the religion that supposedly underpinned them. Because my religion is truer than yours I keep my vow more faithfully; that I keep my vow when you break yours proves that you are a heretic. This is one of the ways in which oaths figure in *Cola's Furie*, where Protestants are repeatedly false. But this cannot quite conceal what the later history of the Confederation bears out, that oaths are metaphysical only to be instrumental, and that the existence of the Oath of Association — made much of in the play — was not entirely a sign of strength. The Confederation brought together men who were not inevitably united but who buried their differences in a speech act.[65]

Micheál Ó Siochrú has recently argued that the Old Irish and Old English leaders had more in common than is usually thought. In his view, a joint Catholic identity had been forged in the decades before 1641. When splits developed in the Confederation they were less along ethnic lines than between a Royalist faction keen to reach agreement with the Old English Protestant leader, Ormond, a pro-clerical party, which came to rally around the papal legate Rinuccini, in Ireland from 1645, and a middle group which held the balance.[66] While Ó Siochrú is

---

[63] For the Scottish national covenant see *The Constitutional Documents of the Puritan Revolution 1625–1660*, ed. by Samuel Rawson Gardiner, 3rd edn (Oxford: Clarendon Press, 1906), pp. 124–34; for the Oath of Association see Gilbert Bellings, *History of the Irish Confederation*, III, 213–14.

[64] On covenanting and federal theology see, most recently, Vallance, *Revolutionary England*, pp. 28–32.

[65] Cf. Beckett, 'Confederation', pp. 31–32; Cregan, 'Confederation', p. 507. The Oath anticipates division and proposes a mechanism for managing it: 'I., A.B., do profess, swear and protest before God, and His Saints, and Holy Angels, that [...] I will not seek, directly or indirectly, any pardon or protection for any act done, or to be done, touching the general cause, without the consent of the major part of the [...] Council.'

[66] Ó Siochrú, *Confederate Ireland*. On the international dimensions of faction, especially the demands of France and Spain, see Tadhg Ó hAnnracháin, 'Disrupted and Disruptive: Continental Influences on the Confederate Catholics of Ireland', in *The Stuart Kingdoms in the Seventeenth Century* (see n. 45, above), pp. 135–50.

persuasive in stressing how social status and economic interest affected the politics of individuals and factions (notably, how much particular landowners stood to gain or lose by staying out as rebels), his playing down of ethnic difference seems more questionable if one arrives at *Cola's Furie* after Shirley and Burnell. The play primarily celebrates the Old English leadership. It does make the Ulster Gaelic general, Owen Roe O'Neill, a conspicuous and valiant figure. It is Theodoric (O'Neill), for instance, who saves the lovely Elleonara from molestation by English soldiers, then almost too promptly marries her — a Catholic Irishman's reply to negative stereotypes of rapacious kerns. Yet Theodoric is a willing implement of the Old-English dominated council; his role is much less heroic than the one attributed to O'Neill in the weightiest, pro-clerical account of the period, *An Aphorismical Discovery of Treasonable Faction* (*c.* 1652–59).

The care with which the play manages such rivalries reveals what is concealed by that aspect of it which most strongly appears to confirm Ó Siochrú's thesis. In its thinly disguised geopolitical setting, *Cola's Furie* recognizes only Lirendeans (Irish) and Angoleans (English). Just as Irish Protestantism is elided into Englishness (a procedure that leaves no room for a Protestant Gaelic leader such as Inchiquin), so the play avers that all Catholics in Ireland are Irish. A member of the clerical faction with an aptitude for literary criticism might have responded with the observation that if religion were the only true good in this play, it would not be seen so actively to determine membership of a political alliance and be so constitutive of an emergent national identity. Characters are preoccupied with land ownership, social status, and fear of extermination; religion emerges as a force contingent upon those other factors, though also, undoubtedly, invested with them. And while the play makes it clear how loyalty to Catholicism drove men to fight, it also helps one see that the potency with which religion joined up the confederacy gave it the capacity to create division. Disputes about what sort of church should be defended or developed would shatter the alliance that Catholicism helped hold together.

The Angoleans, as I have said, show their baseness by breaking their promises. Announcing a pardon for rebels who give themselves up, they betray this with torture and execution. Their leaders offer quarter, then turn a blind eye to massacre. When Cola's lieutenant, Tibernus, instructs his soldiers in such a course, one of them sardonically remarks: 'He speaks like a true zealous protestant' (p. 23). That Catholics would be capable of breaking a promise is on one level so unthinkable as not to be ruled out — inauspiciously, given the disputes about oath-breaking later in Confederate history. When Athenio rallies the leadership he reminds them that

> our quarrell is
> Religious, in maintenance whereof we
> Are already sworne without equivocation.

(p. 19)

The ambiguity of 'religious' (the quarrel concerns religion, maintaining it is a sacred duty), though affirmative at this point, is a reminder that words are slippery, and 'equivocation' part of their nature. When the moderate wing of the Confederation agreed to truces with the Protestant Royalists, in the two Ormond Peaces of 1646–48, the clerical party accused them of taking just such advantage of words. According to the *Aphorismical Discovery*, they evaded the Oath of Association 'by equivocations and mentall reservations, makinge like a Gipsies knott, faste or loose, at theire pleasure'.[67]

Cola himself is more given to passion than equivocation.[68] Since Cola is not just a contraction of Carola, Coote's Christian name in Latin, but a pun on *choler*, the title of the play comes to mean *Anger's Fury*, as Cola is driven, like a Fury in Seneca, up the escalator of his own rage. Yet his downfall is not entirely self-generated, and how it comes about exposes another blind spot in the play. For Burkhead, hating Coote, did not choose to recognize how dishonourable was the plot by Mineus, one of the Catholic leaders, to assassinate Cola — announced with a religious oath:

> Then name of God,
> This night we will advance our forces where
> The besotted tyrant now remaines, if
> We but kill his centrie then, we may more

---

[67] *Aphorismical Discovery*, I, 189; cf. I, 251; II, 38. Owen Roe O Neill can be identified, without name, as 'The Catholicke Generall, to his nation naturall, obseruant of his oath and couenant of Confederacie' (I, 158).

[68] This depiction correlates with other Catholic accounts of Coote, a veteran opponent of Tyrone's rebellion, who responded to the 1641 rising with brutality. Against the view that he was a 'humaine-bloudsucker' (*Aphorismical Discovery*, I, 31) can be set such Protestant praise as *The Latest and Truest Newes from Ireland* (London: printed by H. S. and W. Ley, 1642), 'in truth he is a gallant man, full of courage and good affections' (p. 5) and *The Souldiers Commission* (London: printed by J. H. for T. Underhill, 1658), his 1642 funeral sermon, preached by the gifted poet Faithful Teate, which, like other texts, praises Coote's vigilance regarding catholic plots (sig. D4ᵛ). See also 'An Elegie upon the much lamented death of that famous and late Renowned kn[igh]t and Colonell Sir Charles Coote', preserved in Ormond's papers, and edited in Andrew Carpenter, *Verse in English from Tudor and Stuart Ireland* (Cork: Cork University Press, 2003), pp. 228–30.

> Boldly enter and surprise him napping
> In his bed asleepe.
>
> (pp. 45–46)

Athenio blithely concurs, and this plot becomes the plot of the play.

On the night of his death, Cola is visited, like Shakespeare's Richard III the night before the Battle of Bosworth, by the ghosts of those he has killed. Predictably, he dismisses the vision as 'a plot of some conjuring Papist' (p. 47). Yet for all the machinery of foreboding, Coote is disposed of briskly. In the *Aphorismical Discovery*, his death is tied to the controversy regarding the spiritual power of icons, disparaged by Protestants as idols, and to the domesticated survival of Irish Catholicism after the Reformation — topics that I shall return to. We are told that Coote's son caused 'a great ancient portraiture, or image of Our Blessed Lady engraven in wood, kept with great veneration in the same house since the supression of holy churche in Henry the 8 his time' to be chopped up to make a fire for his father. The moment Coote sat down to warm himself, the Irish launched an attack and he was providentially struck down (I, 32). In keeping with the play's more pragmatic sense of religion, there is no divine framework and no mystery about the agency of death. Cola is merely shot with degrading, anonymous abruptness: 'One meets him and dischargeth a pistoll wherat he falls downe dead' (p. 48).

Cola's nocturnal visions are not the only ones in the play. The Catholic general Abner (Thomas Preston) is haunted in the Low Countries by a group of classical figures who recall him to Ireland. And Caspilona (Castlehaven), in prison, is told by an angel that he will miraculously escape. It is the closing scene, however, that colours the play's politics most strongly with Catholicism in this way. An angel enters to solemn music and calls on Victory (rather optimistically, given the circumstances of the 1643 cessation) to 'Grace this nation with a Crowne, | Of perpetuall renowne' (p. 61). The singleness of 'this nation' is in keeping with the play's confessional definition of Irishness, but this more radically and no doubt unconsciously allows the line-ending to raise, for a moment, the thought that sovereignty inheres in the Irish people, not the Stuart line. There had been talk of Irish separatism in exile circles in earlier decades, but it is symptomatic that, at just this moment, the Lisbon-based, county Cork Jesuit Conor O'Mahony published a *Disputatio apologetica* (1645) which argued that Irish Catholics should shake off their heretic king and find another ruler.[69]

---

[69] For radical contexts see Tomás Ó Fiach, 'Republicanism and Separatism in the Seventeenth Century', *Leachtaí Cholm Cille*, 2 (1971), 74–87. Further instances are cited in Michael

Too bold for the Confederate leadership, O'Mahony's tract was burned by the common hangman and preached against in Kilkenny Castle; but it reflected, despite its Continental formation, the mix of triumphalism and insecurity that characterized Catholic Ireland at this juncture.[70] By dedicating the published text of *Cola's Furie* to the King's envoy to Ireland, the Catholic Earl of Glamorgan,[71] Burkhead was signalling his Old English allegiance to the Crown. He was allying himself with the Ormondists, who would welcome the marquis to Kilkenny in 1646.[72] Yet the terms in which he couches his royalism have an almost Hobbesian, absolute air: ' 'Tis a principle of Nature, that creatures of weake condition, aiming at security, doe direct their course for shelter, to the wings of the more potent, so Principalities and states of inferior note, doe manifest their sollicitude, to gaine the patronage of some Royall Majestie.' The vagueness of 'some' is remarkable. It says, no doubt more clearly than Burkhead himself could hear, that while a nation needed a sovereign there was more than one place in which it could find it.

These issues can be pursued into something like a conclusion by turning to *Titus; or, The Palme of Christian Courage*, a play performed by students of the Jesuit school in Kilkenny. The original may have been in Latin. What survives is a three-page summary, entirely lacking dialogue (the whole artefact is now a *plot*), published in English, in 1644. There is some evidence that it was the

---

Perceval-Maxwell, 'Ireland and the Monarchy in the Early Stuart Multiple Kingdom', *Historical Journal*, 34 (1991), 279–95.

[70] O'Mahony's book, ostensibly published in Frankfurt, but almost certainly produced in Lisbon, contains two texts: 'Disputatio apologetica de jure regni Hiberniae pro Catholicis Hibernis adversus haereticos Anglos' and 'Accessit ejusdem authoris ad eosdem Catholicos exhortatio'. Copies were probably circulating in Ireland by the time *Cola's Furie* was published; action was taken against the work in 1647.

[71] John Lowe, 'The Glamorgan Mission to Ireland, 1645–6', *Studia Hibernica*, 4 (1964), 155–96.

[72] Note the commendatory poem by William Smith ('To my loving and respected friend Mr. *Henry Burkhead* Merchant') prefixed to the printed edition of *Cola's Furie*. This was apparently the William Smith whose association with the Ormond family is explored by Andrew Carpenter in his anthology *Verse in English from Tudor and Stuart Ireland*, p. 273 — cf. his article 'Lost and Found: Tracing Items from a Collection of Verse Presented to James Butler, First Duke of Ormonde', *Butler Journal*, 4 (2003), 481 — and presumably the 'Mr Smith' whose verses welcomed Ormond to the confederate capital in 1646 (see Alan J. Fletcher, '"The Reception of My Lord Ormonde at Kilkenny vpon the First Peace": James Butler's Civic Entry into Kilkenny, 29th/31st August 1646', *Irish Historical Studies* (2007), forthcoming), verses that chime with the subtitle of Burkhead's play when the marquis is asked to 'Pyttye decaying Irelands Myserie'.

custom in Jesuit theatre to distribute a summary of this sort in advance of a performance to advertise the show and help the audience, like a crib;[73] but the publication of this resume by Thomas Bourke of Waterford — printer to the Confederation[74] — makes it natural to assume that the sponsors of *Titus* wanted its story to reach a larger audience than would be gathered in Kilkenny. (Within months, the Jesuits would have their own printing press in the city. Between 1646 and 1649, it turned out dozens of works for distribution throughout Catholic Ireland, until its effectiveness led the Council of the Confederation to com-mandeer it for factional ends.)[75] The Jesuit stamp of the play is clear from such scenes as the one in which St Francis Xavier appears to the protagonist and his family in a vision. More subtle is the way the dominance of the Old English elite among Irish Jesuits[76] informs the play's priorities.

Bourke's little pamphlet sets out the 'Argument' of *Titus* on its title page:

> *Titus* a noble Gentleman more illustrious for his Christian courage, then parentage: was sollicited by the King of *Bungo*, to desert his Religion by severall, most artificious infernall plots, all which he sleighted and dashed with his invincible courage, and generous Christian resolution, whereat the King amazed, restored him to his liberty, wife and children, and granted him the freedome of his Religion, with all his lands and possessions of which before he was bereaved as traitor to the Crowne.[77]

Like *St Patrick*, *Landgartha*, and (more speculatively) *Cola's Furie*, *Titus* was clearly a play with much to offer audiences in the way of intrigue, high morality, and tragicomic reassurance. Since Bourke's summary as a whole shows that the story of Titus was framed by tableaux that depicted in allegorical splendour Divine Love, Faith and Fortitude, and the church both militant and triumphant, yet was punctuated by comic interludes, the drama must have provided a diverse,

---

[73] William H. McCabe, *An Introduction to Jesuit Theater*, ed. by Louis J. Oldani (St Louis: Institute of Jesuit Sources, 1983), p. 124.

[74] Robert Munter, *A Dictionary of the Print Trade in Ireland, 1550–1775* (New York: Fordham University Press, 1988).

[75] James Kelly, 'Political Publishing, 1550–1700', in *The Irish Book in English, 1550–1800*, ed. by Raymond Gillespie and Andrew Hadfield, Oxford History of the Irish Book, 3 (Oxford: Oxford University Press, 2006), pp. 201–02.

[76] Louis McRedmond, *To the Greater Glory: A History of the Irish Jesuits* (Dublin: Gill and Macmillan, 1991), chap. 2; cf. Ó hAnnracháin, *Catholic Reformation in Ireland*, pp. 241, 246, and, on the 'Englishing' of Old Irishmen who became Jesuits, Aidan Clarke, *The Old English in Ireland, 1625–42* (London: MacGibbon and Kee, 1966), p. 23.

[77] *Titus; or, The Palme of Christian Courage* (Waterford: [n. pub.], 1644), text in Fletcher, *Drama, Performance, and Polity*, pp. 302–03.

diverting, at times spectacular entertainment for the troubled, wartime audiences who saw it in performance.

But their troubles were also addressed. Certainly, the Argument's emphasis on 'most artificious infernall plots' is striking. Against all the British Protestant charges of popish plotting, a strain of topicality or, in the Counter-Reformation sense, propaganda in the play intimated that Charles I (the King of Bungo) was a heretic/pagan who had intrigued against Catholic Ireland.[78] That Titus is not highborn, yet is *generosus* (noble) on religious grounds, is consistent with the tendency of Jesuit drama to replace socially elevated Aristotelian protagonists with exemplary Christian believers.[79] This, however, makes it the more telling that the modestly derived protagonist has 'lands and possessions' to be restored. The implicit hope is that Charles will relinquish his claim to estates put in jeopardy by the 1641 rebellion, if not those lost in Ulster after the flight of the Earls in 1607.[80] The play, in other words, may have accommodated the claims of Gaelic Ireland, with its focus in Ulster militancy, yet the constitutional language of the summary — 'liberty'; 'the freedome of his Religion'; 'traitor' — is a clue to its Old English origins.

According to Bourke's title page: 'This history is compendiously set downe by Father Francis Solier, of the Society of Iesus in the *18.* booke of his Ecclesiasticall historie of Japonia, and yeare of our Lord, 1620.' The history of the Jesuit mission to Japan (1579–1651),[81] compendiously recorded by Solier, does provide the

---

[78] Even in Gaelic sources the king was rarely attacked so harshly. For a fierce exception see the anonymous 'An Síogaí Rómhánach' ['The Roman Fairy'], famously translated by Henry Grattan Curran as 'The Roman Vision', in James Hardiman, *Irish Minstrelsy: Or, Bardic Remains of Ireland, with English Poetical Translations*, 2 vols (London: Robins, 1831), II, 307–39, and retranslated in an appendix to Gilbert's edition of *Aphorismical Discovery* (III, 190–96), which denounces, among other wrongs, Charles's persecution of Irish Catholicism: 'It was he who required them to forsake God. | He forbade parish mass-hearing; | He proscribed the Gaelic tongue, | And commanded Saxon speech for all. | By him were mass and music prohibited. | Every horror has been wrought upon Erin; | A perpetual deadly curse is rained upon her; | An atom of what was done would have been woe enough.' (p. 192)

[79] McCabe, *Introduction to Jesuit Theater*, p. 157.

[80] The time scheme of *Titus* is short, but its drawn-out depiction onstage of the mental and physical agonies repeatedly inflicted on the protagonist and his family, the edicts and expropriations imposed upon the faithful (dealt with in the play's comic interludes), must have resonated for contemporary audiences with the experience of decades of religious oppression in Ireland.

[81] St Francis Xavier established Japan's first Christian mission at Kagoshima in 1579; recurrent edicts, directives, and persecutions (including the crucifixion of twenty-six Japanese and foreign Christians in 1597) led to a ban on the faith throughout the country (1614) and extensive oppression.

context for *Titus*, but the protagonist and his story cannot be found in his work.[82] I have discovered the play's source in *A Briefe Relation of the Persecution Lately Made against the Catholike Christians, in the Kingdome of Japonia* (1619).[83] In its basic design *Titus* clearly followed this text closely. To read beyond Bourke's title page, however, into the larger summary which follows, is to notice some telling differences. *Titus*, for example, gave prominence to a topic that was routine in accounts of the Jesuit mission but not included in the relevant episode of the *Relation*: '*Act* I. *Scene* I. Idolatrie stormes at her expulsion out of *Japonia*, and exciteth hell to revenge. *Scene* 2. The Emperor of *Japonia* declareth his affection towards the Idolls, and to this end commandeth a solemne sacrifice. *Scene* 3. The *Bongo's* receive no answer from their gods as they were wont, hence they rage against the Christians'. Idols figure in continental Jesuit as well as English drama.[84] The obvious comparison, however, is with *St Patrick for Ireland*. Much as *Landgartha* rebuts the charge that Irish Catholics are bigamists by showing that, on the contrary, this is the vice of the King of England, so the propagandist strain in *Titus* reverses the claim that Catholics are idol worshippers by imputing that sin to the Japanese. The Irish milieu is crucial; in an English Protestant play, the same scenes would be saying that Charles I's Laudian tendencies were turning him into a papist.

Though Titus opposes idols he is not an iconoclast. In a key scene '*Titus* his wife and familie voweth loyaltie to God before the Crucifix'. Not too much should be made of the connection between this vow and the infrastructure of oath-taking in Confederate Ireland. Expressions of binding faith are common in Catholic prayer books across early modern Europe. More compelling is the presence of the crucifix in this domestic setting. The icon is calculated to distinguish the true, Catholic Christianity of Titus and his family from an heretical

---

[82] François Solier, *Histoire ecclésiastique des isles et royaumes du Japon*, 2 vols (Paris: [n. pub.], 1627–29); Fletcher's attempt to connect *Titus* with the story of Don Paul in this work (*Drama, Performance, and Polity*, p. 194) is properly tentative, and unconvincing.

[83] Morejon Pedro, *A Briefe Relation of the Persecution Lately Made against the Catholike Christians, in the Kingdome of Japonia [...] Taken out of the Annual Letters of the Fathers of the Society of Iesus, and other Authenticall Informations*, trans. by W[illiam] W[right] (Saint-Omer: English College Press, 1619). The subtitle of the play I would trace to another book of Jesuit letters from 1624, João Rodrigues, *The Palme of Christian Fortitude; or, The Glorious Combats of Christians in Japonia* (Saint-Omer: printed by the widow of C. Boscard, 1630).

[84] See, e.g., the 1647 memorandum for a *Judas Maccabaeus* in Cologne, including five or six idols and at least three demountable altars (McCabe, *Introduction to Jesuit Theater*, p. 16) and Fletcher's *The Island Princess* (1621).

British/Irish Puritanism which was as hostile to the crucifix as the Japanese authorities (notoriously) were. The audience at Kilkenny could not have experienced this scene merely as a representation of events in Japan; the symbolic power of the Cross would have drawn them into an involvement more like participation. And it is more largely a measure of the Catholicism of *Titus* that images are potent for good or ill, and not inherently vain. The Japanese idols have been effective in the past, though they prove impotent in the face of Christianity. *Titus* is the product of a culture that refuses to classify its revered icons as idols. While sailing to Ireland from Brittany — the natural route for someone who regarded himself as the new St Patrick[85] — Rinuccini, chased by a Protestant privateer, threw holy water and a picture of St Nicholas into the sea for protection.[86] It worked; he escaped the pirates.

The 1644 summary shows that *Titus* was diversified by three interludes, designed, it seems, to stage lowlife versions of the expropriation that in the main plot deprives the protagonist of his estates. A country clown, hearing that an edict would be issued against Christians — like those against the Catholics of Ireland — attempts to rob a passerby. Soldiers try to pick a doctor's pocket and to force a boy to show them where his mother's purse is hidden. The core of the play, however, is more spiritually engaged. Using threats, deceptions, and torture (another feature of the play that would resonate for Irish Catholics),[87] the King of Bungo seeks to coerce Titus to abandon his religion — so theatrically, at one point, that this *Titus* might be *Titus Andronicus*, or at least *The Dutchesse of Malfy*:

> The King of *Bungo* menaceth death to *Titus* his youngest sonne, if the father abjure not his faith.[...] *Martina* the daughter, biddeth adieu, with mother and brother, assuring them of her constancy.[...] Tidings are brought to *Titus* of his daughters execution, *Martina* the mother of *Simon* is summoned.[...] By the King both are sollicited to desert

[85] Rinuccini believed that he was the first papal legate since Patrick to come to Ireland; Ó hAnnracháin, *Catholic Reformation in Ireland*, p. 93. His formal entry into Kilkenny (November, 1645), where he was met by fifty scholars — presumably including students involved in the performance of *Titus* — armed with pistols, one of whom, garlanded with laurels, recited a eulogy to him, was made through St Patrick's Gate (*The Embassy in Ireland of Monsignor G. B. Rinuccini*, ed. by G. Aizza (= Giuseppe Aiazzi), trans. by Annie Hutton (Dublin: Thom, 1873), p. 90; Fletcher, "The Reception of My Lord of Ormonde"').

[86] Ó hAnnracháin, *Catholic Reformation in Ireland*, p. 244.

[87] The torture of leading Catholics by order of the Lords Justices, after the rising, in Dublin castle, was a keenly felt grievance; cf. the racking scene in *Cola's Fury* (sigs. D2–D3) and the stringing up of Barbazella with burning matches between her fingers (sigs. E4–E4').

their faith, *Simon* scourged.[...] *Titus* is sent for by the King, in whose view supposed heads of wife and children are produced.[...] They are lead from prison before him and a superficiall command given to kill them in his presence, if he persists in his constant resolution.[...] The King amazed at this constancie dismisseth them, freedome of Religion granted with their lives and estates.

The King's amazement was surely infectious. *Titus* gave the young scholars who performed it plenty of opportunity to elicit the *admiratio* which neoclassical commentators prized in drama. For the audience in Kilkenny, the protagonist would have been more exemplary than representative in his endurance. By 1644, Irish Catholics, despite discrimination, torture, and war, had not yet suffered as much as their co-religionists in Japan. If one asks the question, however, to what is Titus constant? the answer the summary gives back has a recognizably Irish accent. For although the play's representation of St Francis Xavier, Faith and Fortitude, not to mention the church both militant and triumphant, connects it with the ethos of the Counter-Reformation,[88] a full-blown post-Tridentine agenda is avoided. The main action deals with a hard-pressed, underground, domestic variety of Catholicism, closer to an Irish survivalist tradition of covert, homely, even (as Rinuccini would see it) slovenly worship — Mass celebrated on the dinner table, and so on[89] — than the splendours of a Continental-style, state-sponsored Catholicism. *Titus* does not present the church as an institution that transmits grace through the sacraments. There is nothing, anywhere in the summary, about catechesis, the parish system, even the role of priests, yet all these were pillars of the Counter-Reformation in Ireland.

In the absence of a full text, one should avoid speculatively exaggerating differences between the framing scenes and the ethos of the Titus narrative. From a dramaturgical point of view, anachronism is a risk, for we are likely, after a century of theatrical naturalism, to underestimate the impact for early audiences of personification allegory (Faith, Fortitude and the rest) and their capacity to translate what is personified across into Titus's experience. The play should not be taken as a drama about individual suffering superficially ornamented with Tridentine pageantry. Historically, too, it should be remembered that, in Kilkenny,

---

[88] The medieval distinction between the faithful in this world (church militant) and those who enjoy the glory of the risen Christ (triumphant) was re-emphasized by the *Roman Catechism* (1566), following the Council of Trent. Cf. R. Po-Chia Hsia, *The World of Catholic Renewal 1540–1770* (Cambridge: Cambridge University Press, 1997): 'The Counter-Reformation Church saw itself as a Church militant and triumphant' (p. 125).

[89] Ó hAnnracháin, *Catholic Reformation in Ireland*, e.g., pp. 104–11, pp. 248–50; on the domestication of the Mass, despite Tridentine priorities, see also Gillespie, *Devoted People*, p. 27.

as in other Irish cities, the Counter-Reformation church (locally advanced by Bishop David Rothe) had in practice been sustained by priests accommodated in the houses of Catholic merchants and gentry, who celebrated Mass in homely settings but made clear their attachment to Rome and the international church. Yet Titus's mode of fidelity, not practically dependent on the clergy, does connect with the long-tested, even indurated belief, predating Trent and reinforced by persecution in Ireland, that Catholicism flourishes in kin-based, custom-led communities, where priests (who might be relatives) distribute the eucharist domestically and eschew public ceremony. It upholds a practice of religion that meshes with the habitus of the Irish family, in its richly interconnected, even rather bigamous, localism.[90]

This version of the old faith was tenacious and it would prove organisationally formidable under the heel of Cromwellian invasion and the eighteenth-century Penal Laws.[91] As Rinuccini quickly recognized, however, it was also politically convenient for the elite, especially the Old English gentry, because by pressing only for toleration of discreet Catholic worship it was less threatening to Charles I (with his need to placate British Protestants) than was the clerical party's insistence on full public recognition. That such light demands are represented even while *Titus* encourages audiences to think of Charles I as a pagan tyrant is not the product of Jesuitical sophistry but a showing through of interests that would become explicit in the collapse of the Confederation so carefully guarded against by, for instance, the construction of *Cola's Furie*. The idea of Titus's estates being returned by the Crown, in particular — a motif not found in *A Briefe Relation* — reflects an Old English willingness to trust even a heretic king of England to give Irish Catholics back their own, as contrasted with a clerical-party desire to take property back from the planters by main force. But it also evades an issue that would bedevil the imminent peace mission of the Earl of Glamorgan: the question of where reinstatement should stop. For the clerical party argued that, as part of any peace settlement, estates taken from Rome during the Henrician Reformation in Ireland which had found their way into the pockets of the Old English gentry should be returned to the church.[92] Consciously or not — presumably the latter — by focusing on a form of reinstatement that all in the Confederation could agree on, *Titus* preserved Catholic unity

---

[90] Bossy, 'Counter-Reformation and the People', qualified by Ó hAnnracháin, *Catholic Reformation in Ireland*, p. 230.

[91] Cf. Bossy, 'Counter-Reformation and the People', p. 169, and Ó hAnnracháin, p. 230.

[92] Ó hAnnracháin, *Catholic Reformation in Ireland*, p. 73, and, for a later phase, pp. 228–29.

while anticipating (hindsight might feel) how the majority of Jesuits would side
with the Royalist-leaning Supreme Council of the Confederation when Rinuccini
split the Catholics by his hard-line demands in 1648.[93]

So we are back with the clutch of issues inaccurately known as 'the British
problem'. The insularity of Ireland that is accented even by Davenport, who
followed Wentworth in wanting the country to be economically self-sufficient,
that is celebrated crypto-nationally (as I have said) in *St Patrick*,[94] and that
emerges more assertively in *Landgartha* and *Cola's Furie*, is plainly a feature
of *Titus*. From one perspective it has unity of place; all its actions happen in
Ireland/Japan. From another, even more propagandist, if Titus (to be reductive)
is Irish and the King of Bungo is Charles I, then two islands, and three kingdoms,
must be involved.[95] This makes sense of the fact that, on the face of it, Titus is
an implausible Irishman because he is surrounded by a population of pagans, not
by fellow Catholics.[96] Of course, even during the period of the Confederation,
some Irish Catholics were oppressed by Protestants in their own communities,
especially in such cities as Dublin and Cork, where Jesuits went undercover — a
missionary church in a Catholic country. That is unlikely, however, to have been
a pressing concern for the audience of the play gathered in Kilkenny. They felt
beleaguered for reasons that would be borne out just a few years later when
Cromwell invaded Ireland. Like *Landgartha*, *Titus* assumes the machinations of
English and Scottish Puritanism, and feels the threat closing in. Even this most
insular-global play, which, looking beyond the archipelago, engaged with the
claims of Rome and the missionary reach of the Counter-Reformation, was unable
to break free of the geopolitical forces that tied the Stuart kingdoms into an
unholy knot.

---

[93] McRedmond, *To the Greater Glory*, pp. 70–71.

[94] See Policy's account of Ireland as 'blew Neptunes round-clipt faire one', and the economic
disquisition which ends the poem, in 'Dialogue', lines 64 and 140–91, and Patrick's praise of
'This nation [...] this great all-nursing Iland' (sigs. I1ᵛ–I2).

[95] Cf. the archipelagic account of '*Iapone*, under which name [are] conteyned diuers Ilandes
lying in the east ocean of the great Kingdome of *China*' which opens 'The Preface to the Reader',
Briefe Relation, p. 19.

[96] The isolation of missionary exposure more readily matches the experience of the English
Catholics addressed by the source translation; see *Briefe Relation*, epistle dedicatory 'To all that
Suffer Persecution in England for Catholike Religion', especially pp. 13–15.

BARE RUINED CHOIRS:
THE MONASTERY AS HETEROTOPIA
IN EARLY MODERN DRAMA

Kristine Steenbergh

H enry VIII's dissolution of the monasteries has been described as an 'act of resumption', a restoration to secular use of both land and buildings once donated to the church largely by laymen.[1] During the Reformation, these formerly religious and self-enclosed monastic sites were sold to private individuals, and put to secular use. During the reigns of Elizabeth and James I, various public and private theatres were housed in former monasteries and their grounds. The question of how early modern plays appropriate and represent monasteries within their texts has so far remained relatively unexplored. This paper examines the representation of monasteries, nunneries, priories, and abbeys on the early modern stage, and investigates how the theatre appropriated for theatrical purposes the sites it inhabited .

In January 1538, John Crayford, a clerk in charge of the dissolution of Titchfield Abbey in Hampshire, sent a letter to the abbey's new owner. Crayford's correspondence offers a glimpse into the niceties of the process of the secular resumption of religious property during the Reformation. In his letter, Crayford

I am grateful to Richard Wilson for referring me to his ideas on the monastery in Shakespeare's work in his British Academy Lecture as well as in his *Secret Shakespeare: Studies in Theatre, Religion and Resistance* (Manchester: Manchester University Press, 2004).

[1] Joyce Youings, *The Dissolution of the Monasteries* (London: Allen & Unwin; New York: Barnes & Noble, 1971), p. 13. Henry VIII ordered the dissolution of monasteries of a yearly value of less than two hundred pounds in the Suppression of Religious Houses Act of 1536; the dissolution of what Joyce Young calls 'the great and solemn monasteries' followed in 1538–39.

recommends the abbey for its excellent potential for conversion into a comfortable private mansion. 'As for pantry, buttery, cellar and larder no man in Hampshire hath better and more handsome couched together', he guarantees.[2] Crayford is at first sight rather pragmatic in his approach to the renovation: 'All the church must [come] down with the steeple', he writes, 'only that portion which is north from the steeple and knit with the dorter to stand, for your dining parlour and chapel beneath, and for lodging above of two stories if you list.'[3] Bringing down an entire church, however, seems not to have been undertaken without controversy. Eamon Duffy relates how the workmen dismantling the rood loft of the priory church of St Nicholas in Exeter were attacked by a crowd of enraged women, 'some with spikes, some with shovels, some with pikes, and some with such tools as they could get'.[4] The women stoned one of the workmen in the tower, and even dealt a blow to one of the city aldermen who attempted to pacify them. It is therefore not surprising that Crayford's letter should gingerly return to this issue of tearing down the church of Titchfield Abbey. He attempts to reassure the abbey's new owner that it does not constitute an act of sacrilege: 'As for the plucking down of the church [it] is but a small matter, minding (as we doubt not but you will) to build a chapel.'[5] Crayford, then, is aware of the possible concerns that accompany the secular appropriation of these 'bare ruined choirs', but seeks to allay them by offering a chapel as alternative, as well as by stressing the abbey's spatial qualities, figuring it as the manor it will soon become. In his *Survey of London* John Stow similarly seems in two minds over the dissolution of the monasteries. Of New Abbey, for example, he meticulously records that it was surrendered in the year 1539, 'the said Monasterie being cleane pulled downe by sir *Arthur Darcie* knight, and other', and how on its site has of late been built 'a large Storehouse for victuale, and convenient Ovens [...] for baking of Bisket to serve her Majesties Shippes'.[6] Yet Stow also expresses his misgivings over the defacement of tombs in former monasteries, and painstakingly catalogues these

---

[2] Letter from John Crayford and Roland Latham to Thomas Wriothesley, 2 January 1538, in Youings, *Dissolution of the Monasteries*, document 37, p. 246.

[3] Youings, *Dissolution of the Monasteries*, p. 247.

[4] Eamon Duffy, *The Voices of Morebath: Reformation and Rebellion in an English Village* (New Haven: Yale University Press, 2003), pp. 89–90. For an excerpt from the Exeter Record Office describing these events, see Youings, *Dissolution of the Monasteries*, pp. 164–65.

[5] Youings, *Dissolution of the Monasteries*, p. 248.

[6] John Stow, *Survey of London*, ed. by Charles Lethbridge Kingsford, 2 vols (1908; facs. repr. Oxford: Clarendon Press, 1971), I, 124–25.

monuments, as if to salvage them from oblivion. As Charles Lethbridge Kingsford notes, Stow

> recalled with regret ancient buildings that had perished in the wreck of change or through greed of gain. He had loved them for their beauty, and, as we may suppose, cherished their memory for the sake of what they symbolized.[7]

This ambivalent position illustrates what Frances Dolan terms the shifting cultural meanings and uses of dissolved monasteries.[8] These shifts form the focal point of this paper. The issue is especially pregnant since the early modern theatre itself made use of dissolved monasteries for the purpose of playing. Indeed, one of the first purpose-built theatres was erected on the grounds of a former monastic site, while the later private theatres of Whitefriars and Blackfriars were both housed in former monasteries inside the city walls of London.[9] The grounds of Blackfriars, nestled in the margins of the city and enclosed by its monastery walls, formed a liberty within the city walls, a site over which the city authorities had no jurisdiction. 'Entering a liberty, whatever its location', writes Steven Mullaney, 'meant crossing over into an ambiguous territory that was at once internal and external to the city, neither contained by civic authority nor fully removed from it'.[10] The ambiguous status of former monasteries rendered them attractive to London theatres, but was not restricted to the paradox of being both part of and external to the city. Former monastic compounds were also ambiguous in relation to their religious past. In Webster's *The Duchess of Malfi* Antonio muses:

---

[7] Charles Lethbridge Kingsford, 'Introduction', in Stow, *Survey of London*, I, p. xxx.

[8] See Frances Dolan, 'Gender and the "Lost" Spaces of Catholicism', *Journal of Interdisciplinary History*, 32 (2002), 643. For Stow's records of defaced tombs, see, for example, his description of Grey Friars: 'The defaced monuments in this church were these. First, in the Quire, of the Lady Margaret, daughter to Philip King of France, and wife to Edward the First, foundresse of this new church.' These words open a list of over two pages in which Stow enumerates the various tombs and monuments, and deplores their demise (Stow, *Survey of London*, I, 317–20).

[9] See also Stephen Greenblatt, *Will in the World: How Shakespeare Became Shakespeare* (New York: Norton, 2004), p. 183. Hunter distinguishes between the first Blackfriars, 'a small "private" playhouse built by Farrant in 1576 in the monastery building of the Black Friars as a showcase for his troupe of choirboy-actors from the Chapel-Royal'; and the second Blackfriars, 'a private playhouse converted by the Burbages in 1596–7, leased to the Children of the Queen's Revels in 1600, and recovered by the King's Men in 1608' (G. K. Hunter, *English Drama 1568–1642: The Age of Shakespeare*, Oxford History of English Literature, 15 vols (Oxford: Clarendon Press, 1997), VI, 547). For the history of Blackfriars, see L. W. Cowie, 'Blackfriars in London', *History Today*, 24 (1974), 846–53.

[10] Steven Mullaney, *The Place of the Stage: License, Play, and Power in Renaissance England* (Ann Arbor: University Microfilms International, 1982), p. 29.

> I do love these ancient ruins.
> We never tread upon them, but we set
> Our foot upon some reverend history.[11]

Dolan similarly stresses that Catholic history lived on inside these religious buildings after the Reformation: 'Since these structures were only gradually emptied, and rarely razed, they were concrete reminders of the ground that Catholics and Protestants shared.'[12] Indeed, according to Wilson, Blackfriars was *literally* shared in such a sense, since it not only sheltered a private theatre, but a secret Catholic community as well. In Wilson's view, monasteries in Shakespeare's plays are similarly represented as reclusive spaces, as 'alternative places to those of the Tudor State'.[13]

While Wilson regards these alternative places primarily as Catholic spaces, what follows offers a consideration of how early modern theatres appropriated monastic spaces in post-Reformation London by representing them in terms rather of liberties, liminal freeholds, or, in Michel Foucault's terms, heterotopias. The London liberties of former monasteries are paradoxically defined by their very lack of definability.[14] They therefore significantly resemble Foucault's description of heterotopias as sites 'connected to all other emplacements, but in such a way that they suspend, neutralize, or reverse the set of relations that are designated, reflected, or represented by them' and as 'places that are outside all places, although they are actually localizable'.[15] Foucault lists prisons, madhouses,

---

[11] John Webster, *The Duchess of Malfi*, in *The Duchess of Malfi and Other Plays*, ed. by René Weis (Oxford: Oxford University Press, 1996), V.3.9–11. Despite the Italian setting of *The Duchess of Malfi*, Antonio's musings on the abbey ruins are strongly connected to the play's post-Reformation English context. On the function of 'Elizabethan and Jacobean stage Italies as imaginary complements to the complex realities of early modern England' with reference to *The Duchess of Malfi*, see Andreas Mahler, 'Italian Vices: Cross-cultural Constructions of Temptation and Desire in English Renaissance Drama', in *Shakespeare's Italy: Functions of Italian Locations in Renaissance Drama*, ed. by Michele Marrapodi, A. J. Hoenselaars and others, rev. edn (Manchester: Manchester University Press, 1997), pp. 49–68.

[12] Dolan, 'Lost Spaces', p. 645.

[13] Wilson, *Secret Shakespeare*, pp. 259–66; Richard Wilson, 'A World Elsewhere: Shakespeare's Sense of an Exit', in *2001 Lectures*, Proceedings of the British Academy, 117 (Oxford: Oxford University Press, 2002), p. 176.

[14] Mullaney, *Place of the Stage*, p. 41.

[15] Foucault, 'Different Spaces', in *Essential Works of Foucault 1954–84*, II: *Aesthetics*, ed. by James D. Faubion (Harmondsworth: Penguin, 2000), pp. 175–85 (p. 178).

museums, and, significantly for our purposes, theatres, as examples of heterotopias. This list can surely be extended to include the sites of former monasteries
in post-Reformation England.[16] According to Foucault, heterotopias are a kind
of realized utopias, characterized by a 'system of opening and closing that isolates
them and makes them penetrable at the same time'. Moreover, they are often
connected to temporal discontinuities, since 'they begin to function when men
are in a kind of absolute break with their traditional time'.[17] The Reformation, of
course, is such a radical break, and the remains of monasteries serve as material
pointers to this discontinuity, as they do for Antonio, who realizes that

> all things have their end.
> Churches and cities, which have diseases like to men,
> Must have like death that we have.[18]

Finally, if, as Foucault argues, such self-enclosed heterotopias can, in the course
of history, be put to new uses, the dissolved monastery in early modern London
is similarly appropriated by the stage for nonreligious, *theatrical* purposes.[19] In
this shift from Catholic religion to public theatre, monasteries are recycled
as theatrical locations that perform a heterotopical function in suspending,
neutralizing, or subverting the relations in the main theatrical spaces of the play.

The Place on the Stage: The Liminality of Monasteries

A monastic building appears prominently in the first act of *Measure for Measure*
(*c.* 1604), in which Lucio visits the convent of the Order of St Clare in Vienna.
The play presents one of the few occasions in early modern drama on which a
monastery is represented onstage as an actual location. When the scene opens,
the audience sees Isabella and the nun Francesca inside the monastery. This
view is actually intrusive because the convent is emphatically represented as a

---

[16] In his 'The Practice of Place: Monasteries and Utopias', *American Benedictine Review*, 53
(2002), 3–26, Philip Sheldrake argues that monasteries which still retain their religious function
should be considered as heterotopias in Foucault's definition. Richard Wilson also applies the
concept of heterotopia to the representations of monasteries in Shakespeare's plays in his *Secret
Shakespeare* (p. 249), but applies the concept in the context of secrecy, of 'recusant culture and
tactics of Catholic survival' (p. 250).

[17] Foucault, 'Different Spaces', p. 183; p. 182.

[18] Webster, *Duchess of Malfi*, V.3.17–19.

[19] Foucault, 'Different Spaces', p. 180

self-enclosed space, with a locked door, and its own 'system of opening and closing'.[20] This episode demonstrates meticulous attention to monastic rules for communication with the outer world: votarists are not allowed to communicate with male outsiders except in the presence of the prioress, and they are not allowed to show their faces while speaking. The convent thus represents a closed-off space accessible only through certain rites of entry, and in so doing functions as a mirror of Viennese society. As Katharine Eisaman Maus writes, the play is concerned with 'general issues about the often-vexed relationship between civic life and human passion'.[21] The urban spaces of the play teem with people who cannot contain their lust. This atmosphere is emphasized by the presence of brothels and other disreputable locations. The convent of the Order of St Clare, on the other hand, is a space of 'strict restraint' and 'renouncement' (I.4.3 and 34), what Foucault terms a heterotopia of compensation, 'creating a different space, a different real space as perfect, as meticulous, as well-arranged as [the remaining space] is disorganized, badly arranged and muddled'.[22]

The staging of this scene has been the subject of much scholarly discussion. In his edition of the play, J. W. Lever suggests that the nun accompanying the novice Isabella would not leave her alone to converse with a man, but would stand aside and wait till the interview was over.[23] His New Arden edition (second series) therefore added the stage direction 'Stands aside', as do Brian Gibbons's New Cambridge edition and *The Norton Shakespeare*, which adds a note that the nun might also exit at this point. These editions also adopt Rowe's eighteenth-century emendation of a stage direction in line 15: 'Enter Lucio', by which Lucio is allowed to go into the convent to converse with Isabella. The convent would thus seem to be located centre stage, with Lucio calling within, and the audience sharing with Isabella and Francesca the sense of being inside its walls.

This insider perspective on a monastic building is exceptional in early modern drama, since monasteries are very seldom physically present onstage as a dramatic location. They are more often referred to, or narrated as locations. Alan C. Dessen's and Leslie Thomson's *Dictionary of Stage Directions* under the heading of 'Places/Settings' lists city, castle, ship, shop, tavern, and tower among

[20] Foucault, 'Different Spaces', p. 183.

[21] Katharine Eisaman Maus, Introduction to *Measure for Measure*, in *The Norton Shakespeare*, ed. by Stephen Greenblatt and others (New York: Norton, 1997), p. 2023.

[22] Foucault, 'Different Spaces', p. 184.

[23] William Shakespeare *Measure for Measure*, ed. by J. W. Lever (London: Methuen; Cambridge, MA: Harvard University Press, 1965).

others, but has no entry for monastery, abbey, cloister, or choir. Of course, this dictionary only sparingly uses evidence from dialogue, since it is based on terms used in stage directions only. The absence of monastic buildings from early modern stage directions is nevertheless significant since it points to the marginal position they occupy on the Renaissance stage.

When a monastery *is* represented onstage, it often occupies a position on the physical edge of the stage, its walls coinciding with the back of the playing area, for example the Abbey of Ephesus in *The Comedy of Errors* (*c.* 1590–93). A similar marginal onstage position of a monastery may be found in the first dumb show of the Inns of Court play *The Misfortunes of Arthur* (1588).[24] Here, three furies rise from under the stage,

> and whiles they went masking about the stage, there came from another place three Nuns which walked by themselves. Then after a full sight given to the beholders, they all parted, the furies to Mordreds house, the Nuns to the Cloister.[25]

The cloister is thus an offstage location, with a door as its only property visible onstage. Yet in these plays the convent is at least physically present; in other plays, monasteries figure only as narrated locations. In Shakespeare's *Titus Andronicus*, for example, a Goth recounts how he saw a ruined monastery that seems to represent a post-Reformation building.[26] 'From our troops I stray'd', the Goth reports, 'to gaze upon a ruinous monastery.'[27] In what seems a tourist outing, this Goth has wandered away from the action of the battlefield to visit a 'bare ruined choir'. The representation of this monastery is thus doubly liminal: situated at the margins of the battlefield, but also absent from the space of the stage, located in the periphery of the play itself.

Monasteries are, in fact, so much a liminal phenomenon that the theatre often employs them as *fictional* retreats. In Massinger's *The City Madam* (1632) Lord

[24] Paul Raffield describes the Inns of Court themselves as an enclosed space physically separate from the city of London, a 'self-governing legal community [that] gave physical expression to a Utopian ideal: an autonomous state governed by the equitable principles of common law ideology'. See Raffield, *Images and Cultures of Law in Early Modern England: Justice and Political Power, 1558–1660* (Cambridge: Cambridge University Press, 2004), p. 1.

[25] *The Misfortunes of Arthur*, ed. by Brian Jay Corrigan (New York: Garland, 1992), first dumb show. All further references to the play are to this edition.

[26] On *Titus Andronicus* and the Reformation, see also Jonathan Bate's introduction to the Arden Edition of the play (London: Routledge, 1995).

[27] William Shakespeare, *Titus Andronicus*, in *The Norton Shakespeare* (see n. 21, above), v.1.20–24.

Frugal informs his family that he will retire into a monastery, only to remain in their vicinity, disguised as an Indian. In *Measure for Measure* the Duke confides that he has sent Angelo strange letters, reporting that he has died, or that he has 'perchance retir[ed] into some monastery'. In *The Merchant of Venice* (1569), when Portia prepares to assume the role of lawyer, she uses a similar excuse. She tells her household that she and Nerissa will retire to 'a monastery two miles off' while their husbands are gone to Venice.[28] In all three cases, the monastery is employed not as an onstage physical location, but as a fictional place, distant from the play's society, and cut off from it, so that the persons who pretend to retire to them cannot be expected to return shortly. Indeed, they are so much marginal to the play as to be a ruse and are introduced as a plot element more than for their religious connotations.

The scene in which Lucio can be heard offstage, calling for Isabella, who is onstage in a space designated as the convent, then, is exceptional. Like Mariana's moated grange, an outlying farmhouse belonging to a religious establishment, the convent is an enclosed female space.[29] Lucio's entry into this female stronghold may be seen to prefigure what is in effect the intrusion of Vienna's disorderly world of sexuality and lust into Isabella's austere and secluded world — Angelo's desire to 'raze the sanctuary' (II.2.175) of Isabella's chastity. The play explicitly contrasts the sanctuary of the convent with the 'waste ground' (II.2.174) of the city of Vienna.[30] The convent functions as a heterotopical site; characterized by strict rules and self-restraint, it serves as a foil to the sexual passions and legal system of the city itself.

In *Hamlet*, the prince notoriously commands Ophelia: 'Get thee to a nunnery.'[31] The nunnery is not invoked primarily for its religious connotations, but for its spatial quality of enclosure, as well as its associations with virginity. Hamlet's directive is motivated by a misogynistic anxiety over female sexuality, for he fears

---

[28] William Shakespeare, *Measure for Measure*, ed. by Brian Gibbons (Cambridge: Cambridge University Press, 1991), IV.2.176. William Shakespeare, *The Merchant of Venice*, in *The Norton Shakespeare* (see n. 21, above), III.4.31.

[29] See Shakespeare, *Measure for Measure*, ed. Lever, note to 3.1.265 (p. 81).

[30] For the convent as a place of refuge in the play and in historical reality, see Maureen Connolly McFeely, '"This Day My Sister Should the Convent Enter": The Convent as Refuge in *Measure for Measure*', in *Subjects on the World's Stage: Essays on British Literature of the Middle Ages and the Renaissance*, ed. by David G. Allen and Robert A. White (Newark: University of Delaware Press, 1995), pp. 200–16.

[31] William Shakespeare, *Hamlet*, ed. by Harold Jenkins, Arden Shakespeare (Walton-on-Thames: Thomas Nelson and Sons, 1982), III.1.121.

that Ophelia might become a breeder of sinners. These sexual connotations of the nunnery are brought into focus by its inherent ambivalent meaning. Since the word *nunnery* could also refer to a brothel, the heterotopical site of the nunnery here also represents its opposite.[32] The 'waste ground' of lust and the 'sanctuary' of virginity contrasted in Angelo's words are here merged into an ambiguous and distorted image of female sexuality. Ophelia, however, does not seek refuge in a heterotopical location. Instead of retiring to the margins of the play, she remains at the centre of the plot, where the crisis at Elsinore forces her to seek exile in a different manner. In Claudius's words, she becomes 'divided from herself' (IV.5.85).

Cloistered Cells: The Monastery as Heterotopia of Deviation

While Ophelia does not follow Hamlet's advice to retire to a nunnery, it is remarkable that many other women in early modern drama disappear from the plot of their plays to seek exile in a cloistered cell. It is worth remarking that these women are initially portrayed as strongly vindictive, only suddenly to abandon their desire for revenge and retire to a convent. Perhaps the most striking of these female characters is King Arthur's wife Guenevora in *The Misfortunes of Arthur*, who is modelled on Clytemnestra. Like her classical counterpart, she has been waiting for her husband to return from the wars; she has committed adultery during this time and craves revenge on her husband for his long absence. Since Guenevora's words are sometimes literal translations of the lines of Seneca's Medea and Clytemnestra, she is portrayed as a classical example of a passionately vengeful spouse. At the close of the first act of the play, however, Guenevora abruptly decides to retire to a convent, and she never returns in the remaining acts. She asks to be conducted 'to the Cloister next hereby' (1.3.76), and says she will there renounce the world. Her sister bewails the change from 'Kingly rooffes' to 'cloistered cells' and laments Guenevora's future separation from her friends, kin, and from the court. What is at issue is the topography of the building. It is an enclosed and isolated space, cordoned off from society. In fact, its representation echoes the 'exile', 'flight', and 'banished state' that Guenevora considered as an alternative to her revenge (1.2.34–47) earlier in the play.

Guenevora's sudden retreat from the play has puzzled critics. Brian Corrigan argues that the play deviates from its sources in this respect, since Guenevora is

---

[32] *OED*, s.v. 'nunnery', 1b. See also the long note to III.1.121 in the Arden edition cited above. The brothel is another institute which Foucault sees as heterotopian.

at this point 'no longer necessary to the plot'.[33] As a vindictive wife, she can no longer be accommodated within a plot that shifts its attention to the struggle between sovereign and usurper in the play. The cloister in *The Misfortunes of Arthur*, then, serves as a heterotopic enclosure of deviant behaviours. Although Guenevora's entry into the convent could be seen as a conversion from her previous vengefulness, the play does not primarily figure her retreat as a religious choice or as a process of reintegration into society. Instead, Guenevora's entry into the convent is represented as an alternative to revenge. When the play shifts its attention from a private marital quarrel to public civil war, the character of the vindictive wife is marginalized in this heterotopia of deviation.

This metatheatrical explanation of Guenevora's exile may seem disingenuous: a woman retreats to a nunnery because the authors no longer need her. I would not dare to propose this idea, were it not that a similar thing happens in Chapman's *The Revenge of Bussy D'Ambois* (1610), where the three vindictive women in the play — who have throughout attempted to incite the Stoical Clermont to revenge — decide to retire to a cloister.[34] Here, as in *The Misfortunes,* the convent becomes an alternative to death. In fleeing thither, the three women say they retreat from a life ruled by wrath and grief, to a passionless world of seclusion. Similarly, Edith in Fletcher's *The Bloody Brother* (1619) is sent to a convent at the close of the play. She is grateful for her exile and promises that 'now [her] fair revenges have their ends'.[35] In these examples, and there are many more,[36] a woman's retreat is represented not so much as a religious choice, but as an escape from the confines of the play, as an alternative to death. Society in these plays can no longer accommodate these vindictive women; the drama cannot reach closure unless these women retire from the centre of the play to marginal cloisters. Like the abandoned monastic sites in the city of London, these religious buildings in the drama function as liberties. Undesirable elements from both the social as well as the plot structure are lodged outside the confines of the play itself. In these liberties, as Mullaney writes, 'we encounter a heterogeneous collection of

[33] See Corrigan's introduction to his edition of *The Misfortunes of Arthur*, p. 23 n. 45.

[34] George Chapman, *The Revenge of Bussy D'Ambois* (1610), in *Four Revenge Tragedies*, ed. by Katharine Eisaman Maus (Oxford: Oxford University Press, 1995), v.5.208–15.

[35] John Fletcher, *Rollo, Duke of Normandy; or, The Bloody Brother* (1619), ed. by John D. Jump (Liverpool: Liverpool University Press, 1969), v.2.166.

[36] Other examples are Camiola in Massinger's *The Maid of Honour* (1621), who according to Bertholdo has every right to be violently revenged on him for his betrayal of her, but retires to a nunnery; and Cimena in Joseph Rutter's *The Cid* (1638), who longs to revenge her father's death, but asks the king's permission to retreat to a cloister.

outcast things, things without a proper place in the customary order of things'.[37] Like London's liberties, these heterotopias of deviation reflect back unto the centre, and comment on a society unable to accommodate vengeful women.

'And here the Abbess shuts the gates on us': The Abbey as Female Stronghold

Although the abbey at Ephesus plays a central role in the final moments of *The Comedy of Errors*, its spatial position is marginal, located at the edge of the stage. The back of the theatre forms the outside of the abbey wall, and the presence of this wall is repeatedly stressed. 'This is some priory', Dromio remarks as he and his master exit from the stage into the abbey.[38] 'Then they fled into this abbey', as Adriana says, 'and here the Abbess shut the gates on us' (V.1.155–57). 'I never came within *these* abbey walls', the other Antipholus declares, perhaps gesturing to emphasize the wall's stage presence (V.1.266, emphasis added).[39] The abbey is clearly marked as an offstage location, separated from the characters onstage by walls and a gate.

The abbey is not the only building to be portrayed in this manner in *The Comedy of Errors*. The scene in which Adriana and Luciana appeal to the Abbess to release Antipholus of Syracuse from within the abbey walls is a visual echo of an earlier scene in which Antipholus of Ephesus stands at the locked door of his own house and appeals to 'Maud, Bridget, Marian, Cicely, Gillian, and Ginn' to let him enter (III.1.31). Both the house and the abbey are represented as female strongholds. The abbey in *The Comedy of Errors,* in contrast to the convents in *The Misfortunes of Arthur, The Revenge of Bussy D'Ambois*, or *The Bloody Brother*, does not function as a remote place of exile for women who stray from the social norm. Instead, the Duke describes the Abbess as 'a virtuous and a reverend lady' (V.1.135). Her abbey does not function as the sink of society, but as a heterotopia of crisis. Foucault defines heterotopias of crisis as 'privileged [...] places reserved for individuals who are in a state of crisis with respect to the society and the human milieu in which they live'[40]. Due to the prevalence of mistaken identities

[37] Mullaney, *Place of the Stage*, p. 55.

[38] William Shakespeare, *The Comedy of Errors*, in *The Norton Shakespeare* (see n. 21, above), V.1.37. All further references are to this edition.

[39] This suggestion is made also by F. Elizabeth Hart in 'Diana and Shakespeare's Ephesus', *SEL*, 43 (2003), 357.

[40] Foucault, 'Different Spaces', p. 179.

in the play, Antipholus clearly finds himself in such a crisis when he enters its gates. In contrast to the nunneries in which vindictive female characters sought permanent exile, the abbey in *The Comedy of Errors* is a temporary sanctuary. The Abbess pledges that she will let Antipholus leave the abbey once she has made him 'a formal man again' with 'wholesome syrups, drugs, and holy prayers'.[41] In the heterotopia of this abbey identity can be restored: it is a location of personal change, an important characteristic of a crisis heterotopia.

Later in the scene, it becomes clear that the abbey functions in a similar way for the abbess herself, too. When she finally escorts Antipholus out of the abbey onto the stage, the play's confusion is resolved as the two Antipholuses recognize each other as brothers. With their restoration to selfhood, the Abbess too regains her identity as a mother. Emilia, as we now learn her name is, implies that her celibate role was thrust upon her by necessity, and she describes her position as an abbess as 'this *fortune* that you see me in' (V.1.362, emphasis added). She too sought refuge from society within the walls of the abbey, and it is only with the rediscovery of her true identity that she can re-enter society.[42] As Jan Frans van Dijkhuizen writes: 'In the closing scene of the play, Emilia [...] discards her role as Abbess. She is no longer the representative of Catholicism in the play [...] but adopts the role of mother instead.'[43] Emilia marks the moment of reunion with her family as a moment of birth:

> Thirty-three years have I but gone in travail
> Of you, my sons, and till this present hour
> My heavy burden ne'er delivered.
>
> (V.1.402–04)

The moment of recognition, when Emilia escorts Antipholus out of the abbey, thus coincides figuratively with the moment of birth of the two twin brothers. The abbey becomes a protective maternal environment into which Emilia withdrew during her long labour, and where she nurtured her sons. The monastery in this play resembles the sacred and forbidden place reserved for women in labour that Foucault lists as an example of a crisis heterotopia.

Similar imagery of birth describes Emilia's invitation of the entire community into her abbey for a 'gossips' feast' (V.1.407). A gossip, of course, is a godparent,

---

[41] Shakespeare, *Comedy of Errors*, 5.1.105–06.

[42] On this rite of passage in *The Comedy of Errors*, *Pericles*, and *The Winter's Tale* in connection to the mythical Diana of Ephesus, see Hart, 'Diana and Shakespeare's Ephesus'.

[43] Jan Frans van Dijkhuizen, *Devil Theatre: Demonic Possession and Exorcism in English Drama, 1558–1642* (Cambridge: Brewer, 2007), p. 67.

but the word is also applied to a woman's female friend invited to be present at a birth.[44] In the context of Emilia's reference to her labours and the deliverance of her heavy burden 'this present hour', the latter definition conjures up the more private and protected environment of a woman's lying-in, the period after giving birth during which only women were allowed into the bedchamber. 'The social space of birth', writes Adrian Wilson, 'was a collective female space, constituted on the one hand by the presence of gossips and midwife, and on the other hand by the absence of men.' He adds that it was

> equally important to demarcate the *physical* space of the birth: to confer upon the room a different character, signifying its special function. This was achieved by physically and symbolically enclosing the chamber. [...] Thus reconstituted, the room became the *lying-in chamber*, the physical counterpart of the female social space to which the mother now belonged.[45]

In *The Comedy of Errors*, the lying-in chamber is represented by the female abbey of Ephesus. The monastery's material, physical features of liminality and enclosure allow it to be appropriated as a lying-in chamber that marks Emilia's transition from abbess to mother.

Where the monastery in *The Misfortunes of Arthur* figured as a female retreat from society, an alternative to death, this abbey is a female stronghold that enables the harmonious ending to the comedy. In finally opening its gates, it breaks down gender barriers when the Duke declares that he, too, will gladly be a gossip at the feast. The abbey in *The Comedy of Errors* is a nurturing, maternal location that finally harbours the entire community of Ephesus within its walls. Like other monasteries on the early modern stage, this abbey is not represented primarily as a Catholic place. Its function is that of a heterotopia of crisis where characters recover their social and familial identities. Randall Martin has argued that the abbey at Ephesus could also represent the Temple of Artemis, traditionally associated with maternal power and child rearing. In a fascinating investigation of the temple in *The Comedy of Errors*, Randall argues that 'Ephesus is a palimpsest of perspectives owned by more than one culture'.[46] It would be reductive,

---

[44] *OED*, s.v. 'gossip', 2.

[45] Adrian Wilson, 'The Ceremony of Childbirth and its Interpretation', in *Women as Mothers in Pre-Industrial England: Essays in Memory of Dorothy McLaren* (London: Routledge, 1990), pp. 68–107 (p. 73).

[46] Randall Martin, 'Rediscovering Artemis in *The Comedy of Errors*', in *Shakespeare and the Mediterranean: The Selected Proceedings of the International Shakespeare Association World Congress, Valencia 2001*, ed. by Tom Clayton, Susan Brock, and Vicente Forés (Newark: University of Delaware Press, 2004), pp. 363–79 (p. 366).

therefore, to identify the female stronghold of the abbey solely with the position of women within Catholic religion, for the play circulates notions of classical deities of maternity as well as early modern conventions of the female space of the lying-in period. The abbey in *The Comedy of Errors* serves as a heterotopia that allows for the circulation and exchange of concepts appropriated from Catholic and classical religion, as well as from spheres of female influence and power.

Conclusion

Monasteries represented on the early modern stage are often figured as marginal locations, enclosed and isolated spaces that serve as heterotopias. Although the Reformation marked monasteries as one of the prime evils of Catholicism, the stage does not portray them as such. Why is this so? I have proposed that it was the theatre's material appropriation of these heterotopical liberties that allowed for a representation of monasteries as heterotopias onstage. The theatre's liminal position within the liberties of the city, inside a building that had lost its Catholic identity, but also outside the influence of the Protestant city authorities, enabled it to take a Janus-faced view of Catholic religion. The monasteries that are figured onstage fulfil a function similar to that of the liberties within the city. No longer represented primarily as houses of the Catholic faith, these locations are not completely evacuated of their religious meaning. Harbouring the socially deviant as well as those in crisis, these offstage locations mirror the society portrayed on-stage, creating a space for the play to come full circle.

To come full circle ourselves, as is only apt when speaking of self-enclosed spaces, let us end where we began — gazing at Antonio's ruined monastery:

> To yond side o'th' river, lies a wall,
> Piece of a Cloister, which in my opinion
> Gives the best Echo that you ever heard;
> So hollow, and so dismal, and withal
> So plain in the distinction of our words,
> That many have supposed it is a spirit
> That answers.

$$(v.3.1-9)$$

The cloister as an echo from the past conjures an image of an older, Catholic culture still powerfully present in post-Reformation literature. The material re-mains of the cloister represent the hollow and dismal relics of that culture, calling to the viewer as a spirit from the past. The echo however, like the mirror that

Foucault evokes in his essay as an image of the function of the heterotopia, is characterized by its 'return effect'. 'From that gaze which settles on me', Foucault writes, 'I come back to myself, and I begin once more to direct my eyes toward myself and to reconstitute myself there where I am.'[47] Similarly, the monasteries represented on the early modern stage should not be read solely as pertaining to an older, Catholic culture. They should be seen also as pointing toward a contemporary reality of secularized religious sites: the monastic liberties that allowed the theatre to engage with the shifting religious and cultural conditions of post-Reformation England.

[47] Foucault, 'Different Spaces', p. 179.

Part IV
Consolation and Remembrance

'These Dear Relicks': Abiding Grief in Reformation England

Andrea Brady

The withering away of purgatory in the folk customs and religious devotions of early modern Britain has attracted a great deal of scholarly attention in recent years. Studies such as Eamon Duffy's *Stripping of the Altars*, Keith Thomas's *Religion, Science and the Decline of Magic*, and Stephen Greenblatt's *Hamlet in Purgatory* have shown that proclamation could not erase from the community's memory and practice those beliefs which served a ritual, social, or emotional purpose as significant as that served by purgatory and the attendant rituals of propitiation. The emotional consequences of death for the survivors, and in particular the religious restraints on their expression of sorrow, have also been the subject of some important critical texts. G. W. Pigman has shown that although a minority of moralists writing in the mid-sixteenth century endorsed Christian-Stoical 'rigorism', the imposition of religious reason on emotion that condemned all sorrow as doubt in the certainty of the resurrection, rigorism remained a 'potent force' throughout the seventeenth century.[1] While some of Pigman's readings of elegies as documents of feeling, rather than as highly social-ized and artificial forms, should I think be challenged, it is also possible to read elegies as another forum for the preservation of consolatory myths such as purga-tory. As such, elegies bear witness to the resistance of the bereaved to constraints on their grieving, to their continued interest in the fate of the body, and to their desire to intervene in the fate of the dead. These secular tributes could fixate on

---

This essay includes some revised material from my book *English Funerary Elegy in the Seven-teenth Century* (Basingstoke: Palgrave Macmillan, 2006).

[1] G. W. Pigman III, *Grief and English Renaissance Elegy* (Cambridge: Cambridge University Press, 1985), p. 27.

the corpse, offering new rituals of propitiation and memorialization, which challenged the radical changes to folk belief presented by the Reformation. While elegies looked to the past, they also looked to the future, and signal in their use of the vocabulary of commerce the effect of emerging discourses on conceptualizations of the value of the individual and her moral responsibilities for her inner life.

In this essay, I turn to the question of 'rigorism', examining the disciplinary teachings of Christianity and Stoicism, and their problematic representation in elegies. These two philosophical systems provide the ideological content for the formal rituals of grieving, including writing elegies and performing lamentations. I briefly sketch the changes to funereal custom caused by the Reformation from the viewpoint of the elegy. Offering an anthropological reading of these texts, I argue that elegies provided the expansion of time, the continued encounter with the corpse during its process of decay, and the combination of expressive mourning and self-restraint which had previously been incorporated into religious ritual. The continued closeness of the dead to the bereaved, and the needs of survivors to address, love, cherish, and placate the dead, are given a home in elegy, which by its artistic form escapes some of the restrictions of rigorism. To exemplify all these themes, I conclude with a reading of the 'Exequy' and 'Anniverse' of Henry King. King's elegies for his wife Anne transplant purgatorial imagery into the increasingly secular and rationalist present through references to the disciplines of accounting and mathematics.

Pigman cites one example of moderation from the mid-century, Hugh Latimer's sermon in 1553, where he notes that

> [i]n the time of popery, before the gospel came amongst us, we went to buriales, with wepyng and wailing, as thoughe there wer no god: but sence the gospell came unto us, I have heard saye that in some places they go with the corses girnyng and fleeryng, as though they went to a beare-baiting: which thing is naught.[2]

Latimer recognizes that the godly enact roles determined by ritual, and argues that changes in faith lead to changes in ritual practice. Some anthropologists have suggested that it is in fact the rituals which *produce* the social order as an apparently external force, rather than the rituals serving an existent social order determined by individual emotional needs.[3] In that case, rituals could determine the magnitude of survivors' bereavement, rather than ritual display resulting

---

[2] Hugh Latimer, *Certayn Godly Sermons, Made uppon the Lords Prayer* (London: printed by John Day, 1562), fol. 105ᵛ. Cited in Pigman, *Grief and English Renaissance Elegy*, p. 32.

[3] *Death and the Regeneration of Life*, ed. by Maurice Bloch and Jonathan Parry (Cambridge: Cambridge University Press, 1982), p. 6.

from pre-social feelings of grief.[4] This view, which is founded particularly in the work of Emile Durkheim, can veer toward the assertion that emotions possess no explanatory or creative power of their own, but are instead inscribed in an obligatory context which eliminates improvisation and spontaneity.[5] To understand the complex interaction between emotional needs and ritual as well as social and ideological determinations in the early modern period, for example, we need to attend to both orthodox and heterodox responses to death, and to the ways that early modern writers adjusted the rituals and rhetoric available to them to serve their own needs.

Latimer's remark exemplifies the Protestant distrust of the theatricality of the Roman Mass which, as Sarah Beckwith argues, was extended to secular theatre.[6] Nonetheless, much Protestant condolence recommends that the bereaved *act* like Stoics: that they can convince others, and eventually themselves, of the uselessness of sorrow through a publicly visible performance of Christian self-discipline. Reformation attitudes toward grief were influenced by scriptural precept (especially Paul's letters) and Calvin's commentaries, as well as Stoicism's adoption of the Platonic attitude of *contemptus mundi* endorsed in the *Phaedo*. These two models, Christian and secular, were not perfectly reconcilable: Calvin's *Institutes* instruct the Christian to eschew Stoic *apatheia* and to submit to the frailty of the flesh, saying, 'The Stoickes in old time did foolishly describe a valiant harted man, to be such a one, [...] as like a stone was mooved with nothing.' However, 'we have nothing to do with that stonie Philosophie, which our master and Lord hath condemned not onely by his word but also by his example.'[7] Like many Protestant moralists, Calvin reminds his readers that Christ himself felt sorrow in adversity, and wept tears of blood during his passion. This example, as well as Paul's direction to the Ephesians (4. 26) 'Be ye angry, and sin not', proved that Christians could curb rather than extinguish their passions without offending God.[8]

---

[4] *Celebrations of Death: the Anthropology of Mortuary Ritual*, ed. by Peter Metcalf and Richard Huntington (Cambridge: Cambridge University Press, 1991), p. 46.

[5] Emile Durkheim, *The Elementary Forms of the Religious Life* (London: Allen & Unwin, 1915), p. 397.

[6] Sarah Beckwith, *Signifying God: Social Relation and Symbolic Act in the York Corpus Christi Plays* (Chicago: University of Chicago Press, 2001), p. 124 and passim.

[7] John Calvin, *The Institution of Christian Religion*, trans. by Thomas Norton (London: printed for John Norton, 1611), III.8.9–11, p. 339.

[8] Francis Bacon, 'Of Anger', in *The Essayes or Counsels, Civill and Morall*, ed. by Michael Kiernan (Oxford: Clarendon Press, 1985), pp. 170–71 (p. 170). See also Henry W. Sams,

More problematic was the 'rigorist' belief that grief revealed a sinful uncertainty about the resurrection. Many examples of this belief can be found in popular drama: in *Twelfth Night* Feste calls Olivia a 'fool' for grieving when her brother is in heaven, while in *The Changeling*, Vermandero reconciles himself to his wife's death because it "Twer sin to wish her in this vale again'. Elegists also made use of it. In his 'Elegie on the Lady Marckham', Donne laments a world eroded by the oceans of death, in which 'even those teares, which should wash sin, are sin'.[9] Fear that grief was a symptom of spiritual doubt is evident in John Coprario's offer after the death of Prince Henry to help readers to

> weep yourselves heartsick, and ne'er repent:
> For I will open to your free access
> The sanctuary of all heaviness:
> Where men their fill may mourn, and never sin.[10]

Notably, this 'sanctuary' could be provided by music. Artistic laments, both musical and literary, could take shelter against allegations of doubt under the aegis of secular forms and rhetoric. Many elegists express their resistance to proscriptions on mourning. An anonymous poet wonders why he should 'grieve, grudge or repine' about the death of his grandson, before complaining that the infant's short life was good enough reason for such feelings. Like many writers, this poet finds a precedent for his resistance in the Old Testament: 'David Mourned for his Adultrous Childe | well then May we for one soe Meeke soe Mild'; mightn't he regret his 'legitimate' grandson?[11]

Scripture's proscriptions on mourning were often debated, and many early modern writers misunderstood Stoicism's response to suffering as *anaesthesia* rather than *apatheia*. Calvin clarified that mourning, a natural response to loss, is fine in moderation. 'They who misuse this testimony to establish Stoic *apatheia*, that is, an iron sensibility, among Christians, find nothing of the kind in Paul's

'Anti-Stoicism in Seventeenth- and Eighteenth-Century England', *Studies in Philology*, 41 (1944), 65–78 (p. 68).

[9] Donne, *The Epithalamions, Anniversaries and Epicedes*, ed. by W. Milgate (Oxford: Clarendon Press, 1978), p. 57.

[10] John Coprario, 'An Elegy upon the Untimely Death of Prince Henry', in *The English Lute-Songs*, ed. Edmund H. Fellowes, rev. by Thurston Dart and Gerald Hendrie (London: Stainer & Bell, [1959]), ser. I.17, p. vii.

[11] 'On the Death of My Deare Grandchild Barnard Corbet, 3 years and [?] old', Oxford, Bodleian Library MS Rawl. poet. 210, fol. 43.

words.'[12] He refers to Paul's advice (I Thessalonians 4. 13), taken by many to for-
bid grieving: 'I would not have you to be ignorant, brethren, concerning them
which are asleep, that ye sorrow not, even as others which have no hope.' Paul's
association of excessive grieving with ignorance is significant. For both the Stoic
and the Christian, moderation and self-discipline were characteristics required
for knowledge, and helped the subject to a universal perspective by eliminating
the distortions of 'emotional' preoccupations. But unlike the Stoics, Christians
held that the passions could be useful. The Jesuit priest Thomas Wright wrote
in *The Passions of the Mind in General*, 'Passions, are not only, not wholy to be
extinguished (as the Stoicks seemed to affirme) but sometimes to be moved, &
stirred up for the service of vertue.'[13] Passionate grief could promote virtuous
introspection and active self-reform.

John Lesly's *An Epithrene; or, Voice of Weeping: Bewailing the Want of Weeping* (1631) shows the complexity of Protestant attitudes toward the justification
of grief. On the one hand, weeping is described as 'the last meanes, by which we
can helpe Soules desperately wicked', an intercessory practice with the living akin
to those sanctioned by the pre-Reformation church.[14] Weeping is also a means
to purify our own souls. To enter heaven, he writes, 'wee must passe through the
Purgatory of Weeping, under the sword that cutteth away the branches of our
corrupt Nature.'[15] Lesly refutes the rigorism which he says is based on the erro-
neous 'Doctrine of *Stoicall Apathy*; That a wise man is not troubled with Griefe
and other Passions; All which Christians must have (for Christ himself had
them) lest they turne *Stoicks*.'[16] By contrast, Christ taught 'by his owne example
to weepe with them that weepe in a moderate manner'; that neither 'after the
manner of mad-men wee should be swallowed up with overmuch sorrow; nor
forget Christian Compassion and Humanity toward the dead, and distressed'.
But, he specifies, 'Nature doth in a sort bidde our Teares, though shee barre our
immoderation: yea, God himselfe allowed his holy Priests to pollute themselves

[12] *Ioannis Calvini in omnes D. Pauli epistolas* (Geneva: I. Gérard, 1551), pp. 481–82;
translated in Pigman, *Grief and English Renaissance Elegy*, p. 137 n. 3.

[13] Thomas Wright, *The Passions of the Minde in Generall* (London: printed by Valentine
Simmes for Walter Burre, 1604), reprinted with an introduction by Thomas O. Sloane (Urbana:
University of Illinois Press, 1971), p. 17.

[14] [John Lesly,] *An Epithrene; or, Voice of Weeping: Bewailing the Want of Weeping* (London:
printed by A. M. for H. Robinson, 1631), p. 14.

[15] [Lesly], *An Epithrene*, p. 43.

[16] [Lesly], *An Epithrene*, p. 25.

in Mourning for their neerest dead friends, except the high Priests.'[17] It is natural to mourn, but not immoderately to 'pollute' ourselves with grief. Commenting on the Thessalonians verse, Lesly clarifies that 'Paul reproveth not all Sorrow, but Heathenish, without hope or measure'. As Barbara Lewalski has pointed out, the Protestant denial of purgatory meant that the departed godly soul could be envisaged as enjoying heavenly glory at once; grief would seem to recall that person from heaven, back to the wretchedness of this life. For this reason, weeping is '[d]iabolical, when a friends departure into Glory is more lamented, then the departure of Christ from the Soule'.

When the Reformers decommissioned purgatory, they put an end to the suffering of the liminal and redeemable dead, but not to the sorrow of the bereaved which mirrored that suffering. It is often claimed that in refuting the doctrine of purgatory, the Reformation denied mourners the consolations of assisting the dead and of sharing space with them. Intermediating between heaven and earth, purgatory was a temporal and spatial realm where the remainders of material life were burned away.[18] For Protestants, this purification of individual souls was displaced to the apocalypse, when the whole world would be renewed: as one elegist writes, 'we must be try'd',

> By flames of fire as gold is purifi'd,
> For my faith teaches me all in this world
> Shall into Gods calcining pot be hurl'd,
> And turn'd into a Calx, from which shall rise
> Another world, too glorious for our eyes.[19]

For all but the most stubborn millenarians, however, this absolute crucible of purification was a long way off, and the intervening time, when the bereaved must wait for death to renew their contact with their loved ones, could seem to stretch out insufferably. The Catholic rituals had reassured the bereaved by commemorating the lived time of their grief, including the gradual decomposition of material remains, the complexities of abiding melancholy, and the guilt of diminished attachments to the dead. Exorcizing the ghosts and disenchanting the world of its dead, the Reformation actually liberated the disciplines of commerce

[17] [Lesly], *An Epithrene*, p. 32.

[18] On purgatory as an 'intermediate' space, see Jacques Le Goff, *The Birth of Purgatory*, trans. by Arthur Goldhammer (London: Scolar, 1984), pp. 225–26.

[19] *An Elegie, and Epitaph for Mistris Abigail Sherard*, Thomason Broadsides, foliated as 669.f.12 92, later as 94.

and accountancy and their rationalization of human time. Peter Marshall makes this Weberian argument when he asserts that

> the doctrinal rejection of purgatory and intercessory prayers translated in cultural terms into a conscious abrogation of the hold of the past, a heedlessness of the wishes of dead ancestors, and a prioritization of resources towards meeting the needs of this world rather than the next.[20]

Rather than assisting the dead person's soul to escape the pains of purgatory, Protestant mourners could only provide the service of a suitable funeral, or a monument in stone or paper, its face turned decidedly toward the present and the edification of the living. These remembrances were often described as 'payments' of the debts of friendship and spiritual fellowship, as for example in the petition at the end of Donne's first *Anniversary*, that Drury

> Accept this tribute, and his first yeares rent,
> Who till his darke short tapers end be spent,
> As oft as thy feast sees this widowed earth,
> Will yearely celebrate thy second birth.[21]

The poem will annually pay the 'rent' on Donne's earthly existence through celebration of Drury's 'second birth'. Again, such financial language reflected not only the Protestant commonplace that temporal life was borrowed from God; it also revealed the growing influence of monetary conceptions of value and labour on the representation of the subject.

It is however acknowledged that early modern folk traditions maintained a version of the idea of purgatory. John Aubrey recorded the 'vulgar' belief in Yorkshire 'that after the persons death, the Soule went over the Whinny-moore, and till about 1624 at the Funerall a woman came [like the *Præfica*] and sang this following Song', 'This ean night' or the Lykewake Dirge.[22] The mortuary customs observed by Aubrey, such as soul cakes, the sin eater, and the offertory, incorporate rituals of hospitality, propitiation, and the symbolic reincorporation of the physical remnants of the dead person which are common to many religious traditions. For Maurice Bloch, such rituals represent the belief that 'the end of the

---

[20] Peter Marshall, *Beliefs and the Dead in Reformation England* (Oxford: Oxford University Press, 2002), p. 107.

[21] John Donne, *The Epithalamions, Anniversaries and Epicedes*, ed. by W. Milgate (Oxford: Clarendon Press, 1978), p. 34.

[22] John Aubrey, *Remaines of Gentilisme and Judaisme*, in *Three Prose Works*, ed. by John Buchanan-Brown (Carbondale: Southern Illinois University Press, 1972), pp. 176–77.

person need not be the end of the constituents themselves', that the constituents of individuality might survive the death of the individual, and that ties between both living and dead individuals are not merely social, but material: they consist of bones, dust, shared biological matter.[23] These rituals mediate between the living and the dead. They allow the bereaved to intervene in the fate of the dead and to personify their memory until the fact of death has become psychologically or socially acceptable. They satisfy needs to acknowledge simultaneously the absence of the person's spirit and the continued presence of his or her physical remains. Catholic customs such as the month's mind, which marked the end of the 'trigintal' period when the soul was believed to linger near the grave, gave institutional recognition to those needs.[24] But the Reformation dispensed with Requiem masses and other traditional intercessory practices and 'superstitious' observances such as 'superfluous' bell-ringing, burning candles in daylight, praying at crossroads, and the use of 'metwands or memories of idolatry at burials'.[25] Funeral ceremonies had been 'so farre abused, partly by the supersticious blyndnes of the rude and unlearned' and by the thirst of the learned for 'lucre', according to Cranmer, that they had to be wholly extirpated.[26] Eventually, the reforming zeal culminated in the short-lived *Directory for the Publique Worship of God*, which outlawed prayers, Scripture reading, and singing at funerals, and required that 'when any person departeth this life, let the dead body, upon the day of Buriall, be decently attended from the house to the place appointed for publique Buriall, and there immediately interred, without any Ceremony'.

Stipulating that they refused funerary ceremony was a mark of Puritan godliness; John Bruen, for example, told his family, 'I wil have no blacks, [...] I love not any proud or pompous Funerals, neither is there cause of mourning, but of rejoycing rather in my particular.'[27] However, these pious imperatives do not

[23] Maurice Bloch, 'Death and the Concept of Person', in *On the Meaning of Death: Essays on Mortuary Rituals and Eschatological Beliefs*, ed. by S. Cederroth, C. Corlin, and J. Lindström (Uppsala: Almqvist & Wiksell, 1988), pp. 11–29 (p. 17).

[24] David Cressy, *Birth, Marriage and Death: Ritual, Religion, and the Life-Cycle in Tudor and Stuart England* (Oxford: Oxford University Press, 1997), p. 398.

[25] Ralph Houlbrooke, 'Death, Church, and Family in England between the Late Fifteenth and the Early Eighteenth Centuries', in *Death, Ritual, and Bereavement*, ed. by Ralph Houlbrooke (London: Routledge, 1989), p. 38. See also Cressy, *Birth, Marriage and Death*, pp. 399–403.

[26] Julian Litten, *The English Way of Death: The Common Funeral since 1450* (London: Robert Hale, 1991), p. 126.

[27] William Hinde, *A Faithfull Remonstrance of the Holy Life and Happy Death of John Bruen* (London: printed by R. B. for P. Stephens, 1641), p. 225.

provide evidence to the actual funeral arrangements made by their executors, and many historians have described the outrage and horror with which parishioners greeted the *Directory*'s order of burial. Judith Maltby argues that there is little evidence that the *Directory* was widely purchased or used in place of the *Prayer Book*.[28] Insistence on strict observance of the rites permitted by the *Book of Common Prayer* (including bell ringing, white vestments, and the funeral sermon) by the laity demonstrates not only that the Protestant Church left room for ritual expressions of love for the dead, but also that these rituals remained popular.[29] According to Vanessa Harding, the Reformation did not change burial practices either, even though it challenged 'the belief that holiness could have a physical location and that association with specific places conferred spiritual benefit'.[30] Ralph Houlbrooke notes that the reformers 'sought to discourage excessive concern for the mortal remains', but that wills and the spread of coffin burial reveal 'a surviving, even growing solicitude for the protection of the corpse'.[31]

In the absence of such pre-Reformation customs as the obit, month's mind or anniversary Mass, poets offer their own rituals of consolation and commemoration, and opportunities to express solicitude toward the mortal remains. Often these make use of the secular consolations of classical myth and of pastoral imagery, which attests to the seasonal cycle of decay and rebirth. Other literary devices and rhetorical strategies for propitiating the dead and consoling the living included encounters with ghosts, admissions of dissent against Christian and Stoic rigorism through the use of *occupatio*, and apostrophes to the dead or the grave. Even the generic properties of elegy helped to expand the time of death and dying into a process. As a genre, the elegy traditionally incorporated condolence — an indulgence of the sorrow of the bereaved, exhortations to resolutions against grief, praise of the dead individual's past life and accomplishments, criticisms of the corruptions of the present age, and expectations of the future, when all the faithful could share in the rewards now experienced by the deceased. These orientations made elegy diachronic, a poetic space in which multiple temporalities were sorted and mixed. Like the funeral, the elegy could expand the instant of biological death into a gradual psychological and social process, treating the

---

[28] Judith Maltby, *Prayer Book and People in Elizabethan and Early Stuart England* (Cambridge: Cambridge University Press, 1998), p. 61.

[29] Maltby, *Prayer Book and People*, pp. 56–63.

[30] Vanessa Harding, *The Dead and the Living in Paris and London, 1500–1670* (Cambridge: Cambridge University Press, 2002), p. 52.

[31] Houlbrooke, *Death, Ritual, and Bereavement*, p. 11.

bereaved as participants in a rite of passage. Elegies describe how the bereaved are separated from the community, distinguished by their grief. Mourners occupy a liminal period during which they are asked to transform themselves, through access to the *gnosis* of virtue and the inevitability of mortality provided by their proximity to death, and are eventually reintegrated into the community through praise and moral behests.

Even the categories which had developed within elegy reflected its ritual status. Julius Caesar Scaliger distinguished three funerary genres: *epicedium*, which is spoken over an unburied body; *epitaphium recens*, written for a recently buried body; and *epitaphium anniversarium*, which commemorates the dead at yearly intervals after death, and so should omit the lament.[32] Henry Peacham also categorized elegy according to its relationship to the corpse:

> The difference between an *Epicede* and *Epitaph* is (as Servius teacheth) that the *Epicedium* is proper to the body while it is unburied, the *Epitaph* otherwise; yet our Poets stick not to take one for the other.[33]

These generic differentiations also show how the elegy accommodated the passage of the funereal time formally. George Puttenham reflected on the residue of a Catholic tradition which shaped the genres: '[T]he lamenting of deathes was chiefly at the very burialls of the dead, also at monethes mindes and longer times, by custome continued yearely.'[34] As these critics reveal, the formal differentiation of elegiac poetry coincides with the temporal process of death and drying of the corpse, and of reconciliation of the bereaved with the community.

Officially, the departed friends were beyond the reach of intercessory prayers, but the elegy could symbolically address the dead under the cover of rhetorical convention. The revised Edwardian Prayer Book of 1552 had signalled this breach in the conversation between the living and the dead by altering the language of the order of burial, so that the corpse was spoken *of* by the minister, rather than spoken *to*.[35] Apostrophes to the dead or the grave were however common in secular elegy. Mark Robson describes this rhetorical figure as attempting 'through

---

[32] Julius Caesar Scaliger, *Poetices* (Heidelberg: Apud Petrum Santandreanum, 1581), pp. 425–26; quoted in Rosalie L. Colie, *The Resources of Kind: Genre-Theory in the Renaissance*, ed. by Barbara K. Lewalski (Berkeley and Los Angeles: University of California Press, 1973), p. 32.

[33] Henry Peacham, *The Period of Mourning* (London: J. Helme, 1613), p. 17.

[34] George Puttenham, *The Arte of English Poesie*, ed. by G. D. Willcock and A. Walker (London, 1589; facsim. edn Menston: Scolar, 1968), p. 48.

[35] Eamon Duffy, *The Stripping of the Altars: Traditional Religion in England c. 1400–1580* (New Haven: Yale University Press, 1992), p. 475.

an obliteration of temporality' to instantiate 'the poem as a happening, as an event in the ever-present "now" of a reading'.[36] Direct address extends the co-presence of the living and the dead in time. Alison Shell has discussed a particularly spooky example of this form of address, in poems of a member of the Feilding family which record the stern warnings of her ghostly husband. The poet — whom she tentatively identifies as Frances Feilding — replies to the 'Dearest Shaede th[at] waitest night and days | about my Bead', protesting that she could not replace him so long as his memory lingers around her physical space. She promises that 'if allteration Bee | tis in my dress, my hart is true to thee'.[37] Her marital bed haunted by her 'soe JeaLous' spectral spouse, this poet cannot be unfaithful. Donne's conceit in 'The Apparition' is here fitted to an actual elegiac context. Drawing on another disciplinary tradition, we might also recall that Freud explains these revenants as manifestations of the unconscious guilt and hostility of the survivor which is projected onto the dead.[38] The Protestant emphasis on the culpability of the living, whose sinfulness brings providential punishment, might magnify that guilt and hostility. Rather than propitiating the dead in purgatory through sacrifices, survivors therefore turn to apotropaic fantasies about earthly visitations.

If visions of the dead may help to articulate psychological responses to death such as guilt and anger, they had also formed part of a pre-Reformation tradition in which the dead regularly appeared, demanding that the living relieve their suffering. Pope Gregory's mother, who haunted him until he said a trental of masses to free her from her crime of infanticide, is only the most famous example of such insistent specters. Recusant Ben Jonson confessed to his former schoolmaster William Camden a dream in which his oldest son, Ben, whom he had left behind in plague-stricken London, appeared to him with a bloody cross engraved in his forehead. Morbid attention to the corpse was typical of medieval representations of death and of Ignatian meditative techniques. While these traditions

[36] Mark Robson, 'Swansongs: Reading Voice in the Poetry of Lady Hester Pulter', *English Manuscript Studies*, 9 (2000), 238–56 (p. 253).

[37] Alison Shell, '"Often to my self I make my mone": Early Modern Women's Poetry from the Feilding Family', in *Early Modern Women's Manuscript Writing: Selected Papers from the Trinity/Trent Colloquium*, ed. by Victoria E. Burke and Jonathan Gibson (Aldershot: Ashgate, 2004), pp. 259–78 (p. 262).

[38] Sigmund Freud, *Totem and Taboo: Some Points of Agreement between the Mental Lives of Savages and Neurotics*, trans. by James Strachey (London: Routledge and Kegan Paul, 1960), pp. 58–62.

lacked institutional sanction in Reformation Britain, they were adapted rather than extinguished. Lewalski has shown that the Catholic meditation manuals (especially the *Imitatio Christi*, works of Ignatius Loyola, Luis de Granada, Gaspar Loarte, and the *Christian Directory* of Robert Persons) circulated widely in England and contributed to the development of a Protestant meditative tradition.[39]

When they directly address the grave, poets usually ask it to preserve the dead from corruption. An elegist for Etheldred, the daughter of his friend Sir Roger Millison, asks the grave to treat 'gently' its 'tender matchless on[e]' who is laid 'in your sluttish bed': 'keepe her from all heats, all stormes, | from corruption, from the wormes', the poem continues.[40] This commonplace contrasts the purity of the virgin corpse with the 'sluttish' grave, capable of enfolding endless generations of bodies. This sexualized imagery is not unusual; in fact, it resonates with the erotic potential of many meditations on the decaying corpse. In some early modern elegies, visions of the dead led not to spiritual chastisement but to arousal. Elias Ashmole writes about a dream of his dead wife, 'Which reunited what death did disjoyne | And made of us Two, One: a second tyme'. This 'scape' of the soul allowed him to 'injoy those Pleasures, which the day conceale', and he admits that 'in Fancy I have more Content, | Then can reallity to some present'.[41] He describes their reunion as a second wedding day: 'Wee met like knowing Paires, whose former Fires, | Kindled new flames to cherish fresh Desires'. But he hastens to add that those desires were 'Chast as the morne that Coyn'd them'. The erotic desire awakened by this dream must be disavowed, since the material reality of the beloved is now unthinkable and she has become pure spirit. He goes on to thank the spirit which 'her Idea brought unto my Bed', and a sense of his heavenly destiny to console him, but in praying 'Let not decaying Tyme | Feede on thy Joyes' he resurrects the disquieting image of her rotting corpse. This consolatory dream represents his wife as a present, physical reality. His memories and love are not yet consumed by 'decaying time', which is now 'decaying' the beloved body on which worms 'feed'.

Several poets use grotesque imagery to reveal their difficulty in conceding that the bonds of marriage had been severed by death, as when Henry King protests in

---

[39] Barbara K. Lewalski, *Donne's Anniversaries and the Poetry of Praise: The Creation of a Symbolic Mode* (Princeton: Princeton University Press, 1973), pp. 77–79.

[40] 'Epitaph. Vpon Mistris Etheldrid Millisont daughter to his worthie freind Sir Roger Millisone of Linton in the County of Cambridge', Leeds University, Brotherton Library MS Lt q 44, fol. 59.

[41] Oxford, Bodleian Library MS Ashmole 36, 37 fol. 234ᵛ.

his 'Anniverse' at being bound 'Living to a Coarse, | And I must slowly wast[e]'.[42] In a later autograph verse miscellany, religious decorum is completely overwhelmed by the romantic and physical ardour of William Tipping for his dead wife Hess. This manuscript includes a large number of elegies, including one 'putt on her Brest in her Coffin'.[43] Tipping attests 'How oft Times I did kiss my deere | when dead I lovd thee soe'. Then,

> I covetted to die
> And to bee buried with thee
> that I by Thee might Lie.
> with waters well perfumd I washt
> thy hands and face my deere
> fower mornings after thou wast dead
> Thee kiss could not forbeare.
> Till in a Coffin thou wst Layd
> And Nayled up from mee.

His poems re-enact these ritual oblations, his final care for the body of his wife, as a way of preventing the final closure of the coffin. Tipping's compulsively repetitive elegies create what Peter Sacks describes as 'a sense of continuity, an unbroken pattern such as one may oppose to the extreme discontinuity of death'.[44]

Traditional Greek lament, Margaret Alexiou points out, also used direct address and appeals by name to the dead, whose 'function was to rouse the spirit of the dead and establish contact'.[45] According to Reformation eschatology, such contact was only possible by the death of the living partner. Sick with grief, Tipping wishes he were in heaven so that he could embrace his wife, not glorify God. Hess seems to have matched his passionate fidelity, nearly failing the test of the good death that would assure him of her election.

> I one expression from her heard
> Im even Ashamed to Tell
> Shee said as mee, her verie soule

[42] Henry King, *The Poems*, ed. by Margaret Crum (Oxford: Clarendon Press, 1965), pp. 72–73. All references to King's poems are from this edition.

[43] Oxford, Bodleian Library MS *Rawl. poet. 101, fol. 15ᵛ.

[44] Peter M. Sacks, *The English Elegy: Studies in the Genre from Spenser to Yeats* (Baltimore: Johns Hopkins University Press, 1985), pp. 23–24.

[45] Margaret Alexiou, *The Ritual Lament in Greek Tradition*, 2nd rev. edn (Lanham: Rowman & Littlefield, 2002), p. 136.

> Shee did not Love soe well.
> [...]
> I Askt her If that Christ shee Lovd
> Could freely to him Goe
> mee Answere made shee freely Could
> If Ide Goe with her too.[46]

This is hardly the stalwart confession of faith required by Protestant *ars moriendi*. By the time he has accepted Hess's death, Tipping despairs at the thought that his excessive mourning had transgressed against God. He 'was an Idolater | as Greate as ere was knowne', he professes;

> To whom my soule did then belonge
> was hard for mee to knowe
> for with my God whom I now love
> I little had to doe.[47]

While Tipping's verses demonstrate how difficult it could be to relinquish attachments in favour of Christian consolation, by their conclusion they also reveal how salutary time could be in forcing grief to relent.

A more famous example of pathological attachment to the dead is the recusant Sir Kenelm Digby, who famously mourned his beloved Venetia for years in verse, letters, religious meditations, commissioned art, and monumental sculpture, and even his own deportment. Two days after Venetia's death, Kenelm 'caused her face to be moulded of by an excellent Master [likely to have been Van Dyck], to have it by that afterwardes painted as she lay dead and cast in metall'. Digby's aim was to preserve her beauty, and to extend the moment of her death until he could deal with it:

> [T]ruly all that saw her lye thus, said she looked (if it were possible) with more lovelinesse then while she lived; onely wannesse had defloured the sprightfulnesse of her beauty: but no sinking or smelling or contortion or falling of the lippes appeared in her face to the very last.[48]

In Kenelm's veneration of his wife, Catholic sainthood and Platonic admiration of beauty give more philosophical justification to his physical desires. When he

---

[46] Oxford, Bodleian Library MS *Rawl. poet. 101, fols 13–14[v].

[47] Bodleian Library MS *Rawl. poet. 101, fol. 27.

[48] Vittorio Gabrieli, 'A New Digby Letter-Book: "In Praise of Venetia"', *National Library of Wales Journal*, 9 (1955), 133–48, 440–62 (p. 132).

first discovered Venetia dead, Digby says he 'knelt downe by her, and with wordes as broken as my thoughts, could not choose but pray to her, her lookes were so like an Angell'.[49] Though later in a letter to his sons he described these ecstasies of grief as shameful, he continued to regard her as 'designed for my salvation: to sett me on fire with her lovelinesse and then to go to a place whither by goodnessee and vertue onely I can come to see her againe'. His wife's physical loveliness, and his sexual desire for her, is his motivation to seek salvation, so that they can be re-united in heaven.

Like Tipping's, Digby's idolization of his wife seems to arise from physical and romantic love rather than the iconology of his own Catholic faith. Yet these poems could be contrasted with the erotic lyrics of John Donne, whose erotic veneration of the lover is streaked through with the gross effects of mortality and with paradoxical references to Catholic hagiography. Digby's elegies for Venetia include one grotesque fantasy about the corruption of her fetishized body. 'You wormes (my rivalls) whiles she was alive' addresses the creatures who now have a freedom for which 'many thousands [...] did strive' in her life: to penetrate her body and wear 'unseemely holes in her soft skinne'.[50] The poem is animated by phallic imagery, morbid sexual curiosity, and possessiveness, and betrays his anxieties about Venetia's reputation. Digby invites the worms to 'taste of her tender body', but asks them not to 'deface' her. They may chew holes in her ears, 'carve' a cross on her breast, and finally 'grave' this epitaph on her forehead: 'Living, she was fayre, yong, and full of witt | Dead all her faults are in her fore-head writ.' Digby gives permission to the worms to penetrate Venetia's body, but refuses to cede his marital property to the grave: instead he imagines stamping his beloved's body, preserved from physical corruption, with his own epigram.

Digby's elegiac representation of grief as a process, mirrored by the process of physical decomposition, is consistent with mortuary rituals in many cultures. Rather than 'an instantaneous destruction of an individual's life', Robert Hertz writes, 'death is to be seen as a social event, the starting point of a ceremonial process by which the dead person becomes an ancestor.'[51] Communal ceremonies

---

[49] Gabrieli, 'A New Digby Letter-Book', pp. 141–43.

[50] The phrase 'the worms thy rivalls' is also used in 'An Elegie on the most beauteous and vertuous Lady the Lady Venetia Digby', by Thomas Randolph, where the worms' rival is Death itself. H. A. Bright, *Poems from Sir Kenelm Digby's Papers* (London: Nichols and Sons, 1877), pp. 26, 29.

[51] Daniel de Coppet, 'The Life-giving Death', in *Mortality and Immortality: The Anthropology and Archaeology of Death*, ed. by S. C. Humphreys and Helen King (London: Academic, 1981),

recognize the gradual relaxation of the bond between the spirit of the dead and his or her body, as well as between the survivors and the dead. Elegies imitate this ritual process in more than just their content: they also transform grief into principled and rational artistry through prosody. Versification forces the poet to contemplate mortality, to order her imagination into rhetorical form, and to bridle her excessive passions with the regularity of metre. Significantly, this metrical discipline relies on time: elegists frequently refer to the time which elapses between death and composition as a necessity for the production of art. Writing poetry allows a writer like Tipping to indulge in long-term reiterations of grief that verge on the pathological, but it also helps to recalibrate time which can seem disordered by death. To conclude, I will look at the second most famous writer of post-Reformation 'Anniversary' poems: Henry King. King's elegies explore death as a process not through reformed or symbolic versions of Catholic rituals, but through the language of accounting. But where for Donne 'even griefe [...] is without proportion' because Elizabeth Drury, the soul of beauty and proportion, is dead, and the 'new Philosophy cals all in doubt', King uses this vocabulary as a way of *giving* proportion to his grief. He explores the time of dying and grieving not by reappropriating religious observances, but by application to the new communal disciplines of economics.

Henry King's poems for his wife Anne (who was buried 5 January 1624) express a desire for death and grief to follow the rules of reason. In his 'Anniverse: An Elegy', written when Anne had 'bin six yeares dead', he wonders

> How happy were mankind, if Death's strict Lawes
> Consùm'd our Lamentations like the Cause!
> Or that our grief, turning to dust, might end
> With the dissolved body of a friend!
>
> (p. 73)

Grief should be consumed as quickly as the decaying body; but its persistence is a consequence of the fall: grief is 'Life's Vocation', the defining characteristic of the human condition, and 'only hee | Is Nature's True-borne Child, who summes his yeares | (Like mee) with no Arithmetick, but Teares' (p. 73). The quantification

---

pp. 175–204 (p. 175). Mircea Eliade writes that 'the onset of physiological death is only the signal that a new set of ritual operations must be accomplished in order to create the new identity of the deceased' ('Mythologies of Death', in *Religious Encounters with Death: Insights from the History and Anthropology of Religions*, ed. by Frank E. Reynolds and Earle H. Waugh (University Park: Penn State University Press, 1977), pp. 13–23 (p. 15)).

of sorrow not only rationalizes psychological time; it also proves the authenticity of human experience, of the self-awareness of a 'true-born child' of nature who takes 'possession of the earth', rather than the delusions of those who count themselves the 'adopted sons' of Fortune. Where sorrow emerges from a recognition of the sinner's fallen condition, it accords with Christian discipline; but were it to remain undiminished by Christian hope, it would betray its irrational aspect.

King's elegy shares with Donne's *Anniversaries* an insight into the way bereavement disturbs the perception of time. Donne writes on Elizabeth Drury that 'Some months she hath beene dead (but being dead, | Measures of times are all determined)'; that is, after the cataclysmic event of Drury's death, all sense of duration is meaningless, unpunctuated by significance. In 'An Exequy To his Matchlesse never to be forgotten Freind', King looks for consolation to the regular return of the sun, which foretells Anne's resurrection. His own individual sense of time has been disoriented, and now goes 'Backward and most praeposterous' (p. 69), not taking him toward their reunion but to a melancholic dwelling on the past. Time's slow passage oppresses him; days seem like years, just as they do to souls in purgatory.[52] He realizes

> How lazily Time creepes about
> To one that mournes: This, only This
> My Exercise and bus'nes is:
> So I compute the weary howres
> With Sighes dissolved into Showres.
>
> (p. 69)

King's sole 'exercise and business' is the computation of 'weary hours', with his sighs and tears as the ticking of his grief's lazy clock, creeping 'about' the clockface. The use of the word *business* in this context of weary time-filling is not coincidental. A. J. Gurevich argues that mechanisms for measuring time developed in the context of urban merchant activity, and represented a form of emancipation from the authority of the church and its cyclical and liturgical time. As cyclical time gave way to linear, 'man for the first time discovered that time, whose passing he had noted only in relation to events, did not cease even in the absence of events.'[53] It became important to *save* time as a source of value to emerging mercantile trades; time began to 'impose its rhythm on [people], forcing them to act more

---

[52] Le Goff, *The Birth of Purgatory*, p. 294.

[53] A. J. Gurevich, 'Time as a Problem of Cultural History', in *Cultures and Time*, ed. by Louis Gardet and others (Paris: Unesco, 1976), pp. 241–43.

quickly, to hurry, not to allow the moment to escape'. Jacques Le Goff agrees that medieval time had been dominated by 'liturgical time, calendar time, the daily routine marked by the ringing of bells, rural time, largely determined by natural rhythms but punctuated by partially Christianized annual rites'.[54] Purgatory was another spatial realm governed by the passage of time.[55]

Gurevich's provocative descriptions of post-medieval time — as autonomous, neutral, 'experienced independently of its real object-related content', a 'pure categorical form' of duration — resonate with King's own relation of his experience of time during this period of mourning. His poem refers to time's autonomy, its lack of regard for his wishes, and its ability to impose its own lagging rhythms on him. King wishes to hurry it onward, to 'empty' it of content so that it matches his 'empty hopes':

> woe is mee! the longest date
> Too narrowe is to calculate
> These empty hopes.
>
> (p. 70)

He complains that, after Anne's death, time marches on inexorably, void of events which might tie his own life to the cycle of nature. He recalls that Anne 'scarce hadst seene so many Yeeres | As Day tells Howres' (p. 69); her lifetime was so brief as to be analogous to the cycle of the day, but he lives out an eternity in her absence. He must await the apocalypse for 'a glimpse of Thee': that day

> Which shall the Earth to cinders doome,
> And a fierce Feaver must calcine
> The Body of this World, like Thine,
> (My Little World!)
>
> (p. 70).

This Donnean paradox, that the world will be cleansed and burnt to cinders by a fire similar to the fever which killed her, releases him to imagine the ecstasies of reunion:

> That fitt of Fire
> Once off, our Bodyes shall aspire
> To our Soules' blisse'.
>
> (p. 70)

---

[54] Le Goff, *The Birth of Purgatory*, p. 290
[55] Le Goff, *The Birth of Purgatory*, p. 229.

While the bliss of the body will begin with its freedom from illness, its end looks like erotic rapture.

King then addresses the grave, switching from these meditations on time to the legal lexis of property ownership. His admission of guilt that he 'could not keep' Anne alive becomes a proud declaration of independence: heaven wills that 'I might not call | Hir longer Mine', so King resigns to the grave all 'My short liv'd right and Interest' in her (p. 70). This boon is surrendered 'With a most free and bounteous grief': he pays his debt to the grave, and to God who leant Anne to him, but his grief is a free gift, the surplus added to the 'right and interest' he relinquishes by necessity. The indebtedness which Marcel Mauss argues characterizes the recipient of a gift now affects the grave: King is in the position to demand something in return. His request is peculiar. He wants a record of Anne's physical 'parcels' to be entered in a kind of apocalyptic account book:

> See that thou make thy reck'ning streight,
> And yeeld Hir back againe by weight;
> For thou must Auditt on thy trust
> Each Grane and Atome of this Dust:
> As thou wilt answere Him, that leant,
> Not gave thee, my deare Monument.
>
> (p. 70)

Fearing the dispersal of his wife's precious remains, King uses the language of 'audits' and 'reckoning' to demand the grave be an honourable trustee of her 'grains and atoms'. Proprietary references recur in his description of 'two Children dying of one Disease, and buryed in one Grave' as unable to 'number many Yeeres | In their Account': life becomes an *account*, a saving-up of goodness to spend on judgement day. The speaker 'discharges' his debt of grief with the meagre consolation that 'Heav'n hath decreed you ne're shall cost mee more' (p. 72): he pays out sorrow in the place of a dowry. In the 'Exequy', mercantile language also displaces his sentimental interiority. Struck by the indifference of the universe to his tears, King ironically adopts the matter-of-fact terms of commodity exchange to signal his defeat.

Le Goff suggests that the medieval conception of purgatory introduced the language of 'calculation' and 'reckoning' into eschatology.[56] The veniality of the dead could be calculated, evaluated, and exchanged for suffrages by the living. The

---

[56] Le Goff, *The Birth of Purgatory*, p. 227.

Reformers' attitude to the resulting commercialization of indulgences which resulted is well known; but Le Goff explores the epistemological consequences of extending mathematical language to the afterlife. He argues that the purgatorial contest for the soul of the elect was 'obviously inspired by judicial procedures and legal ideas associated with this world'; but by the time of King's poem, 'Death's strict laws' had hardened into an absolute decree.[57] Like the natural law of mortality or human law, money is, Georg Simmel writes, 'characterised by [its] complete indifference to individual qualities'.[58] Simmel perceives the influence of money in the emergence of a 'cognitive ideal' which conceives 'of the world as a huge arithmetical problem'.[59] King refers to law and commercial transactions as a way of lamenting the fixed and non-negotiable reality of Anne's death. Like money, death is indifferent — to the individual merits of his beloved wife. However, this calculating mode is not simply a rhetorical expression of those aspects of his grief which resist determination. King's experience of grief as an unyielding duration of empty linear time is a discourse which is produced by the money economy. Simmel continues, 'like the determination of abstract value by money, the determination of abstract time by clocks provides a system for the most detailed and definite arrangements and measurements that imparts an otherwise unattainable transparency and calculability to the contents of life.' It is the existence of that system which enables King to reduce his life, in mourning, to a transparency and calculability consistent with Christian and Stoic rationalism.

Geometry also produces a sense of 'transparency and calculability' in the measurements of space, the other persistent theme in these poems. King imagines time's passage as a journey through space requiring his own physical movement, as he travels toward his wife in time and space. This poetic figuration of time as space replaces the space of duration previously represented by purgatory, which Le Goff has called a 'spatialization' of the ritualistic penitential system of the church. In King's words

> Each Minute is a short Degree
> And e'ry Howre a stepp towards Thee.
> At Night when I betake to rest,
> Next Morne I rise neerer my West

[57] Le Goff, *The Birth of Purgatory*, p. 211.

[58] Georg Simmel, *The Philosophy of Money*, ed. by David Frisby, trans. by Tom Bottomore and David Frisby, 2nd enlarged edn (London: Routledge, 1990), p. 442.

[59] Simmel, *The Philosophy of Money*, p. 444.

Of Life, almost by eight Howres' sayle,
Then when Sleep breath'd his drowsy gale.
(p. 71)

Rejecting the empty, autonomous linear time which has no sympathy for him, King seeks solace in the diurnal cycle which marches him toward his own death. It is a cycle finally complemented by the rhythms of his body itself: 'But hark! My Pulse, like a soft Drum | Beates my Approach, Tells Thee I come' (p. 71). The pulse is the body's timer, ticking out the remnants of life, and also the drum which signals the advancing army, conquering time. The steady beat of his heart reminds him of his own mortality and his creaturely connection to nature. Modulated by feeling and by the rhythms of breathing which also govern prosody, the noise of his pulse — that is, of his own approaching death — might conquer rationalized time.

A lifetime is not available to rational evaluation. When it ends, it is commemorated by grief whose premise is the *opposite* of exchangeability: mourners offer the free gift of sorrow, a surplus which recognizes their indebtedness to God for the loan of the individual, and the impossibility of attributing a true value to his or her life in words, symbols, or gestures. To accept the necessity of death and to give up the passions of grief, the mourner must either submit to the laws of Christian fortitude or Stoicism, or wait out the process of acceptance and healing with the help of communal or private rituals. King's poems use the language of audits, interest, quantifications, mathematics, and measures to reveal the difficulties of overruling sorrow with logic. This new faith in commerce and its brokers, money, and mechanized time, was gradually coming to replace pre-Reformation customs and even the mysteries of religion itself. However, if Le Goff is right in arguing that 'the creation of purgatory combined a process of spatialization of the universe with an arithmetic logic that governed the relationship between human behaviour and the situation of the soul in Purgatory',[60] then King's poems are not so much indicators of a radical break with pre-Reformation traditions, foreshadowing the secularization of culture and the retreat to psychologized interiority in the experience of death, as their natural inheritor.

[60] Le Goff, *The Birth of Purgatory*, p. 227.

'FOR GODS INHERITANCE ONELYE': CONSOLATION AND RECUSANT IDENTITY IN ROBERT PERSONS'S *CHRISTIAN DIRECTORIE*

Kevin Laam

Robert Persons's *The First Booke of the Christian Exercise, Appertayning to Resolution* (1582), begun in the early stages of the Jesuit mission in England but not published until the author was forced into exile at Rouen, did not share the combative spirit of the other works he wrote at the time. Instead it advertised itself as a spiritual salve to Christians oppressed, or otherwise swayed from their faith, by troubled times. In the book's preface he casts no aspersion upon the non-Catholic audience except to say that faith is profitless without charity — and this claim is mitigated with the assurance that God will show mercy on the pious even if their faith is misguided. '[I]f thow be of an other religion than I am', he writes, 'I beseche the most hartelye, that layenge a side all hatred, malice and wrathfull contention, let us joyne together in amendment of our lyves, and prayeng one for an other: and God (no doubt) will not suffer us to perishe finallye for want of right faithe.'[1] God is entrusted to correct the misunderstandings of believers who are sincere in their conviction and diligent

---

[1] Robert Persons, *The Christian Directory (1582): The First Booke of the Christian Exercise, Appertayning to Resolution*, ed. by Victor Houliston (Brill: Leiden, 1998), p. 7. All future references to this work are cited in the text by page number and the initials *CD*. Unless specified otherwise, I use the term *Directorie* to indicate all versions of the text authored exclusively by Persons. Houliston's critical edition works from the 1582 Persons text (with the 1585 and 1607 editions serving to help identify errors), and he includes an apparatus with Bunny's alterations. Since my argument is concerned more with the overall structure of Persons's appeal than with his subsequent efforts at accommodation, I have chosen to use Houliston's edition. My usage of the 1585 edition is limited to the preface, in which Persons outlines his opposition to Bunny's revisions.

in their deeds. Persons may concern himself with setting his readers on the path
toward living virtuously.

Perhaps the safest measure of the book's ecumenical threshold is provided by
Edmund Bunny's Protestant adaptation, which first appeared in 1584. Bunny, an
Anglican minister at Bolton Percy in York, purged the original work of its 'Romish corruptions' and supplemented it with *A Treatise Tending to Pacification*, a
conciliatory appeal encouraging recusants to conform. Yet he was demonstrably
generous in his appraisal of the original. 'As it is set foorth by the Author himself', he writes in the preface, 'if we consider the substance of it, surely it was wel
woorth the labor (a few points only excepted) and much of it, of good persuasion
to godlines of life.'[2] Bunny questions Persons's use of the Vulgate, and flatly
objects to the opinions that are out of keeping with reformed doctrine, but he
shares the Jesuit's emphasis on joining Christians across all manner of belief in
fellowship. The Church of God should be united, Bunny insists, and it avails
neither side to stay perpetually in the business of contention.

This essay proposes that the work is anything but neutral. The attempt at
pacification brings out the polemicist in Persons, and in 1585 he issues a revised
edition of the *Christian Exercise* including, among other changes, a new title —
A Christian Directorie Guiding Men to their Salvation (1585) — and an expanded
introduction condemning Bunny's motives. As Persons saw it, the Protestant was
the latest in an ancient line of heretical tricksters prone to the same specious
tactics: feigning scholastic erudition, removing Scripture from its proper context,
perverting other men's books — anything short of producing devotional works
of their own. Thus, rather than cede Bunny's argument for a unified church,
Persons calls his bluff:

> But what is the cause (thinke you) of this so great and suddaine curtesie which now at
> length M. Buny against al custome of his brethren doth offer unto us? you shal heare it
> uttered (if you please) in his owne wordes, *for by consenting so far with them* (saieth he) *as
> to graunt that we are not both of one Church; we bring our selves to needles trouble. For that
> it is greate probabilitie with them, that so we make our selves aunswerable for to finde out a
> several and distinct Church from them, from which we descende, which hath continued from
> the Apostles age to this present, els that needes we must acknowledge that our Church is sprung
> up of late, or at least, since thers:* This is his confession; which we having heard, we neede

---

[2] Edmund Bunny, preface to *A Booke of Christian Exercise, Appertaining to Resolution, that
is, Shewing How that We Should Resolv Our Selvs to Becom Christians in Deed: by R. P. Perused,
and Accompanied Now with a Treatise Tending to Pacification* (London: printed for Iohn Wight,
1585), sig. A6. *A Treatise Tending to Pacification* begins after the conclusion of the revised *Directorie*, and is paginated separately.

not stande any longer in doubt, wherfore he is become so kinde, as at length to make us al of one true Catholique and Apostolique Church with them, whom hitherto they have detested as the Sinagogue of Antechrist. 3

For the purpose of revealing the latent partisanship of the *Directorie*, the usefulness of the Protestant version is clear: it puts Persons on the defensive, forcing him to articulate the ideological assumptions behind one of his most uncharacteristically evenhanded works. But the bitterness of his response may also be misleading, inasmuch as it sees him coaxed into a pose more familiar to his reputation than to the actual temper of the *Directorie*. The Persons-Bunny feud fails to explain how a work steeped in Ignatian piety and nourished by missionary zeal ascends into the pantheon of Elizabethan devotional literature. The popularity of the *Directorie* outlasts the immediate controversy by generations, going through some fifty editions between 1582 and 1640.[4] While the majority of these editions were Protestant, Catholic books were not infrequently subject to emendation.[5] Bunny concedes a greater interest in ministering the virtues of the national church than in debating theology, hence his formulaic purging of the *Directorie's* doctrinaire 'corruptions'. He is not able nor likely willing to alter the larger framework from which the book derives its sacerdotal authority, and that framework, through all of the text's incarnations, remains fundamentally Jesuit.[6]

[3] Persons, preface to *A Christian Directorie Guiding Men to their Saluation. Deuided into three bookes. The first vvherof appertaining to resolution, is only conteined in this volume, deuided into tvvo partes, and set forth novv againe vvith many corrections, and additions by th'authour him self, vvith reprofe of the corrupt and falsified edition of the same booke lately published by M. Edm. Buny. Ther is added also a methode for the vse of al; with two tables, and a preface to the reader, which is necessarie to be reade* (Rouen: printed by the author, 1585), sig. 19[r-v].

[4] *A Short-Title Catalogue of Books Printed in England, Scotland, & Ireland and of English Books Printed Abroad, 1475–1640*, 2nd edn, rev. and enl., comp. by A. W. Pollard and G. R. Redgrave, begun by W. A. Jackson and F. S. Ferguson, completed by Katharine F. Pantzer (London: Bibliographical Society, 1976), pp. 217–18. The printing history of Persons's text is also summarized neatly in Houliston's introduction to the *Christian Directory*, pp. xxxix–xlvii.

[5] Ceri Sullivan reads Bunny's revision as an illustrative example of Elizabethan editing techniques. See 'Cannibalizing Persons' *Christian Directorie*, 1582', *Notes & Queries*, 41 (239.4) (1994), 445–46.

[6] For a comparison of the similarities and differences between Bunny's *Directorie* and the original, see Robert McNulty, "The Protestant Version' of Robert Parsons' *The First Booke of the Christian Exercise*', *Huntington Library Quarterly*, 22 (1959), 271–300; and Brad S. Gregory, 'The "True and Zealouse Seruice of God": Robert Parsons, Edmund Bunny, and *The First Booke of the Christian Exercise*', *Journal of Ecclesiastical History*, 45 (1994), 238–68. Also valuable is McNulty's 'Robert Parsons' *The First Booke of the Christian Exercise* (1582): An Edition and a Study' (unpublished doctoral dissertation, Columbia University, 1955).

While it is reasonable to suggest that Bunny's revisions make the *Directorie* safe for widespread consumption among English readers, I would suggest that the qualitative attraction of the work hinges on its ties to the *Spiritual Exercises* of St Ignatius. Specifically, Persons adapts Ignatian consolatory techniques into a straightforward model of Christian devotion that fits the practical spiritual needs of English readers. He gives currency to the precepts of Ignatius by situating them in the dramatic setting of recusancy — among the most prominent acts of resistance one could perform in 1580s England.[7] Persons draws his subject from a swath of English society unseen in Bunny's reveries of the most glorious and decorated chapter in the nation's history, untouched by the dividends purported to proceed from living under a sovereign ruler. If the popularity of the work is an accurate indication, the recusant plight resonated with an audience well exceeding the minority of loyal Catholics, giving strength to John Bossy's thesis that the traditional church did more than minimally survive the troubled years of the Elizabethan Settlement.[8] Remarkably, the success with which the *Directorie* renovated the concept of consolation gave early modern readers reason to take a Jesuit controversialist at his word.

The term *consolation* has a history that can be traced back at least to Boethius. *The Consolation of Philosophy* was composed in the sixth century while the author was imprisoned on charges of high treason. A seminal example of the medieval *consolatio*, a philosophic dialogue form in which a despairing protagonist receives comfort by way of allegorical instruction, the work endeared itself to a vast Christian audience with its providential themes.[9] In the late-medieval era, consolation features extensively in *The Imitation of Christ*, the venerable book of mystic piety normally ascribed to the Augustinian monk Thomas à Kempis.[10] The

---

[7] See Peter Marshall, *Reformation England, 1480–1642* (New York: Arnold, 2003), pp. 172–73.

[8] John Bossy, *The English Catholic Community, 1570–1850* (London: Darton, Longman & Todd, 1975), pp. 11–34. See also 'The Character of Elizabethan Catholicism', *Past and Present*, 21.1 (1962), 39–59, in which Bossy evaluates the impact of the new wave of Catholic activists or 'clerks' upon the more domestically inclined 'seigneurial Catholicism' of the aristocratic gentry.

[9] A comprehensive study is Michael Means, *The Consolatio Genre in Medieval English Literature* (Gainesville: University of Florida Press, 1972).

[10] I owe the idea to John W. O'Malley's *The First Jesuits* (Cambridge, MA: Harvard University Press, 1993), which observes the recurrent invocation of consolation in the *Imitation* and the subsequent absorption of the concept into Jesuit orthodoxy. See pp. 19–20, 82–84, 264–66.

third book of the *Imitation* consists of admonitions to 'inward consolation', which denotes the private speech of Christ to the soul: 'Blessed is the soul which hears the Lord speaking within it, and from his mouth receives the word of consolation'.[11]

The biblical roots of consolation can be traced to the book of Jeremiah, which offers a model of devotion that prescribes inward reforms for the degeneracy of Judaic society. Jeremiah hopes to alert his countrymen to the wrath God has sworn upon them (25. 9–11). It is to no avail: the Lord's judgement is that '[t]he sin of Judah *is* written with a pen of iron, *and* with the point of a diamond' (17. 1), and so the fate of its people is consigned to the yoke of Babylon for the next seventy years. Jeremiah urges them to bear it patiently, pledging in the 'Book of Consolation' (30. 1–33. 26) the restoration of the kingdoms of both Judah and Israel as well as the advent of a 'new covenant' predicated solely on direct dealings between the individual and the Almighty. Under the new covenant, human beings shall be accountable for their own actions, not for the sins of their forefathers; lands left 'desolate without man or beast' during the period of exile shall be replenished in full.[12] Jeremiah, for his part, is commanded to claim a stake in these future consolations: first by keeping a physical record of the promises that God has confided to him (30. 1–3), and later by purchasing land that he will be able to redeem when the kingdom is restored (32. 1–44). In the meantime, he encourages the captives of the Babylonian invasion to suppress thoughts of rebellion and to resolve themselves to the 'perpetual desolations' (25. 9) their negligence has brought about. When his prophecies are fulfilled, the two kingdoms together are assured an outcome more glorious than either alone could have imagined.

There is little mistaking that Persons conceives of the recusant population in Elizabethan England as itself the captivity of a new Babylon. A series of proposals introduced in the 1581 parliament resulted in legislation that levied a monthly fine of twenty pounds for refusal to attend church services, steepened the penalties for seditious speech (including death for repeat offenders), and expanded the definition of treason to include any act of converting persons away from the Queen's religion.[13] Catholic books were confiscated in massive numbers,

---

[11] *The Imitation of Christ*, ed. by Albert Hyma (New York: Century, 1927), p. 87.

[12] The phrase quoted is reiterated several times during Jeremiah's prophecy of restoration (Jer. 32. 43, 33. 10, 12), figuratively stamping out the old covenant while heralding the providence of the new.

[13] Patrick McGrath, *Papists and Puritans Under Elizabeth I* (New York: Walker, 1967), pp. 176–77. Also see John J. Larocca, 'Popery and Pounds: The Effect of the Jesuit Mission on

less for errors of faith than for suspected associations of treason.[14] In this climate of mounting persecution, the Jesuit mission was concerned as much with rallying the Catholic faithful as with keeping faith alive for the silent majority whose outward conformity Persons equated to spiritual defeatism.

Bunny's attempts to gloss the situation notwithstanding, the *Directorie* makes no effort to massage the conscience of the reluctant or lukewarm believer, nor to feed the illusion that the odds of attaining salvation are in one's favour. In both its Protestant and Catholic incarnations, the book's confessional outlook is shaped by the assumption that the relationship between the individual and the universe is inherently antagonistic. Early in Chapter 1 Persons asserts that the very act of reading it requires a show of resistance: one must be willing to admit elements contrary to his or her 'present humor or resolution' (*CD*, p. 12) against the warnings of Satan and others that spiritual books only beget feelings of guilt and dejection. From the moment readers accept that worldly wisdom is hostile to their best interests, they may never let down their guard. Chapter 2 of the *Directorie* advises a course of active and vigorous self-reflection, lacking which 'all the foule errors of the woorlde are committed, and many thowsand Christians doo fynde them selves within the very gates of hell' (*CD*, p. 14). That so many who ascribe to the tenets of Christianity are doomed to this fate does not result from deficient or impure knowledge. The 'mysteryes of our Christiane fayth' (*CD*, p. 16), remarkably, are the subject of little contention or confusion. But these mysteries are accepted so lightly, with such little regard for their bearing on our day-to-day lives, that the average believer fails to comprehend how they stage the passage from earth to heaven. Consequently, Christians are saved a scant one per thousand. In this way, Jeremiah's lament for the men of Judah in Jeremiah 12. 11 gains new significance: 'All the earthe is fallen into utter desolation for that there is no man which considereth deeply in his harte' (*CD*, p. 14). Consolation, meanwhile, awaits the few who will give the necessity of God's plan the consideration it deserves.

Penal Legislation', in *The Reckoned Expense: Edmund Campion and the Early English Jesuits*, ed. by Thomas M. McCoog (Woodbridge: Boydell, 1996), pp. 249–63.

[14] Cyndia Clegg, in *Press Censorship in Elizabethan England* (Cambridge: Cambridge University Press, 1997), clarifies three specific offenses for which Catholic books were most commonly suppressed: libel, treason, and writing about the succession (p. 81). Devotional texts were classified somewhat arbitrarily; they might be used to corroborate suspected linkages to seditious activity, deemed seditious in their own right, or simply left alone. See chap. 4, 'Catholic Propagandists: Concerning the Queen's Majesty or the Realm without Licence', pp. 79–102.

As the two poles of affective experience in Jesuit orthodoxy, consolation and desolation are central to the soteriology of the *Directorie*. In the *Spiritual Exercises* of Ignatius, the terms are used to denote not static conditions but opposing movements within the soul — 'consolations' and 'desolations'. Ignatius outlines definitions for each in his 'Rules for the Discernment of Spirits', which aid individuals struggling to make sense of the internal vicissitudes stimulated by performing the Exercises.[15] Spiritual consolation, which occurs under the auspices of the good spirit, encompasses all motions causing the soul to spill over with love for its Lord. These might begin in grief (as when the soul weeps for past sins or for Christ's suffering), but they will always conclude in serenity. Spiritual desolation includes motions to the contrary, such as 'obtuseness of soul, turmoil within it, an impulsive motion toward low or earthly things, or disquiet from various agitations and temptations'.[16] The *Spiritual Exercises* treats some degree of fluctuation between the variant motions as a fact of earthly living; there is no indication that one may be inured from unwelcome advances. To be safe, we should not be deceived by periods of prolonged contentment — this is an avenue to false consolation[17] — but instead equip ourselves to repel the thrusts of the enemy. The tenth rule for discernment of spirits categorically states that happier times are not to be savoured indefinitely but rather spent in preparation for their end. The eleventh mandates a sturdy diet of self-deprivation toward that goal: 'One who is consolation ought to humble and abase herself or himself as much as possible, and reflect how little she or he is worth in time of desolation when that grace or consolation is absent' (*SE*, p. 124). Conversely, when desolation arrives, the soul must recall the resolutions it has made in healthier spirits and have faith in consolations to come. Whatever counsel it receives in the meantime is the work of the evil spirit, contrived in malice and deceit.

[15] O'Malley, *First Jesuits*, p. 44.

[16] George E. Ganss, *The Spiritual Exercises of Saint Ignatius: A Translation and Commentary* (Chicago: Loyola University Press, 1992), p. 122. Future references to this work are indicated in the text by page number and the abbreviation *SE*.

[17] The final rule for discernment of spirits (the eighth rule of the second week) cautions readers to be wary immediately following an experience of consolation, during which 'the soul remains still warm and favored with the gifts and aftereffects of the consolation which has itself passed away' (*SE*, p. 128). The afterglow may be caused by any one of three agents — a good spirit, an evil spirit, or our own dubious judgement — and thus should not be trusted as willingly as consolatory sensations that are experienced without an identifiable cause. In the second rule of the second week, Ignatius establishes that neither spirits nor individual faculties but 'Only God our Lord can give the soul consolation without a preceding cause' (*SE*, p. 126).

The ethic imparted in the *Spiritual Exercises* is one of consummate self-awareness, one that endures the soul's flights into good and evil but insists that they be monitored and managed correctly. This duty is handled jointly by the 'retreatant', or subject of the Exercises, and the director, who assigns them selectively to accord with the specific needs, circumstances, and ability levels of persons under his charge. Before proceeding into the prayers, meditations, directives, and other activities that comprise the four-week curriculum, the text acquaints directors with the varieties of retreatant they can expect to encounter in their work. The director is entrusted to prescribe the Exercises with such discretion as befits not only the particular situation of the retreatant, but more generally the atmosphere of mutual support to which all Christians should be inclined. At the start of the first week of the Exercises, both participants are admonished that 'every good Christian ought to be more eager to put a good interpretation on a neighbor's statement than to condemn it', and that if the statement is made in error, 'one should correct the person with love' (*SE*, p. 31). A free and open exchange between likeminded believers ensures a robust defence against any who would mislead them. Consolations are ultimately the province of the individual soul — the text grants that God's goodness is received best when the retreatant is in seclusion — but in the wider prognosis of Ignatius, they also belong to the collective interest of Christendom.

True to form, the inward orientation of Ignatian piety forms a significant basis for Jesuit evangelical practices in sixteenth-century Europe. John W. O'Malley observes that the Jesuits pushed the concept of consolation 'far beyond confession to a theme that was especially and insistently characteristic of their pastoral ideal. They expected the manifestation of God's presence within the soul to be accessible, in some degree, to all human beings, and thus deemed unconscionable the prospect of allowing godly infusions to go to waste for lack of ministerial support.[18] O'Malley identifies three programmes through which the Jesuit pastoral tradition was institutionalized in the sixteenth century: the ministries authorized by the *Formula of the Institute*, a charter of the society's mission; the spiritual retreat, the setting for which the *Exercises* were conceived; and the schools, which gave the Jesuits a credible stake in public life. All three programmes placed a premium on the necessity of catechetical instruction, particularly for the most delicate constitutions, such as those of children. While catechesis took on an increasingly civic-minded character as the century progressed, the practice was traditionally geared toward strengthening of the individual conscience, or what O'Malley classifies

---

[18] O'Malley, *First Jesuits*, p. 83.

under the heading of late-medieval 'Christianitas'.[19] The Jesuit catechists, represented throughout Continental Europe by such men of renown as Diego Guzmán, Peter Canisius, and Diego de Ledesma, had no shortage of successes to report in Protestant and Catholic countries alike, giving hope to the Society's ambitions of propagating a serious spirituality for believers from all walks of life.[20]

Persons in England is another matter. His *Directorie* retains the ethic of vigilance stressed in the *Exercises* and in the catechetical works, but discards the pretence that a standing army of spiritual battalions is on guard to assist individuals in distress. Having resigned himself to indefinite exile at Rouen, Persons was unable to perform the duties of a priest, catechist, or spiritual advisor for the recusant faithful in England. But he was able to compensate for this failure by diverting his energies toward the composition of spiritual texts. In a September 1584 letter to Pedro Ribadeneira, he writes:

> To do this and a number of other things required for the equipment of this spiritual war, I am obliged to maintain a modest establishment at Rouen, which is a most convenient town on account of its nearness to the sea, so that from there some can make trips to the coast to arrange for boats to convey people across (for they cannot use either the public boats or the ordinary ports that are well known), whilst others take charge of the preparation and introduction into the country of books, written in English, both on spiritual and devotional subjects, and on matters of controversy and in answer to calumnies with which the heretics assail us.[21]

Not only was Persons a prolific author, but he also took an active interest in overseeing the details of production and distribution for his works.[22] Ronald Corthell goes so far as to pronounce Persons's career a 'writer's mission', arguing that Persons knew the extent to which religious authority was configured by contingencies of discourse, not by the significance of any one set of values. For this reason, Corthell argues, Persons was actually emboldened by the fortunes that scattered the mission across several locales. He was an even stronger advocate for the primacy of conscience than if that had been a matter for the institutional centres from which power derived, Rome in particular.[23]

---

[19] O'Malley, *First Jesuits*, p. 87.

[20] O'Malley, *First Jesuits*, pp. 115–26.

[21] Persons to Pedro Ribadeneira, Paris, 10 September 1584, *Letters and Memorials of Father Robert Persons, S.J.: Volume I (to 1588)*, ed. by L. Hicks (Leeds: Whitehead & Son, 1942), p. 236.

[22] See Francis Edwards, S. J., *Robert Persons: The Biography of an Elizabethan Jesuit, 1546–1610* (St Louis: Institute of Jesuit Sources, 1995), p. 41.

[23] Ronald Corthell, 'Robert Persons and the Writer's Mission', in *Catholicism and Anti-Catholicism in Early Modern English Texts*, ed. by Arthur Marotti (Houndmills: Macmillan,

Notably, Corthell does not address the *Directorie* but only the polemical writings of Persons, likely because the book did not overtly entangle itself in debates over ecclesiastical authority. Yet there is arguably more riding on Persons's credentials as a writer in a situation that finds him, to borrow Corthell's phrase, 'doubly decentred' from the seat of rhetorical privilege.[24] As a self-professed peacemaker, Persons must not only put aside his proven polemical talents but also conduct his sacerdotal work outside the setting of Ignatian retreat. The *Directorie* courts an audience of earnest but wearying believers who, lacking recourse to catechetical or supervised models of instruction, required a self-sufficient alternative for their continued resolve. As a writer, Persons can provide this, but he cannot field the diversity of profiles they represent; he cannot extend them the full luxury of the Ignatian treatment. In surrendering his *Directorie* to the discretion of an unsupervised readership, Persons risks isolating the arguments he has conscripted — the *text*, such as it is — in such a way that the agency shared between director and retreatant in the *Spiritual Exercises* is obscured.[25]

Consequently, Persons does not appeal in the *Directorie* to individual recusants. Rather, he mobilizes the more permeable concept of recusant identity for the creation of a devotional programme that assimilates the first week or 'purgative way' of the *Exercises*, in which the individual is cleansed of unruly affections and poised to serve God with selfless dedication.[26] In the *Directorie*

1999), pp. 46–57. Another exponent of the view that Catholic polemicists were served rhetorically by the circumstances of exile is Alison Shell, who surveys some of the more suggestive intersections of Catholic loyalism and English nationalism in *Catholicism, Controversy and the English Literary Imagination, 1558–1660* (Cambridge: Cambridge University Press, 1999).

[24] Corthell, 'Writer's Mission', p. 57.

[25] The challenge facing Persons is not exceptional. In *Dismembered Rhetoric: English Recusant Writing, 1580 to 1603* (Madison: Farleigh Dickinson University Press, 1995), Ceri Sullivan observes among recusant authors a recurring anxiety over the ability of meditative texts to turn out converts. According to Sullivan, Continental writers such as Luis de Granada and Gaspar Loarte (both of whom influenced Persons's vision for the *Directorie*) benefited from the luxury of an audience reasonably schooled in the trade of devotion, whereas their counterparts in England wrote for a group of readers that might at once encompass church papists, curious Protestants, and otherwise faithful Catholics without access to a priest. For a full discussion of the differences between meditation theory in England and on the Continent, see chap. 3, 'Meditation as Deliberative Rhetoric', pp. 40–63.

[26] Houliston establishes the connection between the *Directorie* and the first week of the *Exercises* in his introduction to *Christian Directory*, p. xxxiv.

Persons imbues recusancy with greater urgency than it possesses in the polemics.[27]
For instance, in *A Brief Discours Contayning Certayne Reasons Why Catholiques
Refuse to Goe to Church* (1580), Persons portends that the sufferings of English
Catholics under the yoke of Protestant temporal law will cast a pall over future
generations. The *Directorie*, meanwhile, continues to trade on the estrangement
of Catholics from the national church but ceases to treat their outsider status as
an historical aberration, citing as a fact 'the small number that shalbe saved even
among Christians' (*CD*, p. 23). He betrays greater agitation over the proclivity of
human beings to deplete their mental energies on things of the world,

> which is as muche from the purpose, as yf men beinge placed in a course to runne at a
> golden game of infinite price, (as we are all placed to runne at heaven, as S. Paule sayeth)
> they should leave their marke and some steppe a side after flyes or fethers in the ayre, and
> some other stande styll gatheringe upp the dunge of the grounde: and how were these men
> worthie (trowe you) to receave so great a rewarde as was proposed to them? (*CD*, p. 25)

Here in the third chapter of the *Directorie*, Persons mutes his well-rehearsed
grievances against the Protestant establishment and accuses humanity in general
of losing sight of the end for which it was placed upon Earth. Then, introducing
a refrain that will sound with growing insistence as the *Directorie* progresses, he
exhorts readers to resolve themselves toward salvation while there is still time,
dashing any hope that the Roman Church will re-emerge to dispense consolations
en masse. True believers have no choice but to act in deference to a power higher
than the monarchy or papacy. Neither, it is implied, has done enough to save
individuals from themselves.

Thus Persons brings to bear an extraordinary burden upon the ethic of self-
vigilance fostered in the *Exercises*, fashioning an audience for whom the self is the
solitary vigil. The recusant subject, spiritually abandoned by the English Church
and awaiting reinforcements that may or may not arrive, has no defence against

---

[27] Christopher Haigh, in 'The Continuity of Catholicism in the English Reformation', in *The
English Reformation Revised*, ed. by Christopher Haigh (Cambridge: Cambridge University Press,
1987), pp. 176–208, observes that the annals of Jesuit history tended to create a monolithic
portrait of recusant suffering, which fails to recognize the fairly permeable boundaries of 'formal
recusancy' (pp. 205, 207). Recent scholarship has worked to correct this imbalance: in addition
to Haigh, see Alexandra Walsham, '"Yielding to the Extremity of the Time": Conformity, Orthodoxy and the Post-Reformation Catholic Community', in *Conformity and Orthodoxy in the
English Church, c. 1560–1660*, ed. by Peter Lake and Michael Questier (Woodbridge: Boydell,
2000), pp. 211–36; James McConica, 'The Catholic Experience in Tudor Oxford', in *Reckoned
Expense*, pp. 39–63; and Adrian Morey, *The Catholic Subjects of Elizabeth I* (Totowa, NJ:
Rowman and Littlefield, 1978), chap. 8, pp. 133–55.

combatant spirits besides its own internal faculties. Ignatius anticipates a similar plight in the seventh rule for discernment of spirits for week one, but there is a conspicuous abstraction, bordering affectation, about the course of action he recommends:

> When we are in desolation we should think that the Lord has left us to our own powers in order to test us, so that we may prove ourselves by resisting the various agitations and temptations of the enemy. For we can do this with God's help, which always remains available, even if we do not clearly perceive it. Indeed, even though the Lord has withdrawn from us his abundant fervor, augmented love, and intensive grace, he still supplies sufficient grace for our eternal salvation. (*SE*, p. 123)

Within the complex notion of selfhood that Ignatius posits, the subjective element is demystified — we are seen to act only as freely as our present apportionment of grace will allow. To be consigned to 'our own powers', in his analysis, is a by-product of mental engineering, a self-delusion that will crack once the Lord elects to dispatch his full arsenal of graces. There is never a moment, after all, when the soul is not amply fortified by his presence.

Like Ignatius, Persons recognizes that the self is empowered indispensably by grace. Unlike Ignatius, he allows his reader no relief from this truth. Persons does not have to sell the necessity of internal embattlement to an audience whose loyalties, like his own, are pledged to both the English queen and the Roman Church.[28] Desolation is the default setting of everyday existence for recusants. What limited spiritual sustenance they have Persons imagines to have come overwhelmingly from books of controversy — many authored by himself, no less — that, while requisite to defend the faith, have the collateral effect of throwing spirits into terminal havoc. For the soul thus afflicted, the motions of duelling spirits need not be simulated in the laboratory of supervised retreat. To

---

[28] More decisive displays of loyalty (or treachery, for that matter) were generally not viable for recusants. Arnold Pritchard, in *Catholic Loyalism in Elizabethan England* (Chapel Hill: University of North Carolina Press, 1979), notes that '[t]he Catholic community was never confronted with an obvious choice between violent resistance to the government and oblivion. At each stage of the persecution, accommodation and evasion appeared a more plausible choice than violent resistance' (p. 40). Persons eventually embraces a theory of active resistance, but it does not seem to have been buoyed by any sudden escalation in the threat of Catholic extinction. Holmes, in *Resistance and Compromise*, makes a persuasive case that the Catholic resistance literature that grew to prevalence in England from 1584 to 1596 (including, most notably, Persons's *A Conference about the Next Succession to the Crown of England*) originated from a brief window of Continental support opened by opposition to Henry of Navarre's succession in France. The fashion for resistance theory in England, he claims, was thus 'ideological rather than political' (p. 130).

stir these individuals in a meaningful way, Persons tries at once to relate to their
predicament *and* to interrogate the intensity of their beliefs. He seeks to make
them not simply beneficiaries but unvitiated organs of godly grace:

> Saye at lenght unto thy Savyour, I doe confesse unto the[e] o Lorde, I doe confesse and
> can not denye, that I have not hitherto attended to the thinge for which I was created,
> redeemed, and placed here by thee: I doe see my error, I can not dissemble my greevous
> faulte, and I doe thancke the ten thowsande tymes, that thou hast geeven me the grace to
> see it whyles I maye yet amend it: which by thy holye grace I meane to doe and without
> delaye to alter my course, beseeching thy divine majestie that as thou hast geeven me this
> light of understandinge to see my daunger, and this good motion to reforme the same: So
> thow wilt continew towardes me thy blessed assistance, for performance of the same, to
> thy honour and my soules healthe. (*CD*, p. 26)

Persons compels the reader into a posture of thoroughgoing abjection. He demands full disclosure before God, full acknowledgment of the soul's dependency
on divine assistance — and wields the threat of encroaching time to press his
audience toward these goals. In his view one should not halt to receive a gift of
grace, as there is no telling when God will present it again.

Fundamentally the *Directorie* does not therefore diverge from the *Exercises* so
much as accelerate its devotional curriculum. In chapter three Persons dresses
down his readers in such a way that they may be set to embark at once on a programme of rigorous consideration. He keeps up the pressure in succeeding
chapters, structuring his appeal around the three powers of the soul commissioned
in Ignatian meditative technique: memory, understanding, and will. Memory
generates 'vivid and imaginative reconstructions of the details of scenery and
action'[29] pertaining to subject matter assigned for meditation (sin and hell, in the
first week of *Exercises*). Understanding allows one to deliberate further upon the
scene composed, using the powers of reason. In the *Exercises*, Ignatius supplies the
memory generously with directions for mentally reconstructing the story of the
Fall, creating an itemized account or 'court-record' of one's sins, and conjuring the
torments of hell via the five senses. To aid understanding he suggests questions for
further investigation as well as exercises to assist in organizing one's thoughts.

But the faculty that Ignatius holds responsible for deepening the affections —
the will — is comparatively underwritten in the *Exercises*. This is partially
explained by the fact that all three stages of meditation in the Ignatian tradition
are wired automatically to the affections, as illustrated in the script he advises
exercitants to follow for contemplating the expulsion of the angels from heaven:

[29] W. W. Meissner, *To the Greater Glory: A Psychological Study of Ignatian Spirituality*
(Milwaukee: Marquette University Press, 1999), p. 149.

> My aim in remembering and reasoning about all these matters is to bring myself to greater
> shame and confusion, by comparing the one sin of the angels with all my own many
> sins. For one sin they went to hell; then how often have I deserved hell for my many sins!
> (*SE*, p. 41)

Memory and understanding are designed not to invent knowledge per se but incrementally to enlighten the soul about what it already knows. The actual by-product of their labours — in this case, shame and confusion — is a refinement of the affections. In concert with these two faculties, the will may then be understood mainly as the finalizing stage, in which scenes summoned from the shared spiritual heritage of Christians are etched permanently into the individual consciousness. Ignatius abstains from compartmentalizing the will further through direct exhortation. He trusts that among the three constituent powers of the soul there is sufficient unity of purpose to steer the individual through the purgative process.

Persons adopts a manner that seems overbearing in comparison, still stressing the interconnectedness of the soul's threefold structure but manoeuvring the will deliberately into the foreground. He makes explicit demands that Ignatius subsumes into the greater meditative structure of the *Exercises*, leaving demonstrably more to the obligation than to the discretion of the individual. The fourth chapter of the *Directorie* pleads with the reader who still has not heeded the call to resolution to 'resolve thy selfe to begynne now' (*CD*, p. 36); the fifth laments that 'so fewe are watchfull, and so manie fall a sleepe in ignorance of their owne daunger' (*CD*, p. 51), wishing the reader better fortune. The sixth vows forgiveness for our sins if we 'serve hym whiles he is content to accept of our service', and 'if we would once make this resolution from our harte' (*CD*, p. 64). By the seventh chapter, having recounted the litany of benefits God has granted to his most exalted of creations, Persons can express rightful indignation at the pittance of gratitude tendered in kind. 'There is not so feerse or cruell a nature in the worlde', he pontificates, 'but is mollified, allured, and wonne by benefits' (*CD*, p. 72). Even 'brute beasts' know to give thanks to their keepers. The sinner who has not shown God the same courtesy is pressured to make swift amends:

> Be a shamed then (good Christian) of this thy ingratitude, to so greate, so good, and
> bountifull a Lord: and resolve thy selfe for the tyme to come, to amende thy course of lyfe
> and behavyour towardes hym. Say with the prophet, which had lesse cause to saye so then
> thow. *Domine propitiare peccato meo multum est enim. O lord pardon me myne offence for
> it is greate in thy sight.* I know there is nothinge (o lorde) which dothe so muche displease
> the, or drye upp the fountaine of thy mercye, and so byndeth thy handes from doinge
> good, as ingratitude in the receyvers of thy benefites: wherin hetherto I have exceeded all
> others: but I have done it (o lord) in myne ignorance, not consideringe thy gyftes unto me,
> nor what accounte thow wouldest demaunde againe of the same. (*CD*, p. 74)

The cardinal shame which Persons imputes to his audience is one of ignorance, of failure to recognize what is plain to the most brutish perception: that the Lord's stewardship is deserving of eternal gratitude. Persons imagines the soul to have fallen into such neglect that even this most axiomatic of truths is beyond its comprehension. He takes offence at the notion that the most precious knowledge imparted to human beings might not rouse the emotions but instead produce a middling sensation unworthy of acknowledgment. For this reason, the knowing Christian is cast simultaneously as the worst ingrate. It insults logic to have God's bounty writ large before oneself and still fail to grasp its most elementary implications.

To correct this deficiency, Persons steadily increases the intensity of his arguments. Through the seventh chapter the author's tone has been one of heightening sorrow, and shortening patience, for human beings' rude disregard of the end for which they were given to Earth. Thereafter his rhetoric intensifies sharply: the eighth chapter ushers readers to the moment of their death, the ninth to the midst of the afterlife, and in neither scenario are 'worldinges, and reprobate persons' (*CD*, p. 76) spared the pangs of a debilitating remorse. The dying sinner is overcome with the triple torment of having his soul reft from his body, disuniting from his dearest attachments on Earth, and pondering what will become of himself next. Memory returns to haunt such a man with a vengeful precision: 'For there is not a severe saynge of God in all the scripture, whiche commeth not now to his mynde to terrify hym withall at this instant' (*CD*, pp. 82–83). Understanding illuminates only to incriminate him, as the enemy spirit, hitherto bent on suppressing the truth, 'will now laye all and more too, before our face, amplyfiynge and uringe everie pointe to the uttermost, alleaginge always our conscience for his witnes' (*CD*, pp. 83–84). For the sinner resigned to his deathbed, it is impossible to accept this belated rush of knowledge as anything but ironic retribution. The reader may yet be saved by admitting remorse in the here and now. However mightily the record impugns the man of the world, the shame toward which he wills himself in consequence — and to be certain, it must be *willed* — shall prove his saving grace.

In death as in life, all appeals to memory and understanding in the *Directorie* are repeatedly brought to bear upon a single moment of reckoning when the individual may decide his or her fate. The evidence that Persons has his audience consider is overwhelming, but the options are simple — resolve unto God or resist — and the will casts the deciding vote. At the hour of death, one who has answered the call to resolution 'shalbe at this tyme *beatus vir*, a happye man', while those who have deferred shall amount to 'nothinge els but a heape of all sorowes together' (*CD*, p. 89). The mortal threshold dictates the final form into which the consolations and desolations used to chart the motions of the soul will congeal: sorrow or happiness. If Persons has his way, the latter shall leave the stronger impression on the reader: while he cites fear of punishments as God's most effective tool of persuasion (*CD*, p. 89), and describes them in odious detail in Chapter 9, he pins his greatest hope for inciting readers to amend their lives on the allure of rewards. In the tenth and final chapter of the first part of the *Directorie*, Persons acknowledges that gratitude for benefits received and fear of future sufferings are powerful incentives and 'might well suffice, to sturre up the hart of anye reasonable Christian to take in hand this resolution'. Yet unless he can show this resolution 'to be more gainfull and profitable than any thinge els in the worlde that can be thought of: thow shalt not be bound unto yt for anye thing that hitherto hath bene sayde in that behalfe' (*CD*, pp. 112–13). The author gamely excuses readers from those duties to which he has obliged them by sheer force of reason, betting that by now they have been sufficiently motivated to behold God's majesty with fear *and* hope.

Hence in the tenth chapter, Persons rewards readerly patience and holy living in the same breath. He relents from the browbeating tactics that he has relied upon for the greater part of the book and at last indulges his readers with a preview of the riches they stand to inherit in heaven. It is primarily a conjectural rendering, abetted by contributions from Scripture and the Church Fathers. At the same time it is constrained by the divine kingdom's remoteness to the uninitiated: '[S]urelie no tongue created ether of man or Angell can expresse the same, no imagination conceave, no understanding comprehend it. Christ hym selfe hathe sayd, *nemo scit nisi qui accipit*: No man knoweth it but he that enjoyeth yt. And therefore he calleth it *hidden manna*' (*CD*, 114–15). Happiness is knit so tightly with individual experience that the author can only hint at its magnitude through arguments of proportion, which by his own admission are bound to come up short 'seing that the whole earth put together, is by all Philosophie, but as a pricke or small point in respect of the marvailouse greatnesse of the heavens' (*CD*, p. 121).

Instead of firsthand knowledge of heaven's magnificence, Persons assembles a coalition of prophets to testify on its behalf, including St John the Divine, who relates his vision of the new Jerusalem with architectural precision (Rev. 21. 9–22. 5); Daniel, who beholds God's formidable legion of angels in his dream of the four beasts (Dan. 7. 1–28); and Isaiah, who prophesies that God will join his chosen people in a feast 'of fatt meates and pure wines' (Isa. 25. 6) to celebrate their deliverance from evil (*CD*, pp. 118). Persons's method in bringing together these diverse accounts is to allow fleeting glimpses of majesty, to establish a sparse but essential minimum of continuity between mortal apprehension and the *visio Dei beatifica*, or blessed sight of God, that symbolizes 'the accomplishment and perfection of happinesse' (*CD*, p. 125). The totality of God's magnificence may never be captured in word, vision, or thought. As a writer, Persons's dependency on these tools doubles as a silent admission that he is no better positioned to scale the fabled heights of happiness than the lowliest sinner among his readers. At most he may whet their appetite for heavenly commodities; God alone can succour it.

As he draws the first part of the *Directorie* to a close, then, Persons is cautious not to signal that readers should hasten the course of Providence. Recalling the prophetic counsel of Jeremiah, Persons advises his followers to tend swiftly to their backsliding ways while abiding the injustice around them. He declines to instigate further antagonism between the Catholic faithful and their Protestant oppressors. The closest he musters is to have his readers divert their aggressions toward the conquest of heaven, a suggestion troubled by militant strains but finally admissible under the ethical parameters he has authorized for his subject. The centrepiece of this strategy is to starve the 'spirite of contradiction and contention' (*CD*, p. 5) that has been branded the soul's nemesis since the book's outset. Persons recollects Christ's observation that 'The kyngdome of heaven suffereth violence and men lay handes now on it by force' (Matt. 11. 12) (*CD*, p. 135), setting up a play on words that enables him to rehabilitate the image of a holy kingdom under siege. Heaven *can* be won by force, he explains, but solely 'by force of Gods covenant made with Christians. [...] What soever Christian then, doeth good workes and lyveth vertuouslie, taketh heaven by force (as it were) and by violence' (*CD*, p. 135). Under the terms of the new covenant, no element of coercion is recognized. Force consists in effort duly spent, virtue hard fought, and the spirit whose energies recklessly enflame (rather than enlighten) can no longer be sustained. To separate the good soldiers of Christ from mere rabble-rousers, Persons continues to renovate metaphors of sport and conquest. '[T]his game and gole is sett upp for them that will runne', he proclaims, 'and no man is crowned in this glorie but suche onelie as will fight.' The resolve 'to buyld this tower, and make this warre' requires a combination of virtuosity and force, 'good will and holie manhode' (*CD*, p. 137). Lacking either, no man stands a chance of crossing the threshold of heaven.

Bunny's discomfort with this conclusion is evident. He omits a majority of the discussion of gaining heaven by force from the Protestant *Directorie*, un-wittingly reinforcing the very point that the Jesuit makes. Persons issues the call to resolution specifically to weed out the agitators and pacifiers who vainly seek reprieve from their mortal lot, whether by scheming to storm heaven's gates or simply by presuming them wider than they are. In his analysis, the two factions are not substantially different: years of exposure to conflicting messages 'hath wroght in mens mindes a certaine contempt and carles insensibilitie in thes affaires, esteeming al things to stand vpon probabilitie only of dispute to and fro, and so by litle and litle, doth bring them also to thinke the same of Christian religion it self'.[30] A work of such unabashed sophistry as Bunny's *Directorie*, he implies, is the natural by-product of a society whose judgement has been contaminated by an atmosphere of unrelenting antagonism. Persons, looking to counteract this influence and to re-establish the central core of Christian experience, maintains that a reasoned commitment to God is a stable one; it should neither demand nor allow unreasonable accommodation to fluctuating conditions on earth, friendly or hostile.

Under this logic, the adherence to the doctrine of salvation by faith alone in the Protestant *Directorie* is simply objectionable to Persons. The true abomination of the work is Bunny's overriding desire that the people of England 'be more safely preserved, & more comfortably governed, until the comming of Christ himself',[31] with its tacit assumption that through conformity the rigours of Christianity may be sufficiently domesticated to alleviate the sufferings of the many. The work of Persons throughout the *Directorie* has been to disabuse readers of their sense of entitlement. In Bunny he meets an offender of the most egregious sort, one who vainly expects that through deft engineering on his part a religion of the elect can award salvation by consensus. Persons holds no such illusions. On Earth he presumes only a hostile reception; from God, the minimum grace to let him bear it.

Once readers have been braced to accept desolation as their lot — and grace as its tonic — consolations may be savoured with greater abandon. This is the selling point upon which Persons inaugurates the second part of the *Directorie*, in which the audience is at last poised to make the leap from knowledge to action. It speaks volumes that Persons, after imploring readers to yield their lives wholeheartedly to God, instantly invokes the promise of consolation to ease them into the actual work of their commitment. The second part of the book, which is designated to help individuals overcome excuses or 'impediments' that interfere with their resolution, addresses fears of hardship in the first chapter. In it Persons

[30] Persons, preface to *Christian Directorie* (1585), sig. 20ᵛ.

[31] Bunny, *Treatise*, p. 29.

reiterates the key points of the first part explicitly in terms of consolation, giving hope for the immediate present. Consolation provides an earthly frame of reference for the heavenly delights of which Christians will one day partake. In this sense, it visibly benefits the author: Persons's descriptions of heaven are understandably tentative, but his descriptions of heaven on earth take full advantage of his proximity to the subject at issue. He imbues grace, for instance, with a physicality that would be impossible outside the auspices of consolation:

> David also had proved the force of this assistance, whoe sayde, *I dyd runne the way of thy commaundementes, when thou dyddest enlarge my hart.* This enlargement of hart, was by spirituall consolation of internall unction, wherby the hart drawen together by anguishe is opened and enlarged: when grace is powered in, even as a drye purse ys softened and enlarged by annoynting it with oyle. Which grace being present, David sayed, he dyd not onelye walke the way of Gods commaundements easilie, but that he *ranne them*: Even as a carte wheele whiche crieth and compleyneth under a small burden being drye, runneth merilye and without noyse, when a litle oyle is put unto it. Which thinge aptlye expresseth our state and condition, whoe without Gods help, are able to doe nothing, but with the ayde thereof, are able to conquere and overcome any thing. (*CD*, pp. 143–44)

Through the example of David in Psalm 119, Persons showcases the inner workings of consolation to maximum effect; he represents the passage of grace from its physical inception through its realization in spirited action. In contrast to the sentiment professed in Bunny's treatise, Persons does not locate the best chance for human happiness in the minimization of earthly discomfort. David's consolation is reflected in the desire to bear a burden ever more impressive.

As he advances his thesis that God 'sweetens the yoke' for persons bound to his service, Persons narrows his focus, as if to emphasize not only the bounty of grace but also the privileges of election. Among the most prized of these is a 'hidden and secret consolation' (*CD*, p. 154) through which God reproduces sensations of bona fide celestial bliss in deserving individuals, with the intent of encouraging them to soldier onward in his name. '[T]his is not meate for everye mouthe', instructs Persons, 'but *a chosen moisture layed aside for Gods inheritance onelye*' (*CD*, p. 156). Its effects are so exhilarating 'as to make all those drounken that taste of the same: that is, to take from them, all sense and feeling of terrestriall matters' (*CD*, p. 155). Persons furthermore contends that those newly inaugurated into the guardianship of the Holy Spirit are likely to feel consolation more keenly than their more experienced brethren, as they are the least accustomed to its potency — and the most likely to receive it without interruption, owing to God's careful efforts to discourage backsliding among the most vulnerable (*CD*, pp. 156–57). One recent convert is so smitten that he must plead, '*O Lord retyre thy hand from me a litle, for that my hart is not able to receave so extreme joye*' (*CD*, p. 171).

When consolations threaten to overwhelm human affective capacity, they carry the implication that the scope of happiness on earth does not end with murky premonitions of the afterlife, but more suggestively, with the possibility of a true-to-life paradise on earth. Yet the consolations of the *Directorie* are not mystical ecstasies. More accurately, they are testimonials of life in progress, articulations of the exquisitely finite potential that can be realized in all who are humble and reasonable enough to accept the gift of grace. Such individuals are few in numbers, but that is largely the point: in the manner of Ignatius in the *Spiritual Exercises*, Persons hypothesis is that such a vast gulf exists between the calibre of piety that his reader has supplied, and what God demands, that no one is truly adequate to the challenge. All believers who come into contact with the book sight unseen are typecast as intransigent sinners.

In short, in Persons's judgement, the blight of conformity is so insidious that it requires a self-imposed recusancy from one's governing affections to contend for the prize of consolations. Such logic pointedly controverts Bunny's claim that Catholics are mere shades removed from full participation in God's blessings. Few of either religious persuasion are anywhere close, as far as Persons can see, and the distance cannot be bridged as a matter of quotidian convenience. Otherwise he might heed the Protestant's counsel to have his fellow Catholics in England stay committed but silent on their faith. Instead, Persons stubbornly refuses to mould members of his audience in the image of church papists. He treats them as recusants one and all, and they, in turn, are entered into a confidence of the highest order. With God on their side, they will be consoled.

'THE GREATEST BLOW TO ANTIQUITIES THAT EVER ENGLAND HAD': THE REFORMATION AND THE ANTIQUARIAN RESISTANCE

Oliver Harris

The rise in antiquarian interests and activity in early modern England and Wales was stimulated and given form by a number of factors, including the influences of humanist scholarship, new nationalistic concerns, and a growing regard for lineage; but it was shaped too by the circumstances of the Reformation, which created a potent symbolic divide between past and present.[1] The productions of the movement were many and varied, including not only such published landmarks as Lambarde's *Perambulation of Kent* (1576), Camden's

---

[1] There is an extensive secondary literature on early modern antiquarianism in Britain, but see in particular F. J. Levy, *Tudor Historical Thought* (San Marino: Huntington Library, 1967), especially chaps 3 and 4; May McKisack, *Medieval History in the Tudor Age* (Oxford: Clarendon Press, 1971); J. M. Levine, *Humanism and History: Origins of Modern English Historiography* (Ithaca: Cornell University Press, 1987), especially chap. 3; Graham Parry, *The Trophies of Time: English Antiquarians of the Seventeenth Century* (Oxford: Oxford University Press, 1995); Daniel Woolf, *The Social Circulation of the Past: English Historical Culture, 1500–1730* (Oxford: Oxford University Press, 2003), especially chap. 5; and, on local and regional chorography, S. A. E. Mendyk, *Speculum Britanniae: Regional Study, Antiquarianism, and Science in Britain to 1700* (Toronto: University of Toronto Press, 1989); and *English County Histories: A Guide*, ed. by C. R. J. Currie and C. P. Lewis (Stroud: Sutton, 1994); and Jan Broadway, *'No Historie so Meete': Gentry Culture and the Development of Local History in Elizabethan and Early Stuart England* (Manchester: Manchester University Press, 2006). Biographical details of most of the antiquaries mentioned below can be found in the *Oxford Dictionary of National Biography* (2004). The influence of the Reformation is highlighted in Margaret Aston, 'English Ruins and English History: The Dissolution and the Sense of the Past', *Journal of the Warburg and Courtauld Institutes*, 36 (1973), 231–55.

Britannia (1586), Weever's *Ancient Funerall Monuments* (1631), Spelman's
Concilia (1639), Dodsworth and Dugdale's *Monasticon* (1655–73) and Somner's
Dictionarium Saxonico-Latino-Anglicum (1659), but numerous unpublished
works which circulated in manuscript, and indeed countless further projects,
some of which occupied decades of their begetters' lives, but which never progressed beyond quantities of transcripts, notes, and drafts. There existed, among
the participants in the enterprise, a definite sense of community, of labouring in
a common cause. The most formal embodiment of this notion was the Society of
Antiquaries, active from about 1586 to 1607, and briefly revived in 1614. Less
formal expressions included the clusters of researchers around the great manuscript collections of Archbishop Matthew Parker, Sir William Cecil, John Stow,
and Sir Robert Cotton; the regional antiquarian networks (particularly those
of Wales, the Midlands, and Devon and Cornwall); the local informants who
supplied material for successive editions of Camden's *Britannia*; and innumerable
casual instances of friendly assistance, such as that offered in 1589 to George
Owen from Pembrokeshire, during his first, floundering attempts at research in
London, or that by which in the 1620s the disheartened John Weever was
introduced to a circle of sympathetic scholars and their collections.[2]

The religious loyalties and motivations of this community have recently
attracted some comment, and a case has been made that the retrospection and
nostalgia inherent in antiquarianism tended to dovetail with the religious sentiments of Catholics and conservative Protestants. Mervyn James, writing of
County Durham, points to the Catholic antiquaries William Claxton and John,
Lord Lumley, and the Protestant writers Christopher Watson and Robert Hegge
whose theme was continuity with the Catholic past.[3] Richard Cust similarly
highlights the Catholicism of such Midlands antiquaries as Sir Thomas Shirley,
Thomas Habington, Sampson Erdeswick, Henry Ferrers, and Lord Brudenell:
he argues that, marginalized as they were by the state, Catholic gentry found
provable genealogical status 'the one sure basis on which they could compete
with Protestants'; but he also notes, even among Protestants, a 'marked overlap'

---

[2] Joan Evans, *A History of the Society of Antiquaries* (Oxford: Oxford University Press, 1956),
pp. 8–13; Christina DeCoursey, 'Society of Antiquaries', in *Oxford DNB*; *The Description of
Penbrokshire, by George Owen of Henllys, Lord of Kemes*, ed. by Henry Owen, Cymmrodorion
Record Series, 1, 2 pts (London: Cymmrodorion Society, 1892), pt 1, pp. 370–73; John Weever,
Ancient Funerall Monuments (London: Thomas Harper, 1631), 'The Author to the Reader'.

[3] Mervyn James, *Family, Lineage and Civil Society: A Study of Society, Politics and Mentality
in the Durham Region, 1500–1640* (Oxford: Clarendon Press, 1974), pp. 108–11.

between antiquarianism and religious conservatism.[4] Patrick Collinson, however, is sceptical: he sees a more pluralistic community that could embrace the Catholic sympathies of John Stow, the Protestant fervour of William Lambarde, and the moderate Protestantism of William Camden and Richard Carew, all of whom co-existed amicably within the Society of Antiquaries.[5] Daniel Woolf lists twenty Catholic antiquaries, but also admits exceptions, and concludes that despite the suspicions of popery which sometimes attached to such pursuits, the correlation between antiquarianism and Catholicism was not in fact high.[6] Jan Broadway argues that in the Midlands, Catholics and Protestants were prepared to over-look religious difference, seeing antiquarianism rather as a means of 'bolstering a sense of identity among a gentry community threatened by division'.[7] Graham Parry concedes that many early-seventeenth-century antiquaries had Laudian and High Church sympathies, but again points to exceptions, including those whose interests lay in the history of the law, and whose politics tended toward the Parliamentary cause: when Civil War came, it 'divided the antiquaries as it divided families'.[8] And yet White Kennett, himself a latitudinarian Anglican hostile to both Catholicism and Puritanism, argued in the 1690s that most earlier antiquaries had been 'true Sons and servants' to the Church of England, whose studies had 'settled their judgment, and improv'd their zeal'.[9]

It is clear that no simple equation can be drawn between antiquarianism and religious belief. Certainly many recusants and conservative Protestants can be identified among the antiquaries; but so too, with only a little more effort, can a good number from the radical and Puritan end of the Protestant spectrum, including John Bale, William Fleetwood, John Hooker, William Harrison,

[4] Richard Cust, 'Catholicism, Antiquarianism and Gentry Honour: The Writings of Sir Thomas Shirley', *Midland History*, 23 (1998), 40–70 (pp. 53, 60).

[5] Patrick Collinson, 'John Stow and Nostalgic Antiquarianism', in *Imagining Early Modern London: Perceptions and Portrayals of the City from Stow to Strype, 1598–1720*, ed. by J. F. Merritt (Cambridge: Cambridge University Press, 2001), pp. 27–51.

[6] Woolf, *Social Circulation*, pp. 185–87; see also pp. 62–64.

[7] J. R. Broadway, 'Antiquarianism in the Midlands and the Development of County History, 1586–1656' (unpublished doctoral dissertation, University of Birmingham, 1997), pp. 212–36. See also Jan Broadway, '"To Equall their Virtues": Thomas Habington, Recusancy and the Gentry of Early Stuart Worcestershire', *Midland History*, 29 (2004), 1–24.

[8] Parry, *Trophies*, pp. 17–19.

[9] White Kennett, 'The Life of Mr Somner', in William Somner, *A Treatise of the Roman Ports and Forts in Kent*, ed. by James Brome (Oxford: printed at the Theatre, 1693), pp. 14–15.

William Lambarde, John Norden, Robert Ryece, Thomas Scott of Canterbury, Scipio le Squyer, Archbishop James Ussher, Sir Simon Archer, Abraham Wheelocke, Sir Simonds D'Ewes and William Prynne.[10] And, again and again, we find striking juxtapositions of contrasting religious outlooks. The 'Antiquitas Rediviva' agreement of 1638 brought together, in a scheme for the pooling of efforts and resources, the Catholic Sir Thomas Shirley, the conservative Anglicans William Dugdale and Sir Christopher Hatton, and the Puritan Sir Edward Dering, who would introduce, three years later, the 'root and branch' bill for the abolition of episcopacy into the Long Parliament (though his subsequent ideological swings defy easy labelling).[11] The chief promoter of Dodsworth and Dugdale's *Monasticon anglicanum*, a work seen by some as an apology for Catholicism, was the Calvinist and Parliamentarian Thomas, Lord Fairfax.[12] Sir Robert Cotton, who sat for some thirty years at the heart of the antiquarian project, was committed to the unity of what he called the 'Catholique body of the Church of England', but was on the one hand rumoured to be a 'pontifician' (papist), and on the other said by his Calvinist friend Simonds D'Ewes to be 'a most sound theoretical Protestant'. He may, as a young man, have contracted a (probably irregular) marriage with the sister of a Jesuit, and his son and heir married a daughter of the Catholic antiquary Lord William Howard; he advised James I to treat Jesuits and seminary priests with relative leniency; and he was attended at his deathbed by an Arminian bishop, a Puritan divine, and two moderate Anglicans.[13] Certainly Cotton welcomed scholars of all religious

---

[10] The Devon antiquary Tristram Risdon is said by Gordon Goodwin in the *Dictionary of National Biography* (1896) to have been a Puritan, but no evidence for this claim has been found.

[11] L. B. L[arking], 'On the Surrenden Charters', *Archaeologia Cantiana*, 1 (1858), 55–59; Evans, *Society of Antiquaries*, pp. 21–23; S. P. Salt, 'The Origins of Sir Edward Dering's Assault on the Religious Hierarchy, *c*. 1625–1640', *Historical Journal*, 30 (1987), 21–52.

[12] *The Life, Diary and Correspondence of Sir William Dugdale*, ed. by William Hamper (London: Harding, Lepard, 1827), p. 25n (hereafter *The Life of Dugdale*); N. Denholm-Young and H. H. E. Craster, 'Roger Dodsworth (1585–1654) and his Circle', *Yorkshire Archaeological Journal*, 32 (1936), 5–32; Marion Roberts, *Dugdale and Hollar: History Illustrated* (Newark: University of Delaware Press, 2002), pp. 4, 53.

[13] Kevin Sharpe, *Sir Robert Cotton, 1586–1631: History and Politics in Early Modern England* (Oxford: Oxford University Press, 1979), pp. 108–09; *The Autobiography and Correspondence of Sir Simonds D'Ewes*, ed. by James Orchard Halliwell, 2 vols (London: Richard Bentley, 1845), II, 38–39; Sir Robert Cotton, *Cottoni Posthuma* (London: printed by Francis Leach for Henry Seile, 1651), pp. 109–59. The marriage between Cotton and Frideswide Faunt (sister of the Jesuit Laurence Arthur Faunt) is noted in several Faunt pedigrees by William Burton, whose own

persuasions to his library, even though it led to such prickly moments as an encounter between the Calvinist Archbishop Ussher and the Benedictine monk, Augustine Baker.[14]

Some members of the community were indeed active religious controversialists, and treated antiquarianism as an instrument of debate. Among the Protestants, one thinks in the sixteenth century of Archbishop Parker, John Bale, and the Welsh humanists Bishop Richard Davies and William Salesbury, and in the seventeenth of Ussher, Sir Henry Spelman, and Thomas Fuller, all of whom used antiquarian research to underpin the argument of Protestantism as a return to the purity of a primitive church uncorrupted by Rome.[15] They have their Catholic counterparts, who defended the English Church's long tradition of papal allegiance, in George Lily, Thomas Stapleton, Richard White of Basingstoke, Richard Stanihurst, Lord William Howard and the Benedictines Augustine Baker, John Leander Jones, and Clement Reyner.[16] Others, however, set antiquarian and chorographical activity apart from their religion. William Harrison played down his radical Protestantism in his 'Description of Britaine' of 1577 (published as part of Holinshed's *Chronicles*), though he introduced rather more to the revised edition of 1587.[17] John Norden kept his career as a surveyor,

---

mother was Frideswide's sister: London, British Library (hereafter BL) MS Add. 6046, fols 127ᵛ–28; Staffordshire Record Office D649/4/1, fol. 111; London, College of Arms MS Vincent 11, s.n. Faunt (in narrative form); and see published version in John Nichols, *The History and Antiquities of the County of Leicester*, 4 vols in 8 (London: Nichols, Son, & Bentley, 1795–1811), IV, pt 1, 175. However, Cotton's own personal and genealogical records seem to be silent on the matter, and both he and Frideswide afterward married other people.

[14] *Memorials of Father Augustine Baker and other Documents relating to the English Benedictines*, ed. by Justin McCann and Hugh Connolly, Catholic Record Society, 33 (Leeds: Whitehead & Son, 1933), pp. 112–13.

[15] Levy, *Tudor Historical Thought*, pp. 114–23; Parry, *Trophies*, pp. 134–39, 168–70, 267–74; Alan Ford, 'James Ussher and the Creation of an Irish Protestant Identity', in *British Consciousness and Identity: The Making of Britain, 1533–1707*, ed. by Brendan Bradshaw and Peter Roberts (Cambridge: Cambridge University Press, 1998), pp. 185–212; Colin Kidd, *British Identities before Nationalism* (Cambridge: Cambridge University Press, 1999), pp. 99–122, 162–71.

[16] Levy, *Tudor Historical Thought*, pp. 110–12; M. D. Knowles in *English Historical Scholarship in the Sixteenth and Seventeenth Centuries*, ed. by Levi Fox (London: Dugdale Society, 1956), pp. 119–23.

[17] G. J. R. Parry, *A Protestant Vision: William Harrison and the Reformation of Elizabethan England* (Cambridge: Cambridge University Press, 1987), pp. 150–54, 172, 176, 185–87; Annabel Patterson, *Reading Holinshed's Chronicles* (Chicago: University of Chicago Press, 1994), pp. 64–69.

chorographer, and antiquary so entirely separate from his anti-papist devotional writing that when his religious books met with criticism he was able to deny authorship, attributing them instead to a 'Norden pretender'.[18] Similarly, on the Catholic side, Richard Verstegan, author of a number of polemical and martyrological works, gave his Anglo-Saxonist *Restitution of Decayed Intelligence* (1605) no religious agenda; and, beyond blaming the loss of church brasses on 'the iniquity of this age', Sampson Erdeswick expressed no overtly Catholic sentiments in his 'Survey of Staffordshire'.[19] The discussions of the Society of Antiquaries generally eschewed religious topics, and in 1614 it was explicitly agreed that, 'for avoiding offence, we should neither meddle with matters of State nor of Religion'.[20]

It is certainly the case that many antiquarian writings include expressions of regret for aspects of the Reformation, and that, on occasion, these have their roots in a sympathy and nostalgia for the old forms of religion. There is, for example, little ambiguity in Thomas Westcote's lament at seeing 'the pious devotion of our ancestors ruinated, their godly purposes being abused'; or William Dugdale's characterization of religious houses as 'those signall Monuments of our Forefathers Pietie'.[21] But what is most often being regretted is not theological reform as such, but the cultural and social devastation it had brought in its wake. Arthur Agarde, addressing the Society of Antiquaries in 1600, bracketed the dissolution of the monasteries with two earlier nonreligious cataclysms, the raids of the Saxons and Danes, and the destruction of Anglo-Saxon records and churches by

---

[18] A. W. Pollard, 'The Unity of John Norden: Surveyor and Religious Writer', *The Library*, ser. 4, 7 (1926), 233–52; Frank Kitchen, 'Cosmo-choro-polygrapher: An Analytical Account of the Life and Work of John Norden, 1547?–1625' (unpublished doctoral thesis, University of Sussex, 1993), pp. 147–66; Frank Kitchen, 'John Norden (c.1547–1625): Estate Surveyor, Topographer, County Mapmaker and Devotional Writer', *Imago Mundi*, 49 (1997), 43–61.

[19] Sampson Erdeswick, *A Survey of Staffordshire*, ed. by Thomas Harwood (London: J. B. Nichols, 1844), pp. 250–51.

[20] Sir Henry Spelman, 'The Occasion of this Discourse', in his *Reliquiæ Spelmannianæ* (Oxford: printed at the Theatre for A. and J. Churchill, 1698), pp. 69–70. The one significant exception to this principle was a meeting in 1604 on the antiquity of Christianity in Britain, and even then Arthur Agarde deemed the question 'more proper to be dilated by dyvines than by any other': *A Collection of Curious Discourses*, ed. by Thomas Hearne [and Joseph Ayloffe], 2 vols (London: W. and J. Richardson, 1771), II, 155–72.

[21] Thomas Westcote, *A View of Devonshire in MDCXXX, with a Pedigree of Most of its Gentry*, ed. by George Oliver and Pitman Jones (Exeter: William Roberts, 1845), pp. 145–46; William Dugdale, *The Antiquities of Warwickshire Illustrated* (London: Thomas Warren, 1656), preface, sig. B3ᵛ; and cf. pp. 147, 800–03. See also Aston, 'English Ruins'.

William the Conqueror.[22] Thomas Philipot, in his *Villare Cantianum* (1659) applied the image of a 'ruinous Tempest' or 'Whirl-winde' not only to the dissolution and the more recent Puritan ascendancy, but also (and explicitly reserving judgement on the rights and wrongs of the case) to the suppression of the Templars in the fourteenth century.[23] At the heart of the antiquaries' distress was the fact that the incidental wreckage of religious reform had all too often included their own stock-in-trade, the textual and material relics of the past. In Dugdale's eyes, the suppression of monasteries, hospitals, and chantries was 'the greatest blow to Antiquities that ever England had, by the destruction and spoil of many rare Manuscripts, and no small number of famous Monuments'.[24]

Nevertheless, the antiquaries were able to wage their own rearguard actions against the worst excesses of the destruction, by attempting to save or record antiquities at risk. It is with this campaign of resistance to the collateral damage of reform that the remainder of this essay will be concerned. It will focus on the two areas in which the campaign was waged most assiduously: the salvaging of manuscripts, and the recording of church monuments and glass.

The Rescue of Manuscripts

The dissolution of the monasteries saw the loss of monastic library and service books in their tens if not hundreds of thousands, torn apart for their scrap value or sold overseas.[25] But a significant number were preserved, thanks in part to a

[22] *A Collection of Curious Discourses*, I, 247.

[23] Thomas Philipot, *Villare Cantianum* (London: Godbid, 1659), pp. 221, 283, 301, 327, 329, 352. Philipot's views were conservative, but he was no apologist for Catholicism: see pp. 78–79. The *Villare Cantianum* has sometimes been ascribed to Thomas's father, John Philipot, but, while it draws on John's collections, the final composition appears to have been Thomas's.

[24] Dugdale, *Warwickshire*, preface, sig. B3[v].

[25] C. E. Wright, 'The Dispersal of the Monastic Libraries and the Beginnings of Anglo-Saxon Studies: Matthew Parker and his Circle: A Preliminary Study', *Transactions of the Cambridge Bibliographical Society*, 1 (1951), 208–37; C. E. Wright, 'The Dispersal of the Libraries in the Sixteenth Century', in *The English Library before 1700*, ed. by Francis Wormald and C. E. Wright (London: University of London, 1958), pp. 148–75; R. H. Fritze, '"Truth hath lacked witnesse, tyme wanted light": The Dispersal of the English Monastic Libraries and Protestant Efforts at Preservation, ca. 1535–1625', *Journal of Library History*, 18 (1983), 274–91; Nigel Ramsay, '"The Manuscripts flew about like Butterflies": The Break-Up of English Libraries in the Sixteenth Century', in *Lost Libraries: The Destruction of Great Book Collections since Antiquity*, ed. by James Raven (Basingstoke: Palgrave Macmillan, 2004), pp. 125–44.

positive rescue campaign by a relatively small number of concerned antiquaries. Foremost among these was John Leland, who, while loyally accepting Henry VIII's reforms, took a determined personal stand against the cultural fallout of the reformist agenda. As early as 1533, well before Henry's final break with Rome, Leland secured a royal authorization to visit monastic libraries in order to inspect and record their holdings. Over the next few years, he toured some 140 religious houses, and as the process of dissolution began to take hold, the nature of his task shifted from recording books to removing them, principally for the benefit of the royal libraries, but also for his own collection.[26] While no one else operated with Leland's comprehensive vision and determination, there were other collectors who accumulated books and manuscripts, their number including lay purchasers of monastic lands, and scholars such as John Bale, Robert Talbot, Richard Recorde and John Twyne. Also among them was Sir John Prise, who alone among the functionaries charged with overseeing the process of dissolution took an interest in averting the potential cultural loss.[27]

Although documentation is sparse, there is no doubting the sense of urgency behind some of these salvage efforts. In 1536, Leland appealed to Thomas Cromwell on patriotic grounds, complaining of the plundering of English monastic manuscripts by German scholars, who, 'perceiving our desidiousness and negligence, do send dayly young Scholars hither, that spoileth them, and cutteth them out of Libraries, returning home and putting them abroad as Monuments of their own Country'.[28] His later progress report to the King, the 'New Years Gift' of 1546, is necessarily more circumspect; but when it reached print three years later (by which time King Henry was dead, and Leland himself insane), John Bale added a forthright commentary, recalling how, at the height of the dissolution, purchasers of monastic real estate had

> reserved of those lybrarye bokes, some to serve their jakes, some to scoure theyr candel-styckes, & some to rubbe their bootes. Some they solde to the grossers and sope sellers, & some they sent over see to ye bokebynders, not in small nombre, but at tymes whole shyppes full, to the wonderynge of the foren nacyons.

[26] *The Libraries of King Henry VIII*, ed. by J. P. Carley, Corpus of British Medieval Library Catalogues, 7 (London: British Library, 2000), pp. xliii–xlvi.

[27] N. R. Ker, 'Sir John Prise', *The Library*, ser. 5, 10 (1955), 1–24; Glanmor Williams, 'Sir John Pryse of Brecon', *Brycheiniog*, 31 (1998–99), 49–63.

[28] Anthony Wood, *Athenæ Oxonienses*, 2 vols (London: printed for Thomas Bennet, 1691), I, col. 68; citing 'Papers of state'.

Bale's own faith was zealously Protestant; but he sincerely wished that 'the profytable corne had not so unadvysedly and ungodly peryshed wyth the un-profytable chaffe'.[29]

The aftershock of the breakup of the monastic libraries continued to rever-berate for several decades more. John Dee petitioned Queen Mary in 1557 to establish a great royal library in which manuscripts, now scattered in private hands, could be consolidated: he refers to 'the spoile and destruction of so many and so notable Libraries, wherein lay the treasure of all Antiquity'.[30] Dee's proposal was overambitious, but in Elizabeth's reign more modest programmes along the same lines were initiated by both Archbishop Parker and Sir William Cecil, acting in a private capacity but with the weight of their public status behind them. Bale, writing to Parker in 1560, echoes Dee in referring to 'the lamentable spoyle of the lybraryes of Englande', and tells how he himself had built up his collection during the diaspora: 'Well, only conscyence, with a fervent love to my contray moved me to save that myghte be saved.'[31] Parker, in a letter to Cecil of 1566, rejoices in the rescuing of manuscripts, '[s]o that thei maye be preserved within the realme, & not sent over seas by covetouse statyoners, or spoyled in the poticarye shops'.[32]

England would never again see destruction of the written word on the scale that occurred at the dissolution, and manuscript-based antiquarianism in the late sixteenth and early seventeenth centuries moved into a more measured programme of consolidation, transcription and abstraction. However, the up-heavals of the Civil War and the Puritan agenda for reform brought new threats which were in their way equally disturbing. In the chaos of war, books and documents sometimes became the target of marauding troops, as at Winchester, Lichfield, and Peterborough Cathedrals, where muniment rooms were broken into and ransacked by Parliamentarians: in the last case, the ravagers claimed an explicitly religious agenda, believing that the documents they were tearing up were

---

[29] Bale, *Laboryouse Journey*, sigs. A8, B1.

[30] *John Dee's Library Catalogue*, ed. by Julian Roberts and A. G. Watson (London: Biblio-graphical Society, 1990), pp. 194–95.

[31] *The Recovery of the Past in Early Elizabethan England: Documents by John Bale and John Joscelyn from the Circle of Matthew Parker*, ed. by Timothy Graham and A. G. Watson (Cam-bridge: Cambridge University Library, 1998), p. 17.

[32] Quoted in Wright, 'Dispersal of the Libraries', p. 156; and published with spelling modernized in *Correspondence of Matthew Parker [...]*, ed. by John Bruce and T. T. Perowne (Cambridge: Cambridge University Press, 1853), pp. 253–54.

'the Popes Bulls'.[33] St Mary's Tower, York, used for the storage of the muniments of northern religious houses, was blown up in 1644 during the siege of the city: fortunately, Roger Dodsworth had just finished making extracts from the records, and so preserved much which would otherwise have been lost.[34] In London, the archives of the dissolved Chapter of St Paul's Cathedral were deposited at Scriveners' Hall, where they were further imperilled by the unexpected death of their custodian, John Reading. However, William Dugdale was able to negotiate their transfer ('no lesse than ten porters burthens') to his own keeping; and, having put them into order, to make them the basis of his *History of St Paul's Cathedral* (1658).[35] At the Restoration he was able to return them to the reinstated Dean and Chapter, thanking Providence for making him 'the chief Means of Preserving all those Venerable Chartularies, and Records, belonging to this Ancient and Famous Church'.[36] His rescue effort had hardly been on the same scale as Leland's campaign, but it was in the same spirit, and demonstrates the same imperative to preserve the historical record against the ravages of religious reform.

The Recording of Church Monuments

Among the new tools that became available for antiquarian research in the sixteenth century was a burgeoning awareness of the evidential value of semi-textual and nontextual materials, including coins, seals, archaeological remains and, not least, funerary monuments and memorial stained glass. At the very time that church monuments and glass were beginning to be appreciated as historical documents, however, they also seemed to be in increased danger from the side-effects of the Reformation, including the general neglect of a Protestant culture

[33] [Bruno Ryves], *Mercurius Rusticus* (Oxford: [n. pub.], 1643; repr. London: Richard Green, 1685), p. 151 (*recte* 251); William Dugdale, *A Short View of the Late Troubles in England* (Oxford: printed at the Theatre for Moses Pitt, 1681), p. 559; Francis Standish, 'A Short and True Narrative of the Rifling and Defacing the Cathedral Church of Peterburgh in the Year 1643', in Simon Gunton, *The History of the Church of Peterburgh*, ed. by Simon Patrick (London: printed for Richard Chiswell, 1686), p. 337; Julie Spraggon, *Puritan Iconoclasm during the English Civil War* (Woodbridge: Boydell & Brewer, 2003), p. 209.

[34] Francis Drake, *Eboracum; or, The History and Antiquities of the City of York* (London: printed by William Bowyer for the author, 1736), p. 575.

[35] *Life of Dugdale*, pp. 26–27.

[36] William Dugdale, *The History of St Paul's Cathedral*, 2nd edn (London: Edward Maynard, 1716), p. xxvii.

which no longer welcomed ornament in places of worship, and the more direct assaults of iconoclasm.[37] Official iconoclasm, promulgated by Edward VI, Elizabeth I, and the Commonwealth Parliament, was, of course, concerned solely with religious imagery, though very similar legislation was also introduced by the Commonwealth to extirpate heraldic and other symbols of royalty. In the heat of zealotry, however, such distinctions could easily be overlooked, and, particularly during the Puritan ascendancy and Civil War, tombs and windows that were purely commemorative were wrecked alongside those which bore religious images. In addition, monuments were liable to be despoiled from commercial or utilitarian motives: brass could be melted down, stone slabs reused, and alabaster ground up to make a salve for foot rot in sheep.

Antiquarian writings are filled with expressions of outrage at neglect of this kind, which threatened to wipe individuals and families from the historical record. John Stow characterizes such acts as 'a great injurie both to the living and the dead'; William Burton calls them 'inhumane and sacrilegious'; Thomas Philipot alludes to the 'barbarouse rudenesse of these Times' and the 'Impiety of Sacrilegious Mechanicks'.[38] Stow puts the blame on those 'eyther of a preposterous zeale, or of a greedy minde'; William Wyrley on 'certaine persons, delighting as may seem in noveltie, for they can abide no marke of antiquitie'; and Burton both on 'the vaine and idle conceits of some novelists, who think all pictures in Churches to be Idols, and to tend to Superstition', and on the 'covetousnesse or necessity of some poore Clerkes or Sextons, or the want or poverty of some needy Curates'.[39] John Weever records monuments being

---

[37] For aspects of this topic, see H. F. O. Evans, 'Malicious Damage to Brasses', *Transactions of the Monumental Brass Society*, 10 (1965), 186–91; John Phillips, *The Reformation of Images: Destruction of Art in England, 1535–1660* (Berkeley and Los Angeles: University of California Press, 1973); Jerome Bertram, *Lost Brasses* (Newton Abbot: David and Charles, 1976), pp. 18–28; Margaret Aston, *England's Iconoclasts*, I: *Laws against Images* (Oxford: Oxford University Press, 1988); Eamon Duffy, *The Stripping of the Altars: Traditional Religion in England, c. 1400–c.1580* (New Haven: Yale University Press, 1992), pp. 379–423; Spraggon, *Puritan Iconoclasm*; Phillip Lindley, *Tomb Destruction and Scholarship: Medieval Monuments in Early Modern England* (Donington: Shaun Tyas, 2007).

[38] John Stow, *A Survey of London*, ed. by C. L. Kingsford, 2 vols (Oxford: Clarendon Press, 1908), II, 75; William Burton, *The Description of Leicester Shire* (London: [printed by William Jaggard] for Iohn White, [1622]), p. 97; Philipot, *Villare Cantianum*, pp. 83, 311.

[39] Stow, *Survey*, II, 75; William Wyrley, *The True Use of Armorie* (London: J. Jackson for G. Cawood, 1592), pp. 24–26; Burton, *Leicester Shire*, p. 97. For the authorship of the *True Use*, possibly in fact written by Sampson Erdeswick, see M. W. Greenslade, *The Staffordshire Historians* (Stafford: Staffordshire Record Society, 1982), p. 26.

(to the shame of our time) broken down, and utterly almost all ruinated, their brasen inscriptions erazed, torne away, and pilfered, by which inhumane, deformidable act, the honourable memory of many vertuous and noble persons deceased, is extinguished, and the true understanding of divers Families in these Realmes (who have descended of these worthy persons aforesaid) is so darkened, as the true course of their inheritance is thereby partly interrupted.[40]

James Wright, in the 1680s, suggests that the wreckers of the Civil War years had been minded 'to exterminate the memory of their forefathers, and do what in them lay, that posterity should not know that there ever was a better generation of people than themselves'.[41]

One response was to call on law and authority to stem the depredation. William Fleetwood was a committed Protestant but had strong antiquarian sympathies and later became a respected member of the Society of Antiquaries. In 1559 at Peterborough, as a royal visitor appointed to ensure uniformity of worship, he ordered the restitution of the defaced tomb of Catherine of Aragon.[42] Some thirty years later, William Wyrley urged those in authority to follow Fleetwood's example, and to find a means

that these simple fellowes taking upon them to be reformers, might be reformed themselves, and both kept from destroy[i]ng of good ordinances, and be punished for their offences in that behalfe committed.[43]

Appropriate legislation, as Wyrley acknowledged, did exist. Edward VI's act of 1550 against idolatrous images, and later parliamentary ordinances of 1643 and 1644, excluded the destruction of strictly commemorative memorials. Similarly, a proclamation by Elizabeth I in 1560 positively prohibited, in the interests of protecting the genealogical record and lawful lines of inheritance, the destruction of any monument whose purpose was solely commemorative, and 'not to nourish any kind of superstition'.[44]

---

[40] Weever, *Ancient Funerall Monuments*, 'The Author to the Reader'.

[41] James Wright, *The History and Antiquities of Rutland* (London: Bennet Griffen, 1684), 'The Preface to the Reader'.

[42] Wyrley, *True Use*, p. 25. Cf. P. R. Harris, 'William Fleetwood, Recorder of the City, and Catholicism in Elizabethan London', *Recusant History*, 7 (1963–64), 106–22; and J. D. Alsop, 'William Fleetwood and Elizabethan Historical Scholarship', *Sixteenth Century Journal*, 25 (1994), 156–76.

[43] Wyrley, *True Use*, p. 25.

[44] 3 & 4 Edw. VI, chap.10; P. L. Hughes and J. F. Larkin, *Tudor Royal Proclamations*, 3 vols (New Haven: Yale University Press, 1964–69), II, 1464–68; Spraggon, *Puritan Iconoclasm*, pp. 259–61; Aston, *England's Iconoclasts*, pp. 314–17; F. A. Youngs, *The Proclamations of the Tudor Queens* (Cambridge: Cambridge University Press, 1976), pp. 193–94.

A more practical and realistic response, however, was to create a surrogate record of the monuments before they were lost. There were several distinct methodologies by which this might be accomplished. The first comprised the simple listing of names and sites of burial: the most extensive catalogue of this kind is found embedded in Stow's *Survey of London* (1598), which records the burial places of no fewer than 1775 Londoners of the better sort.[45] A second method, more labour-intensive, involved the full transcription of monumental inscriptions. This practice had its roots in the recording of classical epigraphy by humanist scholars, but was readily adapted to more recent inscriptions, and was given a boost from about 1590 by the late Elizabethan and Jacobean taste for florid literary epitaphs: several such surveys reached print in the early seventeenth century, notably Camden's *Reges, reginae, nobiles* (1600) on the monuments of Westminster Abbey; Henry Holland's *Sepulchraria Sancti Pauli* (1614) on St Paul's Cathedral; Valentin Arithmaeus's *Mausolea regum* (1618), an independent account by a German visitor of the same two churches; Anthony Munday's expanded edition of Stow's *Survey* (1618), which added numerous inscriptions to Stow's original text; and Weever's *Ancient Funerall Monuments* (1631), which supplied over a thousand inscriptions from churches across the dioceses of Canterbury, Rochester, London, and Norwich.

A third method was that of heraldic recording, developed in the first instance by professional heralds on their official visitations, but soon emulated by amateur enthusiasts, such as Humphrey Purefoy, Laurence Bostock, and Robert Kemp, all active in the 1560s and 1570s, and many successors: the resultant records, known generically as 'church notes', normally comprise sketches ('tricks') or verbal descriptions (blazons) of heraldry seen on monuments and in windows.[46] These notes were never intended for publication, though Thomas Churchyard's chorographical poem, *The Worthines of Wales* (1587), John Norden's *Speculum Britanniae: Middlesex* (1593) and William Burton's *Description of Leicester Shire* (1622) all owe something to the genre. Only gradually did the records

---

[45] I take the total from Lawrence Manley, 'Of Sites and Rites', in *The Theatrical City: Culture, Theatre and Politics in London, 1576–1649*, ed. by D. L. Smith, Richard Strier and David Bevington (Cambridge: Cambridge University Press, 1995), p. 41.

[46] For a useful general account, see P. J. Lankester, 'Two Lost Effigial Monuments in Yorkshire and the Evidence of Church Notes', *Church Monuments*, 8 (1993), 25–44. Bostock's collections (relating to Cheshire) are at BL MS Harley 139; Kemp's (Norfolk) at BL MS Harley 901. Purefoy's church notes (Warwickshire and Leicestershire) are copied into BL MS Egerton 3510, a volume compiled by his nephew, William Burton.

of inscriptions and heraldry, and an incipient interest in the sculptural form of monuments, converge. It was therefore not really until the second or third decades of the seventeenth century that surveys of monuments that readily acknowledged all these aspects began to be made, examples being the work of Thomas Habington and Sir Edward Dering.[47]

Many of these projects were undoubtedly driven by the sense, enhanced by the events of the Reformation, of the vulnerability of monumental remains. There is, for example, a telling shift of emphasis in the heralds' visitations, which in the early sixteenth century appear to have been largely focused on defacing and removing displays of unauthorized heraldry, but which after the Reformation became much more concerned with putting on record legitimate displays of arms.[48] A similar desire to create a more durable form of memorial on paper is implicit in Stow's repeated complaints of the destruction of monuments in the *Survey of London*, and in his admission that he had intentionally omitted from his catalogue the tombs of individuals who had themselves been defacers of monuments, and so were 'worthy to be deprived of that memory whereof they have injuriously robbed others'.[49] Henry Holland feared that 'some Monuments of the dead might be defaced, if not quite raced' at St Paul's through Bishop Laud's restoration campaign of the 1630s; but, in publishing a new edition of his survey, trusted that they would be 'preserved hereby to Memorie and Posteritie'.[50]

The most unequivocal scheme of preservation-by-recording was the tour of visits made to major churches by William Dugdale and the arms-painter William Sedgwick during the summers of 1640 and 1641. The initiative was that of Sir Christopher Hatton, who 'timely foresaw the neere approaching storme' — or, more specifically, 'the Presbyterian contagion, which then began violently to breake out' — and

---

[47] Thomas Habington, *A Survey of Worcestershire*, ed. by John Amphlett, Worcestershire Historical Society, 2 vols (Oxford: printed by James Parker, 1893–99), written 1606–47. Dering's church notes for Kent, 1628–37, are at Centre for Kentish Studies U.350/Z.24; and Society of Antiquaries of London MS 497A.

[48] For a pre-Reformation visitation, see A. R. Wagner, *Heralds and Heraldry in the Middle Ages* (Oxford: Oxford University Press, 1956), pp. 139–46.

[49] *The Diary of John Manningham*, ed. by R. P. Sorlien (Hanover: University Press of New England, 1976), p. 154.

[50] H[enry] H[olland], *Ecclesia Sancti Pauli illustrata* (London: printed by John Norton, 1633), sig. A3.

often and earnestly incited me [Dugdale] to a speedy view of what Monuments I could, especially in the principall Churches of this Realme; to the end, that by Inke and paper, the Shadows of them, with their Inscriptions might be preserved for posteritie, forasmuch as the things themselves were so neer unto ruine.[51]

Hatton's fears were swiftly realized, and the tour proved to have been particularly opportune in the cases of Lichfield and St Paul's Cathedrals, both of which suffered grievously over the next few years (Lichfield through military bombardment; St Paul's through neglect and maltreatment), leaving Dugdale and Sedgwick's drawings the only record of many of their monuments. Some of the drawings, along with others newly commissioned, were subsequently engraved by Wenceslaus Hollar for Dugdale's *Antiquities of Warwickshire* (1656) and *History of St Paul's* (1658): the latter publication was, of course, again fortunate in its timing, the Cathedral burning down only eight years later.[52] In soliciting financial support for the plates, Dugdale had once more emphasized the likely survival of paper over stone: 'high time it is to preserve the memory of those worthy persons by these meanes; for Monuments will not doe it soe lastingly'.[53]

There were other projects, too, shaped by the circumstances of Civil War. At Peterborough Cathedral, Simon Gunton, son of the diocesan registrar, had transcribed the monumental inscriptions during his boyhood in the 1620s. The destruction of many of the monuments by Parliamentary troops in 1643 prompted him, now a prebendary of the Cathedral, to use these notes as a starting point for his *History of the Church of Peterburgh*, published posthumously in 1686. William Gray published his short *Chorographia* of Newcastle-upon-Tyne in 1649, 'that those Monuments which these late warrs have obliterated and ruin'd, may be left to posterity'.[54] The anonymous 'Monumenta Eblanae', a survey of church monuments in Dublin probably made in the late 1650s, may have been

---

[51] *Life of Dugdale*, p. 14; Dugdale, *History of St Paul's Cathedral* (London: printed by Thomas Warren, 1658), sig. A3ᵛ; Dugdale, *St Paul's* (1716), pp. xxvi–xxvii. The principal surviving set of drawings from the tour, though it is not complete, is BL Add. MS 71474. Cf. H. S. London, *The Life of William Bruges*, Harleian Society, 111–12 (London: Harleian Society, 1970), pp. 113–15; and Philip Whittemore, 'Sir William Dugdale's "Book of Draughts"', *Church Monuments*, 18 (2003), 23–52.

[52] Cf. Roberts, *Dugdale and Hollar*, especially pp. 18–45, 73–103.

[53] *Life of Dugdale*, p. 280. Similar sentiments appear in several of the Latin aphorisms supplied by donors of plates to the *Monasticon*: cf. Margery Corbett, 'The Title-Page and Illustrations to the *Monasticon Anglicanum*, 1655–1673', *Antiquaries Journal*, 67 (1987), 103–04.

[54] W[illiam] G[ray], *Chorographia; or, A Survey of Newcastle upon Tine* (London: printed by S. B., 1649), 'To the Candid Reader'.

prompted by the devastating wars in Ireland.[55] Matters were not always so straightforward, however. William Somner's *Antiquities of Canterbury* (1640), thoroughly Laudian in tone and intent, was later said to have 'preserv'd the memorial of many Epitaphs, Inscriptions, and proper observations which otherwise had soon been lost to all succeeding ages'.[56] That was quite true; but it may also be recalled that when the uncompromising iconoclast Richard Culmer purged the cathedral in 1643, he himself used Somner's book as 'a card and a compasse to sail by, in that *Cathedral Ocean of Images*'.[57]

The desire to preserve data at risk was not the only motivation behind the recording of church monuments: there was also a simpler and more pragmatic wish to put the information in a more accessible format than that of the monuments themselves. Dugdale tells us that in 1640 he was initially sceptical of Hatton's fears for the future, but he agreed to undertake his tours, 'in order to transmit the Figures of [the monuments] to the View of those, who were never like to see them *in Specie*'.[58] Nevertheless, many sets of transcripts and church notes were indeed made from a conscious desire to preserve on paper what might not survive in stone or brass, and to mitigate the destructiveness of Protestant extremism, civil war and neglect.

Conclusion

The heart of the antiquarian project in the wake of the Reformation was essentially nonsectarian; whatever their personal religious allegiances (which were multifarious), in their antiquarianism most practitioners were driven principally by a desire to celebrate and preserve the record of the past. White Kennett, writing in the 1690s, recalled the timely rescue and recording efforts of Leland, Somner, Dodsworth, and Dugdale, and suggested that they had been the agents of a providence, which had 'often watcht over and preserv'd many monuments of Antiquity, just before the fatal ruine of them'.[59]

---

[55] Dublin, National Library of Ireland, Genealogical Office MS 15; cf. R. Loeber, 'Sculptured Memorials to the Dead in Early Seventeenth Century Ireland: A Survey from *Monumenta Eblanae* and Other Sources', *Proceedings of the Royal Irish Academy*, 81C (1981), 280–86.

[56] Kennett, 'Life of Somner', p. 15.

[57] Richard Culmer, *Cathedrall Newes from Canterbury* (London: printed by Richard Cotes for Fulk Clifton, 1644), p. 22.

[58] Dugdale, *St Paul's* (1716), p. xxvii.

[59] Kennett, 'Life of Somner', pp. 15–17.

It is hardly surprising, of course, that antiquarianism, frequently resurrecting as it did elements of pre-Reformation culture, should sometimes acquire the taint of popery. John Earle's satirical sketch of 1628 suggested that, in the antiquary's enthusiasm for his subject, 'a broken Statue would almost make him an Idolater'; and that '[h]ee will go you forty miles to see a Saint's Well, or a ruin'd Abbey'. In a more serious vein, Thomas Fuller warned in 1642 that

> [s]ome scoure off the rust of old inscriptions into their own souls, cankering themselves
> with superstition, having read so often *Orate pro anima*, that at last they fall a praying for
> the departed.[60]

If Camden met with criticism for what were little more than passing mentions of the Catholic past in the *Britannia* ('[t]here are certaine, as I heare who take it impatiently that I have mentioned some of the most famous Monasteries and their founders'), the same criticisms were levelled with considerably more force at the first volume of the *Monasticon* (1655), a work dedicated in its entirety to monasticism, which was rumoured by some to have been compiled

> purposely to discover the lands sometime belonging to the religious houses in this realme;
> to the intent that upon restoreing the Romish religion, [...] they might returne to their
> former superstitious uses.[61]

But the truth seems to be that many antiquaries, driven though they were by topical concerns such as national identity, or the need to promote the interests of their class, gave little or no consciously religious agenda to their studies. Antiquarianism was a broad church, in which the common factor was a simple fascination with the past and its remains: in John Earle's words, the antiquary 'is one that hath that unnaturall disease to bee enamour'd of old age, and wrinckles, and loves all things (as Dutchmen doe cheese) the better for being mouldy and worme-eaten'.[62]

---

[60] John Earle, 'An Antiquarie', in his *Micro-cosmographie* (London: [n. pub.], 1628), sig. C2; Thomas Fuller, 'The True Church Antiquary', in *The Holy State* (Cambridge: Roger Daniel for John Williams, 1642), p. 69.

[61] William Camden, *Britannia* (London: George Bishop and John Norton, 1607), sig. **; Camden, *Britain*, trans. by Philemon Holland (London: George Bishop and John Norton, 1610), sig. [*5]. *Life of Dugdale*, p. 25n. See also Sir John Marsham's pre-emptive response to criticisms of the work as 'trivial, useless, and no way agreeable to the present Posture of Affairs': Roger Dodsworth and William Dugdale, *Monasticon anglicanum*, 3 vols (London: [n. pub.], 1655–73), vol. I, sig. [D4]; translation from Dugdale, *Monasticon anglicanum*, 3 vols. (London: printed by R. Harbin, 1718), I, p. vi.

[62] Earle, *Micro-cosmographie*, sig. [B8]ᵛ.

Indeed, antiquarianism itself seemed sometimes to take on the characteristics of a secular religion. Peter Clark points to late-medieval fraternities and gilds as precursors of the Society of Antiquaries.[63] Some of the antiquarian lists of burials and monuments, which at first sight appear to be based on personal observation, prove on further investigation to be taken directly from (and arguably to be successors to) medieval imprecatory registers and bederolls.[64] Charles Phythian-Adams writes of the emergence of county history, based on lineage and manorial descent, as 'a retrospective ceremonial substitute for the perpetual chantry' in a 'newly invented cult of the gentle dead'.[65] The analogy can be pushed too far: clearly, most antiquaries were able to hold sincere religious beliefs alongside their devotion to the past. Nevertheless, their dedication to antiquity for antiquity's sake should not be underestimated; and it is worth recalling the words of an anonymous speaker to the Society of Antiquaries in 1600, who averred that 'I reverence [antiquities], as I would revere Adam, if he were alive'.[66]

[63] Peter Clark, *British Clubs and Societies, 1580–1800* (Oxford: Clarendon Press, 2000), pp. 20–25.

[64] Stow, *Survey of London*, I, 319–22; II, 345; Weever, *Ancient Funerall Monuments*, p. 863.

[65] Charles Phythian-Adams, 'Leicestershire and Rutland', in Currie and Lewis, *English County Histories*, p. 230.

[66] Hearne [and Ayloffe], *A Collection of Curious Discourses*, I, 238.

CONTRIBUTORS

Hugh Adlington is lecturer in English at the University of Birmingham. He has published a number of articles and chapters in books on early modern literature, religion, and politics. He is co-editor of *The Oxford Handbook to the Early Modern Sermon* (forthcoming), and is a Volume Editor of *The Oxford Edition of the Sermons of John Donne* (forthcoming).

Andrea Brady is a lecturer in English literature at Queen Mary, University of London. She is the author of *English Funerary Elegy in the Seventeenth Century* (Palgrave Macmillan, 2006) and of several books of poetry, including *Embrace* (Object Permanence, 2005) and *Vacation of a Lifetime* (Salt, 2001).

Frances Cruickshank lectures in early modern literature at the School of English, Media Studies and Art History at the University of Queensland. Her doctoral thesis, which she completed in 2005, is entitled '"The Highest Matter in the Noblest Forme": Religious Poetics in John Donne and George Herbert'.

Jan Frans van Dijkhuizen is lecturer and research fellow at the University of Leiden. He is the author of *Devil Theatre: Demonic Possession and Exorcism in English Drama, 1558–1642* (Cambridge, 2007). His current project, funded by the Netherlands Organisation for Academic Research (NWO), investigates perceptions of physical pain in early modern England.

Oliver Harris was educated at the universities of Oxford and Aberystwyth, and subsequently worked as an archivist. He was awarded his PhD by London Metropolitan University in 2006 for a thesis on aspects of early modern antiquarianism. His publications include papers on John Leland and John Stow.

John Kerrigan is Professor of English 2000 at the University of Cambridge. His books include *Archipelagic English: Literature, History, and Politics 1603–1707* (Oxford, 2008), *On Shakespeare and Early Modern Literature* (Oxford, 2001), and *Revenge Tragedy: Aeschylus to Armageddon* (Oxford, 1996).

Kevin Laam is an Assistant Professor of English at Oakland University. His scholarly interests include early modern lyric poetry and devotional literature. He has written on Thomas Traherne and George Gascoigne.

Claudia Richter is lecturer in English literature at the Freie Universität, Berlin. She is preparing a PhD on violence in early modern drama.

Kristine Steenbergh is lecturer in English literature at the Vrije University, Amsterdam. In 2007 she defended her PhD thesis, entitled *Wild Justice: The Dynamics of Gender and Revenge in Early Modern English Drama, 1558–1642*.

Richard Todd is Professor of British literature after 1500 at the University of Leiden. His publications include *The Opacity of Signs: Acts of Interpretation in George Herbert's 'The Temple'* (Columbia, MO, 1986) and *Consuming Fictions: The Booker Prize and Fiction in Britain Today* (London, 1996). He is assistant textual editor to *The Variorum Edition of the Poetry of John Donne*.

Bart Westerweel is Emeritus Professor of English literature at the University of Leiden and a specialist in early modern literature. His publications include *Patterns and Patterning: A Study of Four Poems by George Herbert* (Amsterdam, 1984) and *Anglo-Dutch Relations in the Field of the Emblem* (Leiden, 1997).

Helen Wilcox is Professor of English literature at Bangor University, Wales. She is the editor of *The English Poems of George Herbert* (Cambridge, 2007), and among her other publications are *Women and Literature in Britain, 1500–1700* (Cambridge, 1996) and *Betraying Our Selves: Forms of Self-Representation in Early Modern English Texts* (London, 2000).

PROTEUS

All volumes in this series are evaluated by an Editorial Board, strictly on academic grounds, based on reports prepared by referees who have been commissioned by virtue of their specialism in the appropriate field. The Board ensures that the screening is done independently and without conflicts of interest. The definitive texts supplied by authors are also subject to review by the Board before being approved for publication. Further, the volumes are copyedited to conform to the publisher's stylebook and to the best international academic standards in the field.

Titles in Series

Image and Imagination of the Religious Self in Late Medieval and Early Modern Europe, ed. by Reindart Falkenburg, Walter S. Melion, and Todd M. Richardson (2007)

In Preparation

Christine Göttler, *Last Things: Art and the Religious Imagination in the Age of Reform*